French Musical Culture and the Coming of Sound Cinema

THE OXFORD MUSIC/MEDIA SERIES
Daniel Goldmark, Series Editor

oxford
music/media series

FRENCH MUSICAL CULTURE AND THE COMING OF SOUND CINEMA

Hannah Lewis

OXFORD
UNIVERSITY PRESS

OXFORD
UNIVERSITY PRESS

Oxford University Press is a department of the University of Oxford. It furthers
the University's objective of excellence in research, scholarship, and education
by publishing worldwide. Oxford is a registered trade mark of Oxford University
Press in the UK and certain other countries.

Published in the United States of America by Oxford University Press
198 Madison Avenue, New York, NY 10016, United States of America.

Library of Congress Cataloging-in-Publication Data
Names: Lewis, Hannah, 1985– author.
Title: French musical culture and the coming of sound
cinema / Hannah Lewis.
Description: New York, NY : Oxford University Press, [2019] |
Series: The Oxford music/media series | Includes bibliographical references.
Identifiers: LCCN 2017057061 | ISBN 9780190635985 (softcover : alk. paper) |
ISBN 9780190635978 (hardcover : alk. paper) |
ISBN 9780190636012 (oxford scholarship online) | ISBN 9780190635992 (updf) |
ISBN 9780190636005 (epub)
Subjects: LCSH: Sound motion pictures—France—History—20th century. |
Musical films—France—History—20th century. | Motion picture music—
France—History and criticism.
Classification: LCC PN1995.7 .L49 2018 | DDC 791.430944—dc23
LC record available at https://lccn.loc.gov/2017057061

9 8 7 6 5 4 3 2 1

Paperback printed by Webcom, Inc., Canada
Hardback printed by Bridgeport National Bindery, Inc., United States of America

CONTENTS

FIGURES

EXAMPLES

ACKNOWLEDGMENTS

I am deeply indebted to numerous individuals who supported me in various invaluable ways as I completed this book. First and foremost, I am grateful to my editors at Oxford University Press. Norm Hirschy provided unwavering support and encouragement from the book's early stages, and the keen guidance of series editor Daniel Goldmark helped shape the project in meaningful ways.

The idea for this book grew out of my dissertation research at Harvard University, which was made possible by the tireless support of my mentors and colleagues. As my advisors, Carol Oja and Sindhumathi Revuluri provided substantial intellectual, moral, and emotional support from the earliest stages of my project, and Alexander Rehding and David Rodowick offered their interdisciplinary, creative perspectives, which influenced my approach in valuable ways. I additionally benefited immensely from the conversations, feedback, and encouragement of other faculty members at Harvard, particularly Carolyn Abbate, Dominique Bluher, Suzannah Clark, Thomas Forrest Kelly, Kay Shelemay, and Anne Shreffler. This book was only possible because of the encouragement of friends whose influence on the project began in graduate school, and who continued to offer crucial feedback and support during various stages of the book's development. Many thanks to Andrea Bohlman, Elizabeth Craft, William Cheng, Louis Epstein, Frank Lehman, and Matthew Mugmon for providing invaluable feedback on drafts of various chapters of this book, and to Glenda Goodman, Lucille Mok, and Peter McMurray, whose input has informed my thinking, and my writing, in countless ways.

Since I have arrived at the University of Texas at Austin, I have been lucky to find the same kind of support and encouragement in my colleagues, especially Charles Carson, Andrew Dell'Antonio, Eric Drott, Robert Hatton, Michael Tusa, and Marianne Wheeldon. Jim Buhler deserves a special thank you for our countless conversations on the transition era and the generosity with which he consistently provided keen, incisive feedback over the past three years. I am additionally grateful to colleagues and friends from various institutions whose conversations and thoughtful questions have in various ways influenced the writing of this book: Michael Baumgartner, Alessandra Campana, Fanny Gribenski, Martin Marks, Emily Richmond Pollock, Colin Roust, W. Anthony Sheppard, and Leslie Sprout.

My research was aided tremendously by the help of numerous librarians and archivists. I am grateful to the staff of the Bibliothèque Nationale de France Département des Arts du Spectacle and Département de Musique, as well as the staff of the Cinémathèque Française. Thanks also to Daniel Brémaud at the Centre National du Cinéma, who made it possible for me to view difficult-to-find films at their archives in Bois d'Arcy, to Francis Malfliet at the Cinémathèque Royale de Belgique in Brussels, and to Bernard Eisenschitz for his help in locating a copy of *Le Chaland qui passe*. Nancy Randle helped me sort through the Jean Renoir Papers in the UCLA Special Collections. I was also fortunate to view a number of film prints at the Harvard Film Archive. At Harvard, the Loeb Music Library staff—particularly Sarah Adams, Joshua Kantor, Kerry Masteller, Liza Vick, and Andrew Wilson—went above and beyond their call of duty helping me find needed resources, and at UT Austin, David Hunter ensured the Fine Arts Library provided me with the materials necessary for my research. I also could not have completed this project without the financial generosity of several individuals and institutions. The Ashford Fellowship at Harvard University supported my graduate work, and at UT Austin, a Faculty Research Award from the College of Fine Arts and a Sarah and Ernest Butler Faculty Development Award from the Butler School of Music supported my work during both the research and writing stages.

None of this would have been possible without the unconditional love and support of my family. To my parents, Jan and Dan, I am grateful for instilling in me, from a young age, the importance of pursuing what you love and approaching the world with curiosity and enthusiasm. My sister, Becca, has inspired me in so many ways, and our shared passion for music and film has profoundly shaped my life both in- and outside of academia. Lastly, I thank my husband and best friend, Ojas Vyas, who has seen me through each challenge and hurdle since the beginning. His love, support, and encouragement have never wavered, and I could not have completed this book without him by my side.

An earlier version of Chapter 6 was published in the *Journal of the American Musicological Society*, 68, no. 3 (2015): 559–603.

ABBREVIATIONS

BNF	Bibliothèque Nationale de France
BNF–AS	Bibliothèque Nationale de France, Département des Arts du Spectacle
BNF–M	Bibliothèque Nationale de France, Département de Musique
CNC à la BNF	Centre National du Cinéma at the Bibliothèque Nationale de France
CNC Bois d'Arcy	Centre National du Cinéma at Bois d'Arcy

French Musical Culture and the Coming of Sound Cinema

Introduction

In the 1930 film *Prix de beauté* (dir. Augusto Genina), a young and beautiful stenographer, Lucienne (played by Louise Brooks), enters the Miss Europe beauty contest against her fiancé André's wishes. She wins, and André delivers her an ultimatum: give up the fame and return home with him for a life of domesticity, or they are through. She chooses him, but, after having experienced a taste of glamour, finds her old life unbearable. She is offered a film contract with "The International Society of Sound Films" (*La Société Internationale de Films Sonores*). Although she initially refuses, the temptation to be a movie star becomes too great, and she ultimately accepts and signs the contract, leaving only a note for André.

Lucienne goes on to make a short sound film. After it is completed, she and the producers screen the film. In the dark projection room, they watch her ghostly image, which stands on a stage in front of a piano, singing to the camera, as it is projected onto the two-dimensional screen. She sings a song called "Je n'ai qu'un amour, c'est toi" (I Have Only One Love, It's You), a simple waltz that she had sung earlier in the film to André when the two were still happy together.[1] Here, the song's lyrics take on a new irony, as one of the producers caresses her hand while she smiles back at him. She watches and listens with delight to her recorded image and voice, the light from the projector flickering on her face as the song fills the room. André sneaks into the projection room. From the back of the room he sees Lucienne acting affectionately toward the producer, just as her filmed image sings "I'll remain faithful to you" (*Je te reste fidèle*). It is too much for him to bear, and he slowly pulls a handgun from his pocket and shoots Lucienne in the back. The producers rush to help her, but it is too late. She collapses to the floor just as her image onscreen begins to sing the song's second verse. The film ends with a shot

Figure I.1: Final Scene, *Prix de beauté* (1930)

of Lucienne's dead body in the foreground, the light from the projection flickering on her face, and her eerie, ghostly onscreen image, still alive and singing (Figure I.1).

Although the tragic ending to *Prix de beauté*'s doomed romance may come across as clichéd and melodramatic to contemporary audiences, this climactic scene is striking in its lurid, fascinating, and strange narrative enactment of technology. It is all the more remarkable given that synchronized sound technology was a new and unfamiliar experience for French audiences, having only just arrived in France one year earlier. *Prix de beauté* conspicuously thematized the brand-new phenomenon of mechanically reproduced synchronized sound. The ability to record the likeness of someone's entire person—both body *and* voice—even in her bodily absence, was both fascinating and unsettling, a source of excitement and anxiety. Lucienne's song, outliving its original source, seems to gain almost magical powers, drowning out any sounds of the characters left in the aftermath of her death and singing directly to André, and, by extension, the film spectator. In its dramatic ending, *Prix de beauté* captured the palpable and pervasive sentiment that cinema would be forever different, now that sounds could be preserved and played back alongside images.

The transition from silent to synchronized sound film was indeed one of the most dramatic transformations in cinema's history, radically changing the technology, practices, and aesthetics of filmmaking within a few short years. While the film industry's transition was swift, however, it was not systematic. The relationship between film and sound—particularly music—had to be negotiated, and the introduction of synchronized sound prompted a range of audiovisual approaches as well as opinions about the new technology and its aesthetic implications. It was a period of bold experimentation, but it was also a time when individuals felt there was something at stake in the artistic directions cinema might take; and they went to great lengths to articulate strong, sometimes conflicting, stances on the role they wanted music to play in the emerging aesthetics of the new audiovisual medium. In the early sound era, many filmmakers tackled theoretical questions about the potential of sound cinema head-on, addressing these questions both in writing and through experiments in their films. Within this heated debate, music became a powerful aesthetic force for many filmmakers.

In *French Musical Culture and the Coming of Sound Cinema*, I show how debates about sound film resonated deeply within French musical culture of the early 1930s, and conversely, how a range of French musical styles, genres, and practices shaped audiovisual cinematic experiments during the transition to sound. From the production of the first domestic sound films in 1930 to the rise of the Popular Front around 1935, sound film in France was a powerful site of aesthetic contestation and negotiation. I analyze films by many of the most prominent directors and screenwriters of the period—including Luis Buñuel, René Clair, Jean Cocteau, Marcel Pagnol, Jean Renoir, and Jean Vigo—alongside a number of mainstream films, lesser known today but equally intriguing in their experimentation. The filmmakers, composers, and critics who created and consumed these early sound films participated in both depicting and actively shaping the diverse soundscape of early 1930s French musical culture, demonstrating music's expressive power in film through their broad range of responses to the new technology.

THE TRANSITION TO SOUND

Although music had long been a part of silent cinema, throughout the first decades of the twentieth century inventors sought a technology that would lead to more precise and standardized musical synchronization. There was little widespread success until the mid-1920s, during a postwar growth in electrical research. The commercial viability of sound film first became apparent with the development of Vitaphone, a sound film technology owned by Warner Bros. and Western Electric in the United States. Warner Bros. first presented Vitaphone to the public in New York City in 1926, through a number of one-reel films and a feature, *Don Juan*, accompanied by a high-profile synchronized musical score. *The Jazz Singer* (1927), the first feature film with directly recorded synchronized dialogue and the film that is still commonly accepted in popular narratives as a turning point in the public acceptance of synchronized sound, appeared a year later. Other American studios quickly followed suit, and by the end of the 1920s the floodgates had opened.

As film historians have well documented, the "transition" period in Hollywood—from 1926 to around 1933—was a time of pronounced experimentation but also of surprisingly rapid aesthetic and economic codification within the American film industry.[2] Within a few short years practically all American films had become "100 percent talkies," featuring recorded and synced dialogue, sound effects, and music. Musical practices, too, shifted significantly in the late 1920s and early 1930s in Hollywood, becoming disrupted and then quickly recodified.[3]

While early sound film in Hollywood has been examined from a range of scholarly perspectives, the transition to sound in France, and the unique interactions between French sound cinema and French musical discourses, remains underexplored. The focus on the transition to sound in the United States reflects a broader scholarly bias toward Hollywood within film studies and film musicology. This bias is not surprising, given that synchronized sound technology was first successfully developed in America and that American production companies played a large role in the international dissemination of sound film technology and aesthetics. However, as a result of this focus on Hollywood, international films are often analyzed within the framework of American cinema, measured against an aesthetic standard that was by no means universal. In the United States, although there were a few outspoken opponents to synchronized sound, the industry adjusted with surprising rapidity, both economically and aesthetically. In France the transition to sound unfolded in fundamentally different ways: it was a hotly and publicly debated topic, eliciting widely divergent artistic responses. Sound cinema incited extensive aesthetic debate and experimentation, as filmmakers and composers attempted to define music's role in the new medium and determine how synchronized sound would affect cinematic style, form, and content. Examining other national filmmaking contexts, including France, complicates the apparent hegemony of Hollywood sound practices that continues to dominate film music scholarship.[4]

FRENCH FILMMAKING BEFORE THE TRANSITION ERA

Although each national film industry responded to the transition to sound in different and interesting ways, France serves as a particularly productive counterexample to Hollywood. France was often considered the medium's birthplace, and from early in its history, cinema had enjoyed a privileged cultural position there, alongside more commercial and popular associations. The country had been one of the international centers of film during cinema's early years, but World War I disrupted France's film industry, which could no longer compete with Hollywood. As a result, filmmakers focused on developing a distinctive French style, leading to a blossoming of experimentation in both narrative and nonnarrative cinematic avant-gardes. This experimental spirit, which was closely connected to musical practices and coupled with a sense of cultural nationalism, would go on to shape French approaches to music in the early sound era in significant ways.

A number of high-profile artistic movements made their mark on French filmmaking in the late 1910s and throughout the 1920s. French cinematic impressionism, which developed in the early 1920s and was led by filmmakers Louis Delluc, Abel Gance, Germaine Dulac, Jean Epstein, and Marcel L'Herbier, focused on using cinema as a means of representing subjectivity, rather than as a reflection of reality. A few years later, the *cinéma pur* ("pure cinema") movement emerged. *Cinéma pur* was a nonnarrative approach to cinema. The movement's advocates (most notably Henri Chomette and René Clair) argued for cinema's uniqueness as related to other artistic media. Rather than treating cinema simply as a tool for representing real life or recording theatrical productions, they used techniques like montage to demonstrate that cinema signified in and of itself. Visual artists from other mediums soon became interested in cinema: perhaps the most famous example is Fernand Léger with his cubist-inspired *Ballet mécanique* (1924). Additionally, in the 1920s, French surrealist artists and writers were among the first to take cinema seriously as a medium, embracing its potential for depicting dreamlike imagery. The lines between mainstream commercial and highbrow artistic filmmaking in France were much blurrier than they were in the United States, as were the lines between cinematic experiments and avant-garde movements in the visual arts.

Music was an important part of the conception of silent cinema in France. Many film theorists compared cinema to music, employing what David Bordwell later coined the "musical analogy."[5] As a time-based medium just like music, film was understood to contain some fundamental similarities, particularly when it came to film "rhythm" (made possible by cutting). Advocates of *cinéma pur* were particularly fond of the musical analogy, using music's abstraction to argue for cinema's similar capabilities. Émile Vuillermoz, a longtime music critic who also became one of France's most vocal film critics and theorists in the 1910s and 1920s, took the analogy perhaps the farthest, when he wrote of cinema:

> This form of development of thought, with its thematic echoes, its conducive motifs, its allusions, its rapid insinuations or slow solicitations, it is exactly like a symphony! The cinema orchestrates images, scores our visions and memories according to a strictly musical process: it must choose its visual themes, render them expressive, meticulously regulate their exposition, their opportune return,

their measure and rhythm, develop them, break them down into parts, reintro-
duce them in fragments, as the treatises on composition put it, through "aug-
mentation" or "diminution."[6]

There were also more explicit connections between modernist musical and
cinematic activities. French modernist composers had long demonstrated an
interest in composing for silent films. As early as 1908, Camille Saint-Saëns
had composed a score for the silent art film *L'Assassinat du duc de Guise*. The
avant-garde followed suit, most notably Erik Satie. In 1924, Satie composed
an original score for the Dadaist film *Entr'acte*, performed between the acts
of his ballet *Relâche*.[7] Members of Les Six had been fascinated with film since
the mid-1910s, and Arthur Honegger and Darius Milhaud both composed silent film scores, Honegger's scores for Abel Gance's films *La Roue* (1923) and
Napoléon (1927) being perhaps the best known. Avant-garde composers also
demonstrated their interest in cinema through references to the new medium
in their live works. Satie's *Parade* (1917), with its reference to the American
film serial *The Perils of Pauline*, is one well-known example. As Scott Paulin
has shown, the internationally renowned silent film comedian Charlie Chaplin
was frequently referenced in the ballets of the Ballets Suédois, including
Honegger's *Skating Rink*.[8] Milhaud's *Le Bœuf sur le toit* (1921) was also inspired by silent film, intended as a film score to a nonexistent Charlie Chaplin
film. Crucial to the "art of the everyday" aesthetic of Les Six, cinema was one
of the forms of popular entertainment that fascinated avant-garde French
composers and served as a source of inspiration in many of their works.[9]

Filmmaking in France was also unique because of its particular network
and distribution of film theory and criticism. Since the 1910s, journals and
newspapers supported a robust film criticism, in both general publications
with devoted film columns and in journals dedicated specifically to film.
Film columns were not unique to France—there is a healthy list of American
periodicals from the 1910s and 1920s devoted exclusively or in part to
films and filmmaking. However, whereas American publications were typically either geared toward industry or fan readerships, French publications
paid much greater attention to broader theoretical and ontological issues.
Filmmakers continuously articulated their theories of cinema as they enacted
them in their films. Composers, musicians, artists, and filmmakers were also
constantly in interaction, reading each other's writings, collaborating, and
attending each other's events. Film critics overlapped with cultural critics of
all kinds, including those involved in theater and the visual arts. Composers,
too, dove into the medium, writing frequently about music's role in cinema.
Many of the earliest film theories emerged from this context. The country was
also home to the first ciné-clubs, which hosted lectures, film screenings, and
discussions. In 1921, an informal group of artists, writers, and professional
filmmakers formed the C.A.S.A. ("Club des amis du septième art"), gathering

regularly at the Café Napolitain to discuss film. Regular attendees of this club included a number of filmmakers, critics, writers, actors, and composers, including Arthur Honegger, Maurice Ravel, Alexis Roland-Manuel, and Maurice Jaubert.[10]

Additionally, the 1920s saw the development of an alternative cinema circuit that screened avant-garde and experimental films, with the Théâtre du Vieux Colombier opening in 1924, the Studio des Ursulines in 1925, and Studio 28 in 1928. Each of these movie theaters paid careful attention to music: at the Vieux Colombier, a chamber orchestra prepared music specially for each program, and the Studio des Ursulines also had a chamber orchestra. A mechanical piano accompanied films at Studio 28.[11]

Thus, perhaps it is not surprising that the transition to synchronized sound in France would prompt a unique intersection of technology, musical modernism, popular music and culture, and the avant-garde. While we must understand the French film industry within its global context, an in-depth examination of French film music on its own terms is a productive means of expanding on, nuancing, and diversifying our understanding of early sound film aesthetics.

MUSIC AND THE TRANSITION TO SOUND IN FRANCE

By the early 1930s, the economic, technological, and aesthetic disruptions in Hollywood caused by the transition to synchronized sound had mainly subsided, as sound and music practices in American cinema became increasingly codified. But Hollywood's transition had global implications. American and German companies held key patents to sound synchronization technology, and members of the French film industry felt powerless to stop these international corporate forces from infiltrating the French market.[12] This pressure from abroad contributed to a deep ambivalence that prevailed among many French directors over the adoption of the new technology. Many critics and filmmakers feared that the dawn of sound film would eliminate the possibility of a French national cinema, on account of the dominance of Hollywood imports.

There were also philosophical objections to synchronized sound. Sound film threatened to destroy France's *septième art*. Sound cinema was, according to some critics and filmmakers, "a savage invention" that threatened to destroy existing cinematic practices.[13] For one thing, critics and film practitioners were concerned that with their reliance on spoken dialogue talkies would lose the purported universality of silent cinema. Additionally, once the debate over the mere existence of synchronized sound subsided, there remained a division of opinion regarding how best to add sound to image. Some spoke out as ardent supporters and others as staunch critics of emergent sound film practices (many of which were borrowed from Hollywood), and a number of French directors made films that resounded both as commercial endeavors and as ideological manifestos on the new medium.

Music became an important point of contestation and experimentation for filmmakers and theorists. In a direct sense, for those opposed to what was seen as a redundancy between sound and image in synchronized spoken dialogue, music had the potential to disrupt or silence the speaking voice. It could move a film away from realism and toward fantasy or abstraction. Characters could sing rather than speak, prompting an especially artificial aesthetic unmoored from the confines of realism. At the same time, it could ground a film in a particular time and place, through realist musical signifiers of cultural groups or environments. Cinema became, in the words of Richard Barrios, "a testing ground,"[14] and filmmakers experimented with questions prompted by the new technology before practices were institutionalized or standardized.

During the transition era, music sometimes took on even greater power as an *idea* than as an actual component of the soundtrack. For many filmmakers and theorists writing in early 1930s France, music was a theoretical concept that sound film could or should emulate in various ways. The musical analogy reemerged in important ways, and music became a powerful metaphor for film theorists attempting to define the new medium. Rather than emphasizing spoken dialogue and realism, for instance, one director suggested that sound cinema could become a "grand visual and sonic symphony."[15] One concept that emerged in France during the transition era was that of *phonogénie*. The neologism was an aural equivalent to *photogénie*, a term that had been coined by Louis Delluc in 1920 to describe the unique quality that people or objects can obtain when they are photographed or filmed, which allowed cinema to go beyond reproducing reality and elevate it to art.[16] *Phonogénie*, coined by director Jean Epstein and used by film composers like Maurice Jaubert, was similarly broad in its scope and concept. It was usually clearer to critics when a soundtrack was "unphonogenic"—most commonly the result of using too full an orchestra or instruments whose registers were difficult to record with fidelity—but some practitioners took care to consider actively what a phonogenic film should sound like.

Discussions surrounding music's role in sound film folded into long-held debates regarding French musical styles and genres. Contestations within France's musical life came to the fore as French filmmaking practices provided a unique context for the intersection of modernist artistic tendencies (including surrealism), popular entertainment (such as cabaret and music-hall), and recording technology. The introduction of synchronized sound technology presented an opportunity for avant-garde and popular genres to interact in new ways, resulting in different aesthetic experiments from those of the 1920s.

During the transition era, a wide range of composers from diverse cultural contexts tried their hands at composition. Some had experience composing for silent films but many worked in cinema for the first time. Many modernist composers were in the same circles as filmmakers and followed trends and debates in cinema closely. The list of transition-era composers includes members of Les Six—Georges Auric, Arthur Honegger, and Darius Milhaud—as well as Jean Wiéner (who was part of Les Six's larger artistic circle); established art composers Jacques Ibert and Henri Sauguet; light operetta composers whose compositions had widespread popular appeal, like Georges Van Parys, Philippe Parès, Raoul Moretti, and Maurice Yvain; and international or émigré composers like Werner Heymann and Hanns Eisler. Thus, the film score in transition-era France exhibited a range of sounds, styles, and compositional approaches.

While there was no specific French "sound" distinguishing French transition-era scoring from film music practices of other nations, early sound films nevertheless reflected national musical priorities more broadly. Just like on the concert stage, neoclassical musical styles were frequently heard on the soundtrack. Orchestration preferences also often distinguished French film scores from their international counterparts. One specific example is the predominance of the saxophone in orchestral arrangements, much more so than in American scores of the same era. Similarly, accordion became a musical marker of Frenchness in film, owing to its importance in popular music styles. Perhaps not surprisingly, French directors were often critical of overly "commercial" uses of music in films—such as song plugging, or cross-marketing of popular music—which they deemed to be too "Hollywood." But French popular music was abundant in transition-era films. French popular dance styles like the *bal-musette* and *java*, and performances by *chanteurs* and *chanteuses* well known for their stage and recording careers made their way onto numerous soundtracks as distinct markers of Frenchness, as Kelley Conway has shown,[17] but also as clever methods of transmedia synergy and cross-marketing (leading to sheet music and record sales), concerns about Hollywood-like commercialization notwithstanding. Additionally, before the transition to sound, composers had also shown a broader interest in mechanical music, writing works for player piano and exhibiting fascination with the capabilities of the phonograph; the interest in composing for sound films stemmed in part from this broader interest in mechanical music. These and other technologies of music reproduction—radios, player pianos—were often featured onscreen in films, as a means of drawing the spectator's attention to the film's recorded soundtrack. These various musical approaches, while in many cases connected to audiovisual practices in Hollywood and elsewhere in Europe, also demonstrate the particular ways in which French musical culture impacted the sounds of French cinema.

The introduction of recording and playback technology also led to changes in who made decisions about sound and music. With synchronized sound, directors could suddenly make musical decisions for their films, and they could conceive of music as an integral part of their overall cinematic aesthetic. Thus, while films are inherently collaborative texts and composers played important roles in developing musical styles in early sound cinema, the artistic decisions made by directors also substantially shaped the cinematic soundscape of the period. Because some directors placed great importance on music as a theoretical concept, I consider the score as a combined product of composers' and directors' creative decisions, which allows me to consider both musical styles and broader questions about how music interacted with the moving image.[18]

COMPETING CONCEPTIONS OF SOUND FILM

Opposing narratives of the early sound era have often described it as either a period of crisis or of continuity.[19] But the reality was somewhere between easy transition and total rupture. As filmmakers sought to establish new audiovisual traditions, sound film was informed by a constellation of related existing practices, including silent film and silent film accompaniment, live theater, various live musical forms (opera, operetta, vaudeville, music-hall), and other media of recorded sound. Communications scholar Carolyn Marvin has suggested that new media "are always introduced into a pattern of tension created by the coexistence of old and new";[20] this was very much the case during the transition era, as filmmakers drew on existing silent film and live musical practices while simultaneously making self-conscious attempts to move away from them. The excitement of synchronized sound partly had to do with its multiplicity of potentialities: musical accompaniment, the audiovisual capturing of live performance, and sound effects, just to name a few. This made the new medium a site of rich creative energy.

Working in the aftermath of substantial technological change, filmmakers' curiosities and anxieties surrounding new media were manifested in an abundant reflexivity within early sound film. Filmmakers, grappling with the cultural and aesthetic implications of the new technology, overtly explored the possibilities of recorded music in film. Rather than hiding or suppressing the technological underpinnings of sound cinema, filmmakers were aware of their technological intervention and often foregrounded the reproduced nature of sound and music, frequently depicting recording technology narratively on the screen, such as in the final scene from *Prix de beauté*. The phonograph frequently became a stand-in for the entire sound film mechanism, allowing directors the opportunity to use recorded sound in a range of contexts: as a magical new tool, as a narrative justification for musical realism, or as an unruly machine. Conversely, sound cinema's aesthetic proximity to different forms of live theater—spoken theater, opera, operetta, musical theater, and vaudeville—was the subject of much debate. Silent cinema had been connected to various forms of live theater since its invention, but in the transition era issues of liveness and mediation came to the fore: in particular, voices onscreen and their relationship to the film's diegetic world became a site of experimentation. Song as a recorded entity became an agent for narrative development and action. By exploring the different ways body and voice could fit together using both recorded sound and image, directors called attention to the cinematic apparatus itself, and the different possibilities it offered that were distinct from live performance. In these ways, the films themselves offered audiences a metacommentary on sound film technology.

There was also a range of approaches to realism versus abstraction in early sound film. At the start of cinema's history, reality and fantasy seemed to be two very separate modes of filmmaking, exemplified in the documentary-style films of the Lumière brothers on the one hand and the fantastical films of Georges Méliès on the other. A strain of silent filmmaking, rooted in pictorial naturalism of the nineteenth century, had already placed high value on cinema's potential to capture reality. In the 1920s, impressionist filmmakers reacted against this style of filmmaking, self-consciously using cinema to represent subjectivity rather than an objective form of reality. The advocates of pure cinema took the idea of abstraction even further.

These long-held debates in French filmmaking were reignited with a new set of challenges in the era of sound. For some film practitioners, the realist potential of sound cinema was its most attractive feature. Sound was a means of expanding cinema's capabilities to reproduce reality, particularly when it came to spoken dialogue. Indeed, the novelty of speech was so pervasive as to be a fundamental selling point for the new medium, and many early sound films focused on spoken dialogue at the expense of other audiovisual possibilities. The predominance of dialogue affected music's role in the soundtrack, in many cases diminishing its importance, particularly in adaptations of theatrical boulevard comedies, where music was rare. This emphasis on dialogue subsequently informed some of the most important theories of film sound and film music, which have focused on an industry that almost always favored realism and narrative clarity.[21]

But other filmmakers of the period wanted cinema to remain a more abstract mode of storytelling. Filmmakers who were committed to developing a cinematic language akin to audiovisual "poetry" avoided the more realist possibilities offered by spoken dialogue. Instead, music became crucial to many filmmakers, figuring prominently into their definition of "poetic" sound film forms. Sometimes filmmakers drew on the "unrealistic" modes of delivery of opera and musical theater, using songs, instead of spoken words, to tell the story; and other times, music covered up or silenced the possibility for other, more realist sounds, prompting visual abstraction that was not bound to speech. These ideas were taken up in a range of genres and forms. Music, as an artificial art form vis-à-vis spoken dialogue, figured prominently into the definition of "artificial," "unrealistic" sound film forms.

Many of the themes discussed here are not entirely unique to France. The French film industry was one of many national contexts with a distinctive response to sound film, a number of which are equally worthy of in-depth study. And no single national film industry was insulated from the international responses around them: the transition to sound in France would not have unfolded in the way it did if not for the mutual influence of Hollywood and Germany's film industry, for instance, or for the number of émigrés in France who brought with them their experience working in the film industries in their home countries. The writings of Soviet filmmakers also impacted French film theorists in formative ways. At the same time, the French response to sound film and the long-term impact of the debates taking place in France during the transition era stand out in many respects. It was a European center for film theory and production, and it remained that way in the later decades of the twentieth century, impacting cinematic practices globally. Many French filmmakers worked in America during World War II, adapting their aesthetics and artistic priorities for Hollywood's more rigid studio system. Perhaps more importantly, the experiments that emerged out of the Nouvelle Vague (New Wave) in the 1950s and 1960s impacted filmmaking on an international scale. And French film theory profoundly shaped the direction of cinema studies in the decades that followed. These aspects of France's cinematic history can be understood as extensions of the discourses and experiments that began in the 1920s and 1930s. By delving into this particular moment in France's musical-cinematic practices, we can not only gain deeper insight into the many, nuanced roles that music played in the transition era but also better understand film music within the broader context of French cinema's global impact over the course of the twentieth century.

FROM THEORY TO PRACTICE

My argument progresses more or less chronologically (but not rigidly so), and each chapter builds on the others thematically, as discussion surrounding film music in France moved from theory to practice. Chapter 1 focuses on the discourse around sound film and examines sound film's arrival in France as articulated by the French press. Before sound film even appeared in France, journalists, composers, and filmmakers weighed in on their opinions about the new form and its possible aesthetic applications. The debates in the French press surrounding sound film's possible applications and the technology's effects on its national filmmaking style reveal how sound cinema, and music's role within it, emerged from a different conceptual model in France than in the United States. Furthermore, they reveal a range of potential applications for the new medium, as understood by composers, directors, journalists, and audiences.

My second chapter turns to avant-garde filmmakers Jean Cocteau and Luis Buñuel, who were both closely connected to French modernist artistic and musical circles. Their controversial early sound films—*Le Sang d'un poète* (1930) by Cocteau and *L'Age d'or* (1930) by Buñuel—brought sound film into the realm of surrealism. In different ways, each film employed music as a tool for audiovisual juxtaposition, pastiche, and shock value. I argue that much of the initial public outrage surrounding these two films was connected to the iconoclastic manner in which their directors manipulated the musical soundtrack. Music's role in the surrealist movement was contested; but instead of demonstrating that there was no place for music in surrealist cinema, these experiments reveal just how crucial music was for a surrealist audiovisual cinematic conception. While these experiments proved short-lived, they offer a glimpse into a style of audiovisual filmmaking that was most closely aligned with modernist musical practices of the 1920s, in terms of the participants involved, their aesthetic priorities, and the institutional structures in which they were funded and supported.

The third chapter focuses on several French-language musical films that were produced by American and German companies but intended for French audiences. Since French production lagged behind its German and American counterparts, many French directors, composers, and actors got their start with German- and American-produced films. One particularly important subset of these international productions was the genre of the *opérette filmée* (filmed operetta). Drawing influence from a range of stage genres from different national contexts, the *opérette filmée* became a successful site of negotiation, both critically and commercially, of international filmmaking styles and specifically French aesthetic concerns. Contributing to a broader critical acceptance of sound film in France, the internationally produced *opérette filmée* makes clear the extent to which musical performance on screen could simultaneously, and paradoxically, be seen to enact an aesthetic specifically designed for a particular national audience *and* make it internationally appealing.

In chapter 4, I focus on the famous debate between playwright Marcel Pagnol and film director René Clair. Pagnol regarded film as a recording medium for live theater, and gained success by writing screenplays that emphasized spoken dialogue and downplayed music's role in the soundtrack. His *Fanny* trilogy epitomized the "recorded live theater" approach to sound cinema, which was pervasive, and incredibly popular, during the early years of sound film, even while *théâtre filmé* was frequently disparaged in the press. Clair, on the other hand, feared that realistic sound would threaten cinema's poetic potential. His first sound films of the period served as both critiques of existing practices and alternative models for film's sound–image relationship. His second sound film, *Le Million* (1931), relied heavily on live musical-theatrical forms, namely opera and operetta, bringing opera and sound film closer together and forcing the two genres to confront each other in their similarities and their differences. The debate between Pagnol and Clair, which was expressed both in the press and in their films, reveals diverging approaches to sound film, the aesthetic connections and tensions between live theater (straight theater and operetta) and cinema, and music's importance in articulating those tensions.

Recorded sound and music—particularly diegetic music—also offered new tools and possibilities for representing reality. Chapter 5 focuses on the role of diegetic music in early poetic realist films. Poetic realism, the filmmaking genre that emerged out of the politics of the mid-1930s, had its roots in transition-era films by directors such as Jean Grémillon, Julien Duvivier, Jacques Feyder, and perhaps most notably, Jean Renoir. The soundtracks of these filmmakers tended to favor a "realistic" incorporation of music into the narrative, an aesthetic decision grounded in a broader preference for direct re-cording in France, and frequently featured popular songs and street musicians to enhance the realism of a film's setting. But diegetic music in early poetic realist films was often multivalent: it contributed to a film's realism, but it also revealed the emotions or thoughts of characters, provided narrative commen-tary, and at times went against the expectations of a scene's mood or actions. Considering diegetic music in early poetic realist sound films problematizes the presumed "realism" of their soundtracks, showing the ways in which audi-ovisual realism and stylization worked hand in hand.

In my final chapter, I focus on one particularly well-known case of con-flict surrounding a film's music: the 1934 film *L'Atalante*. The second collabo-ration between experimental French filmmaker Jean Vigo and film composer Maurice Jaubert, *L'Atalante* has become an international favorite of film lovers. But its initial release was disastrous. As Vigo was on his deathbed, the film's distributors, finding *L'Atalante* narratively incoherent, attempted to make it more broadly accessible: they edited the film substantially, replacing parts of Jaubert's score with the popular song "Le Chaland qui passe" and renaming the film after the hit tune. The distributors' changes subtly altered an im-portant narrative subtext of the film: its reflexive fixation on synchronized sound film, expressed through its focus on musical playback technologies—phonographs, radios, and music boxes—and their ability to captivate. I trace the differences between the two versions of *L'Atalante*, arguing that Vigo's fascination with mediated music and its ability to create a magical cinematic world, and the distributors' attempt to fit the film's music into a commercially successful paradigm, reflect continuing concerns from both sides about how mediated sound would affect French cinema in the mid-1930s.

Many of the most innovative early sound films are often given the pejora-tive title "transitional." Transitional moments are messy. They are difficult to make sense of, because artists were often struggling to make sense of their own moment even as they participated in it. It is more straightforward to understand "mature" technological or musical practices once these messy moments have stabilized. Indeed, this period of filmmaking opened up many possibilities, but the possibilities narrowed significantly once sound film aesthetics became more fully standardized. As such, the films that do not fit into a particular evolution of sound and musical practices tend to be understood as aesthetic anomalies or teleological dead-ends, appearing before the standardization of classic cinema in the United States and France.[22] But the moment of technological change prompted a period of rich creativity and experimentation that was particularly widespread. These figures, their films, and the discourse on music and image they were contributing to the debate reveal alternative directions that the sound-image relationship might have taken. While these concerns were expressed most emphatically in the years immediately following the adoption of synchronized sound, the implications of these debates continued to shape musical cinematic practices of the later twentieth century. Furthermore, the stakes of these debates during the transition era have resonated with each new moment of widespread technological transformation, as artists again confront the old and new in a struggle to redefine their practices. The films created during this crucial aesthetic juncture force us to reconsider our assumptions about the relationship between music and the moving image, reminding us of its malleability, particularly during moments of technological change, and providing us with opportunities to challenge our understanding of how genres, media, and artistic forms relate to one another.

CHAPTER 1

Imagining Sound Film

Debates in the Press

In late 1928, Alexandre Arnoux, writer and editor of the new weekly cinema journal *Pour Vous*, traveled to London to see the first talkie projected in Europe. Reporting back to his readers, he expressed concerns about the new technology's effect on the future of cinema:

> I love the cinema deeply. Its play with black and white, its silence, its rhythmic chain of images, and its relegation of speech—that old human enslavement—to the background, seemed to me to be the promises of a marvelous art. And here comes a savage invention to destroy it all. Forgive my bitterness, my unfairness. After having worked so hard, hoped for so much, for film to ultimately return to a formula as hackneyed as the theater, to be defeated by the tyranny of language and of noise, exacerbated again by a mechanical intermediary![1]

Arnoux was far from alone in this sentiment. Two years earlier, in 1926, *Don Juan*, the first commercially successful synchronized sound film, appeared in the United States. By the end of 1928, sound film's future had become more or less a certainty in Hollywood, as studios rapidly made the technological changeover and theaters rushed to wire for sound.[2] But the French public had barely begun to experience sound film firsthand, and there were many reasons—nationalist, economic, and aesthetic—that filmmakers were concerned about French cinema's future.

Arnoux went on to suggest that the cinema was at a crossroads: "We can't stay indifferent. We are witnessing a death or a birth, impossible to tell which. . . . *Second birth or death?* That is the question that is facing cinema."[3] This statement was a call to arms: French filmmakers could work to keep cinema alive and play an active role in shaping the future of the medium. French critics quickly and prolifically articulated their thoughts in the press, aiming to make aesthetic sense of the new technology; and the tone and language they used to express their opinions reveals just how high the stakes felt for many involved. In these first years when French sound film was struggling to find its voice, the press was anything but silent.

With great concern about developments in Hollywood, journalists, composers, and filmmakers alike spilled ink on the subject of sound cinema before the technology had even arrived in France. As French audiences began to be exposed to foreign sound films and directors in France experimented with making sound films of their own, critics continued to write prescriptively about the new form, articulating what they believed sound film should and should not be. This particular kind of working-out of aesthetic questions in print was unique to the French film industry for two important reasons. First, France observed the early stages of Hollywood's adoption of synchronized sound from afar, giving critics the opportunity to comment on the technology well before most filmmakers and audience members had any firsthand exposure to synchronized sound.

Second, unlike Hollywood, whose publications on film were mainly limited to trade journals (such as *Film Daily* and the *Journal of the Society of Motion Picture Engineers*) and fan magazines (including *Photoplay* and *Variety*), many French publications devoted extensive space to discourse on film aesthetics—including *Cinémagazine, Mon ciné, Ciné-Miroir, Cinéa-Ciné pour tous, Pour Vous, Cinémonde*, and *La Revue du cinéma*, as well as other publications not devoted exclusively to film, like the cultural journal *Comœdia* and many daily newspapers—giving a range of stakeholders a platform for articulating new theories of sound film. The sheer quantity of discourse from this era is astounding, as indicated by an examination of the extensive clippings found in the Auguste Rondel collection at the Bibliothèque Nationale de France.[4] Critics, directors, screenwriters, playwrights, musicians, and composers all contributed to these discussions in the press. In these accounts, the potential energy of the industry on the cusp of adopting synchronized sound is palpable, in both its excitement and its anxiety.

Amid these debates about synchronized sound, music became a powerful metaphor. Many critics, particularly silent directors, frequently returned to what David Bordwell has called the "musical analogy," a concept commonly used to describe silent cinema by French impressionist and Soviet filmmakers interested in the nonrepresentational possibilities of cinema.[5] The return of the musical analogy was a response to the heightened realism brought to cinema by recorded synchronized dialogue and the perceived threat of theatrical conventions on the new medium. Advocates of *cinéma pur* in particular believed that the new sound film should emulate music's abstract, poetic qualities. Though the particulars of the musical analogy in an audiovisual context were not fully defined, its predominance in discussions of the aesthetic possibilities for sound film's future points to the importance of the *idea* of music in the early discourse surrounding sound cinema. The soundtrack could also turn directors into composers, allowing them to manipulate sounds (and images) to "compose" a film's soundtrack as if it were a musical score. Musicians and composers, too, expressed their opinions on sound film. Many musicians were concerned about the future of their livelihood, as synchronized sound threatened to eliminate the live theater orchestra. At the same time, modernist composers were intrigued by the invention, considering it not just a new technology but also a new musical medium, bringing with it its own distinct compositional concerns.

This chapter examines the debates in the French press surrounding sound film's possible applications, the technology's effects on national filmmaking practices, and music's role in defining these parameters. I focus on 1928 through 1930, the earliest years of widespread French engagement with discourse on sound film, and a period before the French film industry itself had adjusted to changes happening abroad. These debates reveal how the new medium was by no means a fixed entity for composers, directors, journalists, or audiences in France during its early years. They also demonstrate how sound cinema was built from a different model and framework for cinema in France than in the United States, reflecting different aesthetic priorities. Furthermore, they provide a glimpse into a broader range of possible applications for sound in cinema, at least as understood by French filmmakers and musicians.

SOUND FILM COMES TO FRANCE: STRUGGLE, AMBIVALENCE, DEBATE

The French reaction to sound film was intertwined with the broader international economics of synchronized sound. By 1929, as American companies turned their attention to producing sound films, they saw Europe, particularly France, as an available market: installing sound equipment and distributing sound films in countries that had not yet developed the technology to do so themselves promised to be a lucrative endeavor. The United States had dominated world markets since World War I, and American companies' patents on sound synchronization technologies gave them a distinct advantage over the film industries in other countries. In early 1928, the American companies ERPI and RCA gained control of the American patents to sound synchronization technology and soon turned their eyes toward Europe. Engineers from two European companies, the mainly Dutch-owned Tobis and the German company Klangfilm, were concurrently developing competing sound synchronization technology. In 1929, these companies merged to create the conglomerate Tobis-Klangfilm, aiming to corner the European market and shut out their American rivals. Through patent disputes, Tobis-Klangfilm attempted to stall the installation of American sound equipment in European studios and movie houses, hoping to obstruct what they saw as an inevitable "talkie invasion" by American studios.[6] French producer Léon Gaumont attempted to counter with his alternate sound synchronization system, but it did not gain enough commercial traction to stop Tobis-Klangfilm and RCA's proliferation.

In the summer of 1930, representatives from Tobis-Klangfilm and members of the American film industry conferred on neutral ground in Paris. An international cartel was established during this "Paris Agreement," and the German and American companies decided to split up much of the world for patent rights and charge film companies royalties for distribution within each territory. France was excluded from the Paris Agreement entirely: the United States and Germany dictated the terms of exchange, economically exploiting other countries.[7] Moreover, Hollywood's vertically integrated studio system contributed to its rapid transition and codification of practices after the introduction of synchronized sound; but French production companies were much smaller, and relied on different freelance workers for each film, which meant that studios in France were much slower to standardize, setting them even further back in adjusting to sound. As a result, sound films initially arrived in France primarily through an influx of American- and German-made films into the French market.

Thus, the transition to sound was imposed on French filmmakers, resulting in deep ambivalence by many French directors over cinema's transformation.[8] Film historian Dudley Andrew asserts, "there was concern about the kinds of films being made. The French were, in general, stridently opposed to the very existence of the sound film, if for no other reason than that it meant further dominance of themes and styles by Hollywood. For the first few years these fears were absolutely justified."[9] Sound film appeared to be a strong arm of American imperialism, seeking to wrest aesthetic control of cinema from French filmmakers. For these reasons, many French critics and film practitioners were apprehensive about sound film's arrival. Behind the surface of aesthetic conversations lurked economic and nationalist concerns: many critics believed that something as commercially motivated as Hollywood's conversion to sound could not be good for the art of cinema.

French audiences were exposed to sound cinema in small and inconsistent doses, another factor that delayed France's widespread adoption of synchronized sound. The first sound films screened in Europe were in London in 1928. Some French writers and directors made the trek to England in order to observe firsthand the technology that had already garnered considerable attention in the press. Soon after (by late 1928), the first feature-length sound films began to appear in Paris.[10] Gaumont presented the first French sound film, *L'Eau du Nil*, a silent film with a postsynchronized score, in 1928, before any American sound films were screened in France. The first American sound film to arrive in France was the MGM film with a postsynchronized score,

Ombres blanches (*White Shadows of the South Seas*), in November 1928 at the Madeleine-Cinéma; *Les Ailes* (*Wings*) soon followed.[11] On January 26, 1929, *The Jazz Singer* (known as *Le Chanteur du jazz*) premiered at the Aubert-Palace, and was a huge success.[12] The French film industry, temporarily in crisis, produced only fifty-two films in 1929, compared to ninety-four in 1928; many were silent films that were already in production before the changeover. The first French-language talking film, *Les Trois Masques*, was filmed in England and premiered in 1929. By the end of 1929, French talkies were beginning to be made in French studios; the film *Chiqué*, a half-hour-long boulevard comedy, was the first French-language talkie to be filmed in France. By 1930, the majority of films coming from the French industry were sound films.[13] But French movie theaters were not yet consistently wired for sound; the cost of installation was often prohibitive, and many movie theaters, particularly in rural areas, were still showing silent films into the mid-1930s.[14] For the first few years, therefore, the French public was exposed to a hodge-podge of talkies and postsynchronized films from the United States, France, and other parts of Europe, many hastily produced, with no unified audiovisual aesthetic approach. But aesthetic debates about sound film had started even before international economic factors came into play.

CRITICAL CONCERNS: REALISM, THEATER, AND THE SPOKEN WORD

The subject of sound film was discussed in France as early as 1927, before it had even found secure footing in Hollywood. News and secondhand accounts of the American talkies arrived in France before any films actually did, giving French critics plenty of time to express their thoughts about the new medium before experiencing it firsthand. Therefore, the first discussions about sound film in the press were purely speculative, based not on experience but on conjecture. That did not stop writers from contemplating the possible benefits and drawbacks of sound cinema and realism, the new medium's relationship to silent cinema and to live theater, and the power of the spoken word on the recorded soundtrack.

It is important to mention that writers discussed both the *film sonore* and the *film parlant*, a technical distinction with aesthetic significance.[15] A *film sonore* ("sound film") was a film with a postsynchronized soundtrack, where music, sound effects, and sometimes dialogue were added to a silent image after filming. A *film parlant*, or "talking film," recorded dialogue at the same time as the image. By about 1930, most films combined the two practices, but they were still understood to have distinct aesthetic possibilities. In the press, writers sometimes singled out *films sonores* or *films parlants* for discussion, but the two were often conflated.

Some critics were excited by sound cinema's prospects. In June 1929, several months after the first sound films were screened in Paris, filmmaker Jacques Feyder expressed an optimistic perspective on the new medium, declaring that the talking film "is unquestionably the future of cinema, both commercially and industrially, everywhere and very soon. . . . But I'll go further: the sound film permits all the possibilities of a broadened cinematographic 'art,' finally delivered from intertitles, augmented by every sonorous emotion."[16] For Feyder, silent film was an "incomplete instrument," and sound film completed it:

> To cinematic rhythm, which is still essential, have been added and blended the innumerable rhythms of the sounds of music and speech; infinite conjugations which are making of the sound cinema a complete mode of expression of an unlimited richness, a spectacle with more numerous possibilities than silent cinema, theater, and music hall combined.

For Feyder, sound film offered far more possibilities than silent film, the addition of the soundtrack adding new artistic dimensions to cinema that surpassed all existing art forms. Feyder's excitement led him to Hollywood, where he worked on his first sound films, moving there in 1929 and not returning to France until 1933.

Many of the most enthusiastic proponents of the new technology were playwrights and stage actors, eager for the possibilities of permanence that sound film offered for live theatrical forms. Playwright, actor, and director Sacha Guitry, for instance, explained,

> Until now, I was only interested in a very few films. But I believe that the coming of sound film is something very important. Important for everyone: first, for film actors, who, if they find themselves incapable of interpreting dialogue for films effectively one day, can be replaced by stage actors the next. For the public, for whom talking cinema will bring all at once the voices and the performances of actors who they never could go and hear in the theater. Finally, theater directors who put on mediocre plays will have to defend themselves against very strong competition.[17]

Guitry's perspective may seem unsympathetic toward both film and theater personnel, but for Guitry, sound film's ability to disseminate recorded theatrical performances to a broader public could also offer a healthy dose of competition to live theater, from which both live and recorded forms would benefit in quality. Playwright Marcel Pagnol, one of the subjects of chapter 4, also praised the audiovisual recording capabilities of sound film for the theater: "From now on, we can achieve effects that have been unattainable onstage."[18] Guitry and Pagnol's remarks anticipated an influx of theatrical adaptations for the screen that would begin in 1929 and continue well through the transition era. Indeed, the adaptation of stage productions—realist and naturalist dramas, vaudeville farces, operettas, boulevard comedies, and music-hall performances—became a widespread and long-standing practice in the French film industry following the introduction of sound film, as I discuss in greater detail in chapters 3 and 4.[19] They highlighted the unity between body and voice, newly possible with synchronized sound, and they provided the film industry with numerous ready-made stories and scripts that could be lucratively adapted for the screen.

But not everyone shared Feyder's, Guitry's, and Pagnol's enthusiasm for sound film. For others, talkies' aesthetic proximity to live theater was detrimental to cinema's ontology. Giving precedence to spoken dialogue at the expense of the visual, relegating the image to a subordinate role, would undermine cinema's status as a primarily mute art form. It seemed neither desirable nor inevitable that the French industry would adopt the new technology. Critic François Mazeline felt this sentiment so strongly when he wrote in 1928 that he assumed (or perhaps pleaded) that French audiences would not accept sound film:

> The dreadful monster has been born. Already in the United States, and soon in France, projection apparatuses, synchronized with phonographic playing devices, will be installed.
>
> The Cinema is, by definition, a mute Art. It is a sort of ideographic writing; the opposite of the spoken word. To create a talking cinema is to create a bad rival to theater for poor neighborhoods. . . . The future of talking cinema is therefore limited. The monster is inoffensive and powerless.[20]

Mazeline simultaneously feared sound film's power and believed French filmmakers and audiences would not accept its intrusion into their filmgoing experience. *Ami du peuple* critic L. P. also saw theater and cinema as incompatible:

> Cinema is the art of movement.
>
> Theater is the art of the spoken word.
>
> Allow me to explain: in theater, only the spoken word is important. All the rest—mise-en-scène, the actor's performance, etc., only serve to showcase the spoken word.
>
> However, the spoken word is the enemy of movement.[21]

Although L. P.'s definition of theater may have been reductive, for this critic and many others, theatrical adaptation was synonymous with overreliance on the spoken word, which would result in reduced camera movement and render sound film less "cinematic." This concern was not unfounded: in many of the earliest sound films, cameras had to remain more or less static, with minimal editing, in order for voices to be captured by the microphone.

Not only did spoken dialogue bring sound film into the realm of theater, it also imposed a degree of realism not previously required of film. For many directors, particularly those who were interested in *cinéma pur*, film's dreamlike qualities could only be brought out by eschewing realism. They valued cinema as a poetic, abstract form, in many respects a visual equivalent to music; and with dialogue, cinema would lose this possibility. Avant-garde filmmaker Robert Desnos wrote, for instance,

> Talking film has been discovered and it announces to us a complete transformation of cinema.
>
> Cinema! It should be entirely at the service of dreams. Here it will fall into the hands of bad literature and of realism.[22]

Impressionist director Marcel L'Herbier was also concerned about the future of cinema with the addition of audiovisual realism. In January 1929, he confessed in the film journal *Mon ciné*,

> Talking film, as it exists at the moment, interests me little. The faithful reproduction of an actor's words or the entrance of a locomotive into a station doesn't have any genuine artistic value.... Cinema has become—with much struggle—an original, independent art.... It would be disastrous if our taking advantage of technological progress set us back, artistically speaking.[23]

For L'Herbier, audiovisual realism went against the grain of cinema's art, which had taken decades to establish. Filmmaker Henri Chomette agreed, and was also concerned that synchronized sound would invert the sound-image hierarchy, where the image would play a lesser role than spoken dialogue. He claimed in 1929,

> It is certain that, thanks to talking film, we will want to record plays, operettas, and music-hall revues and proceed in this way toward a sort of vulgarization and artistic diffusion of certain works. This could be of considerable commercial interest, but, in my opinion, the future of talking film isn't that. Just because we can now join word and sound with image, let's not commit the error of quickly relegating the image to the role of the poor parent. A filmed and sonorized piece of theater, it will only be a "dialogue accompanied by images," where everything is sacrificed for dialogue.[24]

Chomette and his brother, René Clair (discussed at length in chapter 4), both feared that spoken dialogue would cause cinema to lose its capacity for poetry.

Not only did the talkies relegate the image to a secondary role, the spoken word also threatened the perceived universality of cinema, a crucial characteristic of the *septième art*. Because spoken dialogue by its very nature reduced a film's audience to those who spoke a particular language, talkies would make the international dissemination of films much more difficult. "The film must remain mute," implored poet Benjamin Fondane in 1930. Speech "created gulfs early on between individuals," and would do so again if talkies successfully overtook silent cinema.[25] Dialogue limited a film's potential to reach across national borders and language barriers.

For all of these various reasons—sound cinema's perceived proximity to live theater, the intrusion of audiovisual realism into what was considered a poetic form, the reduction of camera movement, and the loss of universality—many viewed the arrival of synchronized sound to France with suspicion, even fear. Dialogue was the enemy, and silence was golden. Lucien Wahl succinctly summed up this sentiment when he proclaimed, "Cinema is always pure when it shuts up!"[26] Yet, by 1929, the adoption of sound film in France seemed inevitable. How, then, could the spoken word be minimized in the talkies, if sound film was coming to France whether people liked it or not?

THE MUSICAL ANALOGY

For many filmmakers concerned about cinema's future, music was the antidote to speech. If sound film could aspire to the poetic abstraction of music, it could avoid the potential pitfalls of spoken dialogue. Many returned to the "musical analogy," first articulated by French impressionist and Soviet filmmakers (such as Gance, Epstein, L'Herbier, Delluc, and Eisenstein) in the 1920s. In the silent era, the musical analogy was used to compare "pure cinema" with abstract art, highlighting cinema's nonrepresentational qualities like motion, rhythm, and composition of the image, and elevating the form to the status of art. The musical analogy was also used to stress film's temporality, emphasizing cinema's structural and formal features beyond narrative realism, including montage. As David Bordwell suggests, music was "a model of how formal unity can check, control, and override representation."[27] The musical analogy in film was part of a long-standing discourse elevating music as a nonrepresentational art form that reached back to the nineteenth century.

The musical analogy resurfaced frequently, in ways both implicit and explicit, in the early years of sound. Critics and filmmakers frequently employed musical metaphors in describing their ideal artistic applications of sound film technology, using words like "compose," "orchestrate," and "symphony" to describe a model for cinema's audiovisual construction, and drawing on Romantic notions of music's universality and grandiosity as aspirational qualities for the sound film. For these critics, such values were in direct opposition to spoken dialogue. Filmmaker Abel Gance predicted, in 1929, that after a period of painful experimentation and failure, a true, universal cinematic art would emerge:

> The dialogue film will not be the death of the art. I dare to predict this: for a fairly long time, world cinema will painfully try, with some true gains, to rejoin the ranks of universal music and spoken drama. But from this revolution will be born, as almost always, an assembly of better things. . . . I intentionally exclude the dialogue film from this future cinema, but I passionately call for a grand visual and sonic symphony that, thanks to synchronization will have captured universal movement and sounds, to offer our ears and our eyes wonders, like a magnificent and divine gift.[28]

Gance's dismissal of the talking film reflected a broader preference for *films sonores* over *films parlants* by many French film practitioners. In the *film sonore*, unlike the *film parlant*, the entire soundtrack—sound effects, music, and sometimes dialogue—could be assembled into a more abstract unified entity, unfettered by the restrictions of realism placed on the soundtrack in a *film parlant*. The *film sonore*, in Gance's opinion, held the possibility for a "grand visual and sonic symphony," restoring cinema back to the realm of art. But the next year, he suggested this could be accomplished even with dialogue: "dialogue, once harmonized with all the sounds of nature and life, gradually will become a *new language*, a mode of expression of rhythms and truths which the cinema will have built up over a thirty-year period."[29] As long as dialogue was just one of many available options for sonic expression on the soundtrack, a film could develop a universal audiovisual language.

One means of creating a sound film with musical qualities might be to "compose" a film as one would write a symphonic work, bringing together disparate audiovisual materials, including image, sound effects, music, and even dialogue, to create a poetic, structurally unified whole. Jean Epstein suggested filmmakers could construct the soundtrack as silent filmmakers had once constructed the image alone:

> The black and white visual cinematography earned its true place, understood its role: to oppose, then reunite, very simple images according to rhythms, a joining together that adds meaning. The role of sound film seems to me to be just as much in the writing of evolving sounds, of their meaningful groupings, their composition and relationship, their separation and connection.[30]

Epstein's description of assembling a soundtrack could be a description of the compositional process: writing evolving sounds and structuring and grouping them in meaningful ways. L'Herbier perhaps took this idea the furthest when he claimed sound cinema's musicality was even superior to absolute music, granting music a newly indispensable role in cinema:

> Music and cinema will function hand in hand, will be bound by a contract that unites them on the same filmstrip. Music, which will become an integral part of the film, will be made for it.
>
> Then we will arrive at a "superior music," a veritable ORCHESTRATION OF LIFE.[31]

If orchestrated like a symphony, L'Herbier claimed, sound film could even surpass music in its musicality. In fact, L'Herbier enacted this concept when he called his first sound film *L'Enfant de l'amour* (1930) "une pièce cinéphonique." The credits list that it was "composed and directed" (*composée et réalisée*) by him.

Proper incorporation of music into an audiovisual aesthetic could help elevate the whole form. Impressionist silent filmmaker Germaine Dulac understood music as an important tool for returning cinema to the realm of universal art (in contrast with dialogue, which limited a film's audience by language).

> Isn't the Art of cinema the art of visual beauty in combination with movement and with light? Their joining with the spoken word is to destroy cinema in its most profound sense. It's a regression, not progress.
>
> Idiomatic expression in use in each country is a moral border. . . . If the time comes when our images will be dependent on the spoken word, something I can't imagine, cinematic spectacles will be incomprehensible for many. . . .
>
> But the biggest progress will be, if not the spoken film, then the musical film. Harmony of sounds. Two profoundly human and international modes of expression, going beyond the frontiers of language. As much as I condemn the talking film, I will greet with enthusiasm the arrival of the musical film.[32]

Dulac believed emphatically that music would be the saving grace of sound film. She intentionally compared the musical film and the silent film as "two profoundly human and international modes of expression," drawing on the perceived universality of music as something worth emulating in the sound film. Dulac's parameters for a musical film were not about any specific film musical genre; instead, she seemed to define a particular approach to the materials of sound film that played with their heterogeneity in "musical" ways. In a practical sense, this often meant a film that emphasized a musical score over speaking voices. Along these lines, director Henri Diamant-Berger suggested the spoken word "is not indispensable to cinema. I prefer music for it. Film is a visual symphony and words don't follow its rhythm with any useful cadence. Film goes much better with an orchestral development than with words."[33] Both Dulac and Diamant-Berger implied that a musical score could help make an entire film more "musical."

At times these prescriptions for sound film aesthetics are cryptic and vague. Indeed, it is difficult to pinpoint how many actual sound films would have fit into these writers' criteria as successes. Regardless, the musical analogy was a multivalent rhetorical strategy. It posed an alternative to spoken dialogue, limiting the impact of the spoken word by relegating its role on the soundtrack. It elevated sound cinema as a "universal" art form akin to the symphony. It gave directors permission to manipulate sounds and images as if they were composed, constructing film in a poetic and "musical" manner. And it presented an early articulation of the concept of audiovisual counterpoint, the idea that soundtrack and image could function in independent but related ways.

MUSIQUE MÉCANIQUE: MUSICIANS AND COMPOSERS SPEAK

Discussions of music in early sound film extended beyond the realm of metaphor. Musicians and composers, too, weighed in on music's role in sound cinema. The fact that film music would no longer be played live, but instead recorded and played back, in mechanical synchronization with the image, required a new conceptualization of music's role in film. This change represented the end of many film musicians' livelihoods, and the Syndicat des Musiciens warned of the dangers of *musique mécanique*. At the same time, French modernist composers, as well as many directors, were intrigued by the possibilities for music composition offered by the new technology, seeing in it the potential for new musical opportunities and challenges. The mechanical nature of the soundtrack was precisely what appealed to composers: it had the potential to elevate the importance of the musical accompaniment in the overall conception of the film, and it offered a new set of compositional challenges as a novel mechanical musical medium.

Syndicat des Musiciens

Just as musicians' unions in the United States protested the talkies' use of "canned music," French musicians' unions fought the elimination of live musicians in movie houses. In the United States, unions began to fight the elimination of their jobs across the country. Beginning in mid-1928, as an increasing number of studios began wiring for sound, the American Federation of Musicians launched extensive advertising campaigns against losing the "human element" of music in the filmgoing experience.[34] Their protests hit their peak in 1929 and continued through 1930. In France, the Syndicat des

Musiciens followed suit. The French unions voiced their concerns around the same time, beginning in mid-1928, but their tactic was more preemptive, as they began to observe the consequences of sound cinema for their American counterparts and attempted to prevent similar outcomes in France. One reporter anticipated what he deemed to be a potential crisis for film musicians, calling sound film a "menace" for musicians:

> [I]f even one more spectator is able to conceive of film without music, the first experiences [of sound film] will greatly concern the musicians' syndicate. We have already pointed out many layoffs of orchestra musicians, and if we consider that workers of this genre are no fewer than ten thousand in Paris alone, the gravity of this possible crisis becomes apparent.[35]

For the Syndicat des Musiciens, the arrival of synchronized sound signaled not just an aesthetic threat to French cinema but also a peril to their profession. In an interview in *Soir*, M. Berthelot, secretary of the Syndicat, shared his concerns: "Mechanical music is more than a danger for us. If it develops, it will become a true catastrophe for us. . . . Will the cinema, which had offered many opportunities for us, now discard us? The only place that remains for us is theater and music-halls."[36]

But the stakes could be even higher, for sound film set a precedent. If technological developments continued to privilege recorded music, mechanical music threatened to replace live music entirely. In December 1928, in *Ciné-Journal*, the Syndicat des Musiciens wrote,

> A great danger (perhaps the greatest since professional musicians have existed) threatens the corporation.
> Mechanical music is trying to take the place of direct, human playing. All are threatened, already cinema orchestras are removed and replaced by soundtrack apparatuses. Others will follow.
> No musician, no conductor should remain indifferent in front of such a threat.
> If soundtracks continue down this road, a repertoire will be created that, one day, will almost completely replace orchestral playing.[37]

By 1930, however, the Syndicat's strategy shifted. It was clear that no matter how loudly musicians protested, they would not be able to fight the tide of recorded musical soundtracks. If music were to remain mechanical, it should at the very least be French. In January of 1930, the Syndicat published the following resolution:

> Considering that foreign sound films and talkies are presented to the French public in foreign languages and with a musical accompaniment almost exclusively consisting of foreign music;

Considering that, a marked exclusion of French language and music, on French soil, if it were to become widespread, would constitute a grave offense against French art and culture:

We put forward the following resolutions:

1: Talking films presented in France should be in French.

2: A significant amount of musical accompaniment of synchronized films presented in France should consist of French music.

And having decided to adopt all useful measures, we appeal to the powers of public opinion, in order to prevent cinema in France from becoming an instrument of intrusion of foreign expressions into a national culture.[38]

In this plea for a French national cinema, the Syndicat put French music on the same plane as French language in its importance as an expression of national cultural identity. This rhetorical strategy was in tension with those who argued for music and sound film's universality, but it revealed music's perceived role in preserving a national cinematic style. Though the Syndicat did not have much sway on how sound films and their soundtracks were disseminated in France, it reflects the extent to which the musical future of sound film was intertwined with, and integral to, the future of the entirety of France's national cinema.

Compositional Possibilities

The mechanical music of the soundtrack might have made musicians wary, but it intrigued composers and directors. It even had the potential to improve cinema: now music would be an immutable part of the cinematic experience. Filmmaker Léon Poirier articulated his hopes that, rather than destroying film music, the new technology would improve it. Sound film would, according to Poirier,

> merge with music. It will . . . enrich film with new sounds, it will supplement instrumental resources and thus obtain a noticeable improvement in the musical atmosphere of a film. It will without a doubt be genuine progress, lasting progress surviving the blustering period that we are currently suffering.[39]

Marcel L'Herbier expressed similar optimistic sentiments for music in sound film, writing, "orchestral recording will be of crucial interest," and not just for composers. "Directors will be very happy that, thanks to sound film, their works will be automatically projected in all movie theaters with an unchanging, original, musical adaptation."[40]

French modernist composers were excited by the possibilities of the new technology. Some, like Arthur Honegger and Darius Milhaud, had already composed silent film scores. But sound film was a new medium for composition, with a novel set of possibilities and interesting challenges. The immutability of the soundtrack offered composers an outlet for composition that guaranteed a certain quality of performance and a wider distribution than silent film. Milhaud, who saw and heard the second Vitaphone feature film *The Better 'Ole* in New York in 1927, was excited by the experience, writing that from the moment he heard Vitaphone, he "was convinced of the great possibilities of this new way to use music for the movies."[41] In *La Revue du cinéma*, he commented,

> Sound film is only at its beginning, but already its application is of considerable importance. What happened before when a composer wrote a special score for a film? Only several large movie houses could have a significant enough orchestra to perform it, then, in smaller cities, the film would be played with a nondescript adaptation and the score would disappear forever. Thanks to sound film, it will be recorded forever and will play everywhere along with the film. What huge distribution![42]

Milhaud was excited by the recorded nature of the soundtrack, which allowed greater permanence of composers' musical scores and guaranteed distribution as wide as the film's itself. When Georges Auric first saw *White Shadows in the South Seas*, a 1928 MGM postsynchronized sound film (equipped with a recorded synchronized soundtrack with music and sound effects), his reaction to the film and its score was mixed, but he also saw in the technology a great potential for composition:

> Music and cinema here harmonize with each other for the first time in an absolute way thanks to synchronism of the screen and the musical performance. This is the first point—and we will understand its importance. Secondly, the elimination of the orchestra pit allows a projection that is completely direct and near to the spectator, at the same time that it finally gives the composer the certainty that he is not wasting his time and efforts if he attempts what was until now a difficult enterprise of completing or adapting a score. Lastly, and to finish, a new *style*—and it's this point that was of the highest interest with this first "soundtrack"—a style where the composer will surpass "absolute music" without needing to submit to the demands of light comedy or lyric drama.[43]

In addition to being excited about the more "direct" relationship of sound film scores with their audiences, Auric suggested that sound film technology necessitated an exciting "new *style*." Critic Émile Vuillermoz wrote that he could even soon "envision the practical utilization of a concert or a recital given via sound film," which would give musical performance primacy over the image.[44]

Furthermore, sound film granted the composer complete control over his or her score, since it necessitated a definitive performance that was recorded to fit directly with the image. Milhaud envisioned two possibilities for synchronized scores, one where a composer's work created the structure for the film, and another where the film was the inspiration for the composer:

> 1st, a filmmaker composes a film, like a choreographer of a ballet, to a musical work already written. In this case the musician doesn't have to worry about the film.
>
> 2nd, a musician writes a score for a preexisting film. In this case, it's a completely new compositional technique to study.[45]

Milhaud likely had the *film sonore* in mind when he made this categorization. The *film sonore* encouraged an uninterrupted musical score that could potentially have enough structural cohesion to stand on its own, even if it was designed to fit with specific images. Whether the music came first or last, the recorded musical score's fixity ensured its close relationship with the image would be preserved.

Milhaud had tried his hand at the second possibility earlier that same year at the Baden-Baden music festival, composing a score for Alberto Cavalcanti's 1927 short silent film *La P'tite Lili*. Organized by Paul Hindemith, the Baden-Baden festival had focused on film music for the past few years, and in 1929 devoted its attention to music for sound films.[46] Cavalcanti's film was a visual illustration of a popular song of the same name from 1900, written by Louis Bénech and Eugène Gavel, and Milhaud drew on the popular song in his score, making reference to its refrain.[47] He composed the score with the idea of the microphone in mind: he avoided the oboe, which was understood to be picked up poorly by the mic, and only used flute and percussion sparingly. The soundtrack was recorded and synchronized using the Tobis sound system.[48] This type of film score—a score added for a sonorized version of a silent film— did not outlast the first years of the transition. But it seemed to be a promising possibility for composers during sound film's arrival in France, offering the unique challenge of fitting music precisely with moving images without having to compete with other components of the soundtrack or risk being edited or cut in postproduction.

Jacques Ibert had a diverging perspective on how the score should relate to the rest of the film. He believed a sound film score should not be created before or after the images, but instead required a close collaboration between composer and director:

> The collaboration with the composer must be strict, the score should be born at the same time as the images: why would the composer not help the director, just like a scriptwriter? These suggestions could enrich the work, amplify the

conceptions of the director; passivity is habitual, but the collaboration must be active.[49]

In other words, the composer could become a true collaborator in cinema, rather than someone whose contribution only came separately and after the fact. This kind of close collaboration would guarantee that music was of equal importance to the images in a film. Arthur Honegger, too, pointed out the importance of suitable music, developed in tandem with the film's images: "the score for the film must evolve parallel with it, wed to its rhythm image by image, press on its effects at the opportune moment."[50]

Composers would be required to think about timbres and sonorities differently when recording a soundtrack, which offered both exciting new possibilities and potential challenges. Honegger suggested that in the sound film, "our momentum won't be stopped by the impossibility of obtaining new sonorities from an orchestra."[51] But some sounds recorded better than others. Émile Vuillermoz cautioned composers, "it will be necessary to select with greater care the orchestral timbres that aren't all reproduced with the same perfection. The kettledrum, for instance, creates painful resonances that would be good to correct. On the other hand, instruments like the flute, the harp, the violin and the cello are translated with a perfect purity."[52] The full symphony orchestra posed potential problems. In 1930, Milhaud wrote about hearing *The Better 'Ole* in New York in 1927, describing music that had "deluged our ears with a dull confused sound, a sort of tonal fog," and stating that the mistake had been "the use of the full orchestra."[53] *Comœdia* critic R. L. agreed, stating that the sound film offered exciting artistic possibilities, but that the sound of the orchestra posed problems:

> The "talking film" reproduces not only the human voice but also music and, in a nutshell, all sounds.
>
> Of course, and this is the interest of the invention: diverse sounds are brought together in perfect synchronism with the images of the film. . . .
>
> Less favorable to me was the use of "talking film" for orchestral adaptation. Music heard in this way sounds too brutal.[54]

These perceived "problems" of the symphony orchestra led composers to be cautious about their instrumentation in early sound film scores, and, as discussed in the following chapters, composers often opted for (or were encouraged to opt for) smaller chamber ensembles. As microphone technology improved in the years following, orchestra size became less and less of a problem. Nevertheless, the concern about timbre in sound film reflects the broader sense in which the technology of synchronized sound was, for many, not merely a recording medium but also a compositional tool.

The soundtrack also facilitated its own new approach to composition, for directors as well as composers, one that expanded compositional boundaries. Germaine Dulac predicted, "through sound film, we will achieve a new music. Frequently orchestral scores go poorly with the projections they accompany. . . . However, there is drama and poetry in noise. Now we can make a double film that will be a musical film, by other means than what we would ordinarily call music."[55] Filmmaker and musician Jean Lods, in a newspaper interview, took the idea of sound film as a tool for composition even further. His discussion of its compositional possibilities seems to hint at a conception of sound film as proto–*musique concrète*, when he compared sound film to an earlier electronic musical invention, the Theremin:

> Remember the amazing demonstration by the Russian inventor Theremin, at the Opéra, the man who used musical waves to create a veritable sonic "bath" with miraculous accents and tonalities. Sound film will permit us to bathe the film in this kind of musical atmosphere . . .
>
> The result: joy for the composer to *construct* his music, by splicing pieces of film.[56]

Although very few composers took advantage of this kind of physical manipulation of the soundtrack for compositional purposes, this type of experiment did emerge a few years later in Maurice Jaubert's reversal of the soundtrack in Jean Vigo's 1933 film *Zéro de conduite* (discussed more fully in chapter 6) and Arthur Hoérée's splicing of recordings of acoustic instruments to create sounds of a storm for Dmitri Kirsanoff's 1934 film *Rapt*. Though the number of subsequent films in this vein was minimal, an experimental approach using technological manipulation of sound seemed to be a distinct possibility for composers working in the new medium.

CONCLUSION

The debates in the French press surrounding sound film's possible applications reveal how the new technology, even after its widespread acceptance in the United States, was by no means settled. Sound film could be recorded theater, it could be a mode of musical dissemination, it could be a vehicle for sonic experimentation, or it could be something new and as yet undefined. As the French film industry moved from theory to practice, film practitioners remained divided over the broader aesthetic implications of adding sound to cinema. Many continued to write about the proper use for sound film technology well into the 1930s.

The musical analogy in an audiovisual context shaped some of the most daring early French sound film experiments. However, there was no true consensus as to what a "musical" sound film should look and sound like. Precisely because of the vagueness of the concept, the plea for a "musical" approach to sound film simultaneously could encompass many or none of the experiments that would take place in the French film industry in the years that followed. However, it generally revealed the experimental, modernist spirit present in artistic circles frequented by both filmmakers and musicians, which had a significant bearing on early audiovisual cinematic experiments.

Furthermore, although many French composers did indeed write music for early sound films, the role of audiovisual "composer" often fell to the director, who typically had control over when and how music was used. In fact, directors were responsible for some of the most innovative audiovisual experiments involving musical soundtracks in the first years after sound film arrived in France. Some of the boldest approaches to composing the sound-track came from experimental directors Luis Buñuel and Jean Cocteau, the subject of the next chapter.

CHAPTER 2

Surrealist Sounds

Film Music and the Avant-Garde

A man kicks a violin lying on the street. A woman sensually sucks on a statue's toe while an offscreen orchestra plays Wagner's *Tristan und Isolde*. A triumphant trumpet fanfare punctuates a poet's suicide. Accompanied by a drumroll, one child throws a snowball that kills another, and a jaunty, upbeat musical theme underscores the boy's slow death. These audiovisual events were just a few of the most iconic and iconoclastic cinematic moments from *L'Age d'or* (1930) and *Le Sang d'un poète* (1930), two of France's earliest domestic sound films. They are surreal. They seem to emerge out of a dream, ignoring logic, rational thought, and accepted social behavior. They could be expressions of someone's unconscious, bearing the marks of free association and juxtaposed sounds and images that seem less strange when taken one at a time, but when put together are bizarre, unsettling, and even shocking. These scenes use music in various ways for shock, social critique, and commentary on the artistic process.

L'Age d'or and *Le Sang d'un poète* were nothing like the imported sound films French audiences had already seen, either in content or in the context of their production. Both were directed by figures who were closely connected to French avant-garde artistic and musical circles: Luis Buñuel, the Spanish filmmaker who had shocked French audiences in 1929 with his silent surrealist film *Un Chien andalou*, directed *L'Age d'or*, and Jean Cocteau, writer, playwright, and frequent collaborator with Erik Satie and Les Six, directed *Le Sang d'un poète*. Both projects were commissioned by the Vicomte Charles de Noailles, which sheltered their directors from normal box office concerns and gave them the freedom to bypass, for the most part, the constraints of commercial cinema. And, at a crucial juncture in France's nascent sound film production, both brought surrealism, an avant-garde artistic movement that originated in France and became prominent in the late 1920s, into the realm of sound film for the first time.

While surrealist cinema had flourished in the late 1920s, its future in sound cinema was uncertain. Music's role in the surrealist movement had been fraught and contested since the movement's beginnings in the early 1920s. The stance of the "official" surrealist writers was staunchly antimusical, and to many surrealists, music seemed to violate surrealism's philosophical and aesthetic principals. This antimusical stance made the very concept of surrealist sound film problematic. Could music play a role in this new audiovisual form? How would the dream logic established in silent surrealist cinema remain with the heightened realism of synchronized dialogue and the presence of a recorded musical soundtrack?

But sound cinema allowed filmmakers to renegotiate music's role in surrealist film. At a time when the potential energy of sound film was at its height, music became a crucial tool in Buñuel and Cocteau's early conceptions of surrealist sound cinema. Buñuel was a Surrealist with a capital "S": he was actively involved in the official surrealist movement and *L'Age d'or* was received as a surrealist film when it was first released. Cocteau, on the other hand, was never accepted by the surrealist movement. Yet many of his projects bear the markings of surrealist artworks—dream logic, unusual juxtapositions, and stream of consciousness—even if they were not accepted by the official movement. Both Buñuel and Cocteau adopted radical approaches to the soundtrack and to the relationship between music and image in sound film. Instead of demonstrating that there was no place for music in surrealist cinema, their experiments proposed a French surrealist sound cinema that was as musical as it was visual.

Both films had inauspicious beginnings. Buñuel's antibourgeois and antireligious film scandalized viewers, and not long after it was released, the film was banned by the Censorship Commission. One scene in Cocteau's film offended his patrons, and the film was not publicly screened until 1932, two years after it was completed. The imagery, political content, and unsettling narratives of these films were the obvious reasons for their controversy. But their soundtracks were just as radical: in different ways, each film employed music as a tool for creating new sound–image relationships, pastiche, and shock value. They not only commented on their political and artistic climate but also made a statement about the role the soundtrack should play in experimental film.

The audiovisual aesthetic proposed by these two films is the subject of this chapter. After introducing the principles of the surrealist movement and its intersections with music and cinema, I discuss the contexts in which these two films were created, the artistic agendas of both Buñuel and Cocteau, and the sound and music in each film. Buñuel incorporated preexisting classical works—including Mozart, Beethoven, and Wagner—into *L'Age d'or* and juxtaposed them with absurd, and at times offensive, images. Cocteau asked composer Georges Auric to compose a score for *Le Sang d'un poète* and proceeded to cut it up and reorder it at will, an experiment in "accidental synchronization" (*le synchronisme accidentel*) and a means of avoiding explicit musical signification. But both directors went beyond mere audiovisual juxtaposition of unexpected elements. Both films experimented with film rhythm and pacing, with alternating between synchronism and audiovisual counterpoint, with subverting musical meaning, and with layering audiovisual expectations. I suggest that, although the musical scores of both films may not sound surrealist on their own, their unique audiovisual juxtapositions make them so. Buñuel and Cocteau's approaches to the soundtrack were different in many ways, but when examined together, we can begin to see the various audiovisual elements that constitute surrealist sound cinema. Their films also point to the inherently surreal characteristics of sound film itself, characteristics that in later years most mainstream filmmakers would try their hardest to erase any traces of.

Audiovisual experiments this radical were short-lived in France, but *L'Age d'or* and *Le Sang d'un poète* offer a glimpse into a style of sound cinema that was most closely aligned with modernist musical and artistic practices of the day, in terms of the participants involved, their aesthetic priorities, and the institutional structures in which they were funded and supported. And, though their most obvious influence did not emerge until years later, *L'Age d'or* and *Le Sang d'un poète* put into practice some of the ideas most strongly articulated by the critics and directors discussed in chapter 1, particularly the musical analogy, reconfigured for sound cinema. Although the distribution of these two films was limited at the time, the films themselves were high profile, and some of the innovations explored in *L'Age d'or* and *Le Sang d'un poète* would find their way into mainstream French sound film practices in the years following, impacting the direction of French sound cinema during the transition era.[1] This brief but productive intersection between avant-garde cinematic and modernist musical practices opened up a new definition of *audiovisual* surrealism, constructed around the new technology of synchronized sound.

SURREALISM, CINEMA, AND MUSIC

Surrealism, in the words of André Breton, one of the movement's founders and spokesmen, is "pure psychic automatism, by which one proposes to express, either verbally, or in writing, or by any other manner, the real functioning of thought. Dictation of thought in the absence of all control exercised by reason, outside of all aesthetic and moral preoccupation."[2] The term *surréalisme* was coined by Guillaume Apollinaire in 1917 to describe Erik Satie's ballet *Parade*, but the official movement formed in 1924 with the publication of Breton's first surrealist manifesto.[3] It became the first major visual art and literary movement to take cinema seriously as a medium. Coming of age as the earliest generation to grow up with motion pictures in their daily lives, surrealist artists embraced the new form; as Robert Short has argued, the modernity of the movies was part of their appeal, as cinema was "as yet unencumbered with the baggage of an artistic tradition."[4] They also saw in cinema a potential for blurring the boundary between reality and dreams, a central tenet of the surrealist philosophy. Furthermore, the surrealists found that, according to Short, "movies were a perfect 'anti-culture' and their mass appeal was a distinct plus."[5] These would become the central components of surrealist cinema: visual representation of the irrationality of dreams, the unconscious (particularly thoughts that are violent, grotesque, or sexual in nature), the liberation of repressed desires, and the rejection of societal norms that served to repress these unconscious desires.[6]

Several surrealist films emerged in the mid- to late-1920s, including Germaine Dulac and Antonin Artaud's *La Coquille et le clergyman* (1928), Man Ray and Robert Desnos's *L'Étoile de mer* (1928), and Man Ray's 1929 *Les Mystères du Chateau de Dé*. The most notorious surrealist silent film was Buñuel and Salvador Dalí's 1929 film *Un Chien andalou*, and Buñuel and Dalí were the first filmmakers officially embraced and welcomed by the surrealist movement (though Dalí's association with the movement was short-lived). The film embodied the antibourgeois, irrational elements of surrealism, its embrace of the unconscious (particularly regarding sexual desire), its fascination with death, and its shock value. In this moment immediately preceding the arrival of synchronized sound in France, the connection between cinema and surrealism had been established and seemed well on its way to consolidating into a larger cinematic movement.

Music, on the other hand, had no official place in surrealism. The surrealist movement was at times indifferent to, at times quite critical of, music as an art form. Breton in particular was outspoken in his dislike of music, writing in his 1928 book *Surrealism and Painting*,

> Auditive images . . . are inferior to visual images not only in clarity but also in strictness, and, with all due respect to a few megalomaniacs, they are not destined to strengthen the idea of human greatness. So may night continue to descend upon the orchestra, and may I, who am still searching for something in this world, be left with open eyes . . . to my silent contemplation.[7]

Breton's distaste for music stemmed in part from personal politics, particularly his intense dislike of Cocteau, who had closely aligned himself with modernist musical experiments in interwar Paris. According to Cocteau biographer Francis Steegmuller, Breton's dislike of Cocteau was "almost maniacal."[8] Moreover, there were no French composers who were willing to carry the torch for surrealism. Satie, who had been associated with the Dada movement, sided with Dadaist Tristan Tzara's faction when the Dadaists and surrealists split. Breton had defended Satie's music in *Littéraire*, and he felt betrayed that this admiration went unreciprocated by Satie.[9] Breton turned to Georges Auric, a composer initially sympathetic to the surrealist movement, and he was the only musician Breton named in the *Manifesto of Surrealism* in 1924. But Auric's relationship with Cocteau proved stronger than his connection with the surrealists, and he ultimately did not become the musical ally the surrealists had hoped for.

But the surrealists' aversion to music went much deeper than Breton.

Surrealism is defined by its play with meaning, often through dream logic, which is built upon illogical juxtapositions. But meaning must be clear in order for its distortion to be legible, and music rarely offers such clarity. As Italian artist Giorgio de Chirico, who was an influential figure for the surrealists, wrote, "One never knows what music is about, and after all, having heard any piece of music, whether by Beethoven, Wagner, Rossini, or Monsieur Saint-Saëns, every listener has the right to say, and can say, what does this mean?"[10] Or, as Daniel Albright has succinctly suggested, "[i]t is impossible to disorient unless some principle of orientation has been established in the first place."[11] Jean-Paul Clébert, in his *Dictionnaire du surréalisme*, goes so far as to bluntly claim, "there is no surrealist music."[12]

If any musical style might be incorporated into surrealism, the art of the everyday embraced by Les Six—called the "cult of the commonplace" by Richard Taruskin and "lifestyle modernism" by Lynn Garafola—was particularly suitable for the kinds of juxtapositions and plays on semantic logic that surrealism required.[13] Some have argued that much of Les Six's music could be considered surrealist, and such multimedia works as Poulenc's *Les Biches* (1924) and *Les Mamelles de Tirésias* (1945), Milhaud's *Le Bœuf sur le toit* (1920), and Cocteau's and Les Six's collaborative *Les Mariés de la tour Eiffel* (1921) are some of the most frequently cited examples. Albright suggests that there is a substantial body of surrealist music, mostly consisting of music that sets surrealist texts. His definition also includes examples that are musically conservative but semantically dissonant, featuring disorienting pastiche or juxtaposition.[14] Poulenc's music, in particular, has been interpreted through a surrealist lens, which Taruskin has linked to the 1920s French modernist cult of the commonplace:

> The essential surrealist *musical* device, as Poulenc (following Satie) demonstrated
> again and again, was to surround the extravagant dream-imagery [of text or

scenario] with a music that sounded insistently "normal" and commonplace in its evocation of the familiar music of one's surrounding "lifestyle." . . . Poulenc affirms the special role music can play in the surrealist collage by utterly banishing anything exotic or otherwise extraordinary from his range of stylistic reference. The music [of *Les Mamelles de Tirésias*] does not try to compete in incongruity with the stage antics, but of course in context its apparent ordinariness is the ultimate incongruity.[15]

This style of audiovisual surrealism relies on the seeming detachment between the music and its images or texts, or, to use a film music analytical term, music's anempathetic qualities, in relation to the images.[16]

Whereas Poulenc's technique was to create incongruities between everyday musical styles and surrealist texts or scenarios, Taruskin argues that Milhaud's polytonal compositional style itself was surrealist, "juxtaposing simple melodies and chords in novel combinations that acquired their piquancy precisely from the recognizability of their homely sources," which was "another case of a calculated incongruity that replaced everyday reality with an alternative or magical sur-reality by building fancifully on the real listening experience of real audiences."[17] This brand of musical surrealism is more difficult to identify: as Christopher Schiff suggests, "while dissonance may be a combining of two incongruous elements that have a mentally bestowed affinity, it is not necessarily surreal, for all harmonic music would then be surreal, since it all relies on some dissonant tension to give it direction."[18]

Whether or not surrealist music is easily recognizable as such, or even possible by either of these definitions, music was actively excluded from the official surrealist movement. For these reasons—ignorance of music by the surrealist writers, Breton's personal dislike of Cocteau and his circle, and the more broadly perceived impossibility of surrealist music—any official surrealist sound cinema would seemingly not allow music an influential role.

Music was by no means absent from the exhibition of surrealist silent films, but it was not seen as an integral part of the surrealist cinematic aesthetic. Perhaps one of the most famous early film scores was Satie's music for René Clair's film *Entr'acte*. Shown between the acts of Satie's ballet *Relâche* performed by the Ballets Suédois in 1924, the film, featuring a scenario by Dadaist artist Francis Picabia, was an important precursor to surrealist cinema. The film, too, featured unusual juxtapositions and dream logic, and some have considered the film, and by extension Satie's score, to be surrealist. Others align it more closely with the Dadaist movement, from which surrealism emerged, which was less focused on dream logic and more interested in *instantanéisme* and absurdity.[19] When Man Ray debuted his 1926 Dada film *Emak Bakia*, live musicians played tangos, popular French music, and the "Merry Widow Waltz," alternating with jazz recordings.[20] Buñuel himself experimented with music during the premiere of *Un Chien andalou*, where he played records behind the screen (discussed in more detail later in this chapter). However, no one else commented on his musical choices at the time. No other surrealist director seems to have dictated what music should be played for his or her films. The experimental cinema houses in Paris—the Théâtre du Vieux Colombier and the Studio des Ursulines—had small chamber ensembles that would prepare music specially for each program,[21] but no extant records indicate what kinds of music they played for screenings of surrealist films. If there was music accompanying any of the films, no one seems to have made any mention of it or considered it an integral part of the surrealist cinematic experience, further evidence of the perceived insignificance of music for surrealist cinema.

But sound film no longer allowed surrealist directors to leave musical decisions to chance. Any silence on the matter would result in literal silence in the theater. Buñuel and Cocteau, therefore, had to make conscious decisions about the music on their soundtracks. They also had to contend with what Mary Ann Doane and Rick Altman have called the "material heterogeneity" of the sound film medium.[22] In other words, Cocteau and Buñuel had to decide for themselves how sound and image, as well as the various categories of available sounds (dialogue, sound effects, and music) would fit together in the newly audiovisual medium. They both embraced the form's material heterogeneity, testing the limits of sound film's capabilities for combining music, sound, and image.

FUNDING SOUND FILM: THE NOAILLES

As we saw in chapter 1, by 1929, the French public was beginning to experience sound film firsthand, primarily via Hollywood and German imports. French-language sound films were soon released, but nearly all were made in England or Germany, not on French soil. French studios were still rushing to equip themselves to produce domestic sound films. Additionally, exhibition practices had not yet caught up with the demand for sound films, and in 1929, many theaters still lacked sound synchronization systems, and in those theaters equipped with sound, a range of systems were in use.[23] The year 1929, therefore, was a crisis year for French filmmaking and the normal channels in which films were produced and distributed.

The financial and creative impetus behind the first surrealist sound films, therefore, came from an unlikely source: the wealthy patrons Vicomte Charles de Noailles and his wife, Marie-Laure. The couple was known for funding avant-garde artists and projects in the late 1920s. They were friendly with a number of prominent artists, poets, and musicians in Paris—Marie-Laure had even been romantically involved with Cocteau briefly when she was younger—and they aimed to support modernist artistic works.[24] The couple had turned their salon into a private screening room, and they had the capability of playing sound films before many cinema houses in Paris. They had already funded several films in the late 1920s, commissioning a new film for Marie-Laure's birthday each year. When they approached Buñuel and Cocteau, they provided very few financial or creative constraints. Therefore, during a time when making sound films was extremely costly and studios were unlikely to take serious risks, these privately funded projects became some of the most audacious sound films yet.

L'AGE D'OR

Luis Buñuel was a logical choice for the Noailles when they first sought to fund a sound film project. The Spanish-born filmmaker had moved to Paris in 1925. After working as an assistant for French directors Jean Epstein and Marcel L'Herbier, Buñuel and Dalí caused an uproar with *Un Chien andalou*, their 1929 *succès du scandale*. If the Noailles wanted to fund a project that would cause controversy and generate artistic conversation, their choice of Buñuel promised to do just that. When they invited him to make a short sound film, they initially suggested he collaborate with Stravinsky. Buñuel declined to work with Stravinsky, disliking his aesthetic priorities.[25] Noailles still agreed to fund his film, giving him complete creative autonomy over all aspects of production, including the soundtrack.

   Though *L'Age d'or* was his first sound film, Buñuel was no novice when it came to music. Musically trained from a young age, Buñuel played the violin and banjo and collected American jazz records.[26] He famously described that, during the premiere of *Un Chien andalou*, he watched behind the screen, playing records to accompany the film, alternating between Wagner's "Liebestod" from *Tristan und Isolde* and Argentine tango.[27] (This accompaniment was added to a sonorized version of the film for a rerelease in 1960, overseen by Buñuel.) The effect is that of a wildly fluctuating mood and tone: the protagonist couple's relationship alternates between almost sublime and practically comic, as the musical style switches suddenly and drastically. Given Buñuel's musical knowledge, the effect was intentional, even if the exact timings were indeterminate. Although the surrealists may not have paid much attention, and although this musical accompaniment may not have been a part of screenings between the premiere and the film's later sonorization, Buñuel's live performance of a recorded soundtrack would have had an important effect on the viewer's understanding and interpretation of the images.

   L'Age d'or was to be another collaboration with Dalí, and the pair spent a week at Cadaques in late 1929 working on the script. They met again in Paris in early January 1930. But they did not work as harmoniously as they had the previous year, and personal tensions put an end to the collaboration. While the extent of Dalí's contribution to the screenplay in the early stages of the project is disputed, by the time shooting began the project was fully under Buñuel's control. He and his crew shot the film in early 1930 at the Billancourt studios in Paris over the course of three weeks, and exterior scenes were shot in Catalonia and the outskirts of Paris. Buñuel selected preexisting musical works for the film's score, and operetta and film composer Georges Van Parys contributed a brief *paso doble* called "Gallito" for the end of the film, though he is only credited as "X."[28]

L'Age d'or's Scandal

On June 30, 1930, the Noailles hosted a private screening at their house, attended by their close friends. They organized another private screening on October 22, at the Cinéma du Panthéon, in Buñuel's absence (three hundred guests were in attendance, including Cocteau and Picasso).[29] But the Vicomte's aristocratic friends were shocked and offended. According to Buñuel, Noailles stood at the door shaking hands of the guests, who left in silence.[30] The next day, Noailles was expelled from the Jockey Club, and the Church threatened to excommunicate him. The real outcry, and the moment that cemented the film's infamy, however, came a month later. Studio 28 began to screen the film once the theater was equipped for sound, premiering it on November 28, 1930. Though the sound system malfunctioned on opening night, the first few screenings passed without much comment.[31] Then, on December 3, 1930, a group of right-wing protesters disrupted the film's screening, throwing ink on the screen, tearing up the theater's seats, and destroying an exhibition of surrealist paintings in the foyer.[32] The extreme-right groups were upset at the film's antireligious content, but they also likely targeted Buñuel because of his foreigner status. On December 11, the film was banned by the Censorship Commission, and all copies were seized the following day. Although the film was not publicly screened for another forty years, the surrealists were quite pleased by the affair and defended the film in a lengthy manifesto. The drama surrounding its censorship created just the kind of artistic scandal they desired, and they wholeheartedly embraced the film.

It is not surprising that *L'Age d'or* caused such a scandal, given its blatant and scathing critiques of contemporary values, bourgeois culture, and the Roman Catholic Church. The film focuses on the unbridled lust between a man (played by Gaston Modot) and a woman (played by Lya Lys), depicting their continued thwarted attempts to be together. The couple has no concern about moral or social taboos, and they attempt to make love during a religious ceremony, a bourgeois party, and an orchestra concert. Their love is never consummated, resulting in continued frustration on the part of both the man and the woman. Unfolding through a series of vignettes, only some of which relate directly to the couple, the film is interspersed with shocking and absurd images. It opens with a prologue consisting of found footage from a science documentary about scorpions, presented in the manner of documentary newsreels. Soon after, we see a number of bishops reciting a mass on top of some rocky cliffs; but next time we see them, they have transformed into rotting corpses. Buñuel also shows us a cow on the woman's bed, a man shooting his young son to death on the lawn during the party, and Modot pushing a blind man to the ground to take his taxi. The film ends with an extended reference to the Marquis de Sade's *120 Days of Sodom*: the intertitle describes an orgy in a castle that has just come to an end, and we see the participants emerge, one of whom looks like Jesus Christ. In the time span of an hour, *L'Age d'or* attacked the religious traditions and social mores of most of its audience. But the film was just as audacious in form and content as it was in subject matter. This is all the more surprising, considering it was one of France's first sound films, when filmmakers still felt limited by primitive sound editing and mixing technology. Buñuel used a remarkable range of techniques in order to disrupt expectations of realism, including conflicting messages given by sound and image, an unusual musical structure, and a multivalent use of preexisting musical excerpts.

L'Age d'or and Synchronized Sound

Jean-Paul Dreyfus, in his review of *L'Age d'or*, noted, despite his positive impressions of the film, that it was technologically primitive:

> One of the things people have reproached Buñuel with quite readily in his new film is its technical poverty. Once and for all, let's not go on worrying about technique! Let's grant it its place, which is completely mechanical and artificial. It's not the unsurpassed technical perfection of American films that, to my mind, determines the quality of the American cinema; and, for that reason, it has never touched me very deeply. Once more *L'Age d'or* verifies this opinion—that one willingly overlooks a deficiency in technique in order to follow a wonderful "story" impatiently. If it's true of certain parts (notably, the soundtrack added after the shooting), if it's true that *L'Age d'or* smells of cardboard, if the photography is poor, if the silent scenes follow the sound scenes in [a] disagreeable style . . . , if there are one or two slow sections in this feature-length film, none of that can harm or prejudice the spiritual perfection of the film.[33]

In other words, Dreyfus suggested the film succeeded *despite* the technological limitations imposed by synchronized sound. Indeed, sound recording and synchronization technology would become more sophisticated over the following years, resulting in greater fidelity and flexibility in shooting sound sequences. Buñuel himself later recounted that the sound was synchronized, "not like now, but by guesswork."[34] However, *L'Age d'or*'s soundtrack contains such a striking range of sonic techniques and kinds of audiovisual relationships that any apparent "mistakes" were anything but accidental. Quite the opposite: Buñuel's soundtrack reveals a sophistication not common in early sound films in France, even those of a few years later.

Buñuel's early shooting script indicates he was thinking about the interaction between sound and image from the conception of the project. He included some dialogue (although the dialogue changed between his shooting script and the final film), and made indications of other kinds of sounds. For instance, he specified that sound would instigate the important conflict of the film, as the couple would be first introduced not visually, but by Lys's pleasure shriek, which interrupts an official ceremony marking the founding of Rome ("Suddenly, screams are heard coming from behind the crowd, right at the back. Everyone turns around to see what is going on.").[35] Other indications include detailed descriptions of speaking voices, such as the voice of the governor giving his speech on the rocky cliffs as "squeaky and unintelligible,"[36] and Modot's reciting of his document of diplomatic immunity from the Minister "in the sing-song voice of school children when they recite the multiplication table."[37] Though Buñuel made many changes from the original shooting script, it was clear he was thinking about the possibilities for sound from the very start. Whether it was preplanned or ad hoc, Buñuel had tight control over the soundtrack. Any abrupt shift in the representational functions of the soundtrack, any artificial and mechanical element that struck Dreyfus as a result of poor technology, was almost certainly an intentional means of unsettling and disrupting any impression of reality within the world of the film.

In *L'Age d'or*, asynchronous sound is an important tool for distorting reality. This approach was a bold statement in 1930, given the novelty of synchronized spoken dialogue. Indeed, within the film itself, Buñuel directly remarked on sound film technology and its ability to manipulate and mislead, commenting on synchronized sound as a tool for surrealism. In one of the few dialogue scenes, Lys sits speaking to her mother in the drawing room about hiring musicians for their upcoming orchestra concert. She says:

> We went out together in the morning, and we already engaged four of them. There was a small one who sang like the others, and he had a small moustache. Only the pianist was missing. But they suggested a priest who plays the violin very well. In my opinion, with those musicians we will have enough, because six of them playing close to the microphone make more noise than sixty placed ten kilometers away. It's true that a lot of sound gets lost in the open air, but we could seat the guests close to the orchestra. What do you think?

This statement is clearly absurd: six musicians could never be mistaken for a sixty-piece orchestra, even with a microphone, and at the same time, an amplified small ensemble would be better heard than a full ensemble ten kilometers away. Buñuel mocks the widespread concern with recording fidelity and the microphone that was typical of the early years of synchronized sound, and iconoclastically suggests technology as a (partial) replacement for great musical works. But this comment, which was present in his early shooting script, also points to sound recording technology's ability to manipulate reality and deceive. The monologue suggests that sound in film is not a trustworthy representation of reality, even when sound and image seem to go together on the surface. Indeed, this comment explicitly points to the material heterogeneity of sound film, the fact that sound and image are recorded separately, and thus need not create an illusion of organic unity. It also suggests a degree of excitement about the possibilities of recording technology, precisely *because* sound film allows for the disjunction between image and soundtrack, which aligns perfectly with surrealist distrust of reason and perception. Later, a small ensemble (though not as small as six musicians) *does* stand in visually for a full symphony orchestra.

Throughout the film, Buñuel experiments with a range of manners in which sound can enhance and subvert signification. Sounds have a range of meanings, and throughout the film they do not mean the same thing or even create the same world of representation. Some scenes feature directly recorded synchronized dialogue, but these "realist" scenes are few and far between. The infrequency of dialogue scenes makes realism just one of multiple sonic options, no more privileged than any other. Other scenes feature important sync points, almost always as a representation of violent acts on the part of Modot, who transfers his sexual frustration into physical violence. He kicks a dog, stomps on a beetle, pushes a blind man to the ground, and slaps the Marquise after she spills wine on him. Other violent acts are similarly represented sonically: the groundskeeper shoots his son twice, and both shots are heard clearly.

Other scenes allow for more flexible relationships between sound and image, granting sound symbolic import. These scenes, in their audiovisual construction, are the most obviously surreal. In the scene where we are first introduced to Lys and Modot, the crowd attempts to interrupt their aggressive lovemaking, accompanied by the Prelude from Wagner's *Tristan und Isolde*. Modot is seen in close-up. He has a vision of Lys sitting, impeccably dressed, on a toilet.[38] Then, the image cuts to a toilet with burning toilet paper beside it, then dissolves to a shot of hot lava pouring out of a volcano. At this moment, the music cuts out and we hear the sound of a flushing toilet. The lava becomes a visual metonymy for the flushing excrement that the sound has already made clear.[39] The music resumes while the image of the lava continues, before we are again shown a close-up of Modot's face (Figures 2.1a–d).

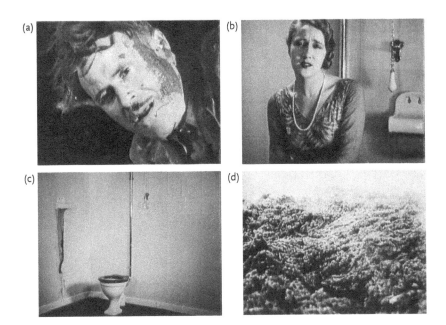

Figures 2.1a–d: Visual Metonymy for Flushing Toilet, *L'Age d'or* (1930)

In a later scene, Lys goes into her bedroom to find a cow sitting on her bed. She shoos it off as casually as if it were a dog. During this scene, we hear the cow's bell ring, and the bell continues to sound long after the cow disappears out the door. Lys sits down at her mirror, and the image cross-cuts to Modot, who is being led by two policemen. The shot cuts back to Lys, who is dreaming of her lover, and we hear nondiegetic musical accompaniment begin to play. At the same time, we hear a dog bark, which appears at first to have no diegetic source. The image cuts back to Modot, who is walking past a barking dog, and the sound becomes diegetically justified. The cow's bell continues to ring throughout. Buñuel adds a final layer onto the soundtrack: the sound of blowing wind. The source of this sound becomes justified when we see Lys's hair blowing in the wind, as well as clouds that appear in her mirror, though these are not grounded in realism (Figure 2.2). In this complex sonic layering, Buñuel combines the diegetic sounds from both Modot's and Lys's environments, to connect them sonically rather than spatially. On top of this, he adds the fantastical wind sound, which connects their realities with their dreams.

The climactic scene of the lovers' encounter in the garden during the orchestra concert is perhaps the film's most adventurous instance of asynchronism between sound and image. The conductor begins playing the "Liebestod" from *Tristan und Isolde* (discussed in greater detail later in this chapter) as the two embrace. Modot must attend to a telephone call. When Modot returns, they resume their lovemaking, and the two speak to each other without opening their mouths. Though the image places the couple in

Figure 2.2: The Dream World Reflected in the Mirror, *L'Age d'or* (1930)

the garden, their conversation appears to be occurring in a bedroom: Lys says "I was just falling asleep" as she stares at Modot, her face appearing to age suddenly. Modot then asks where the light switch is, and Lys responds that it is at the foot of the bed. The two, now seen together (and Lys again her young age), sit side by side in wicker chairs embracing, but their conversation indicates the couple is trying to get comfortable in bed together (Modot suggests she move her head closer, as the pillow is cooler). The image is quite tame, especially considering how ravenous their embraces were earlier in the film. This scene may represent telepathic communication, some kind of reverie, or perhaps an indication that the image is not depicting the truth. Indeed, the specificity of the conversation makes it clear that the image is purely a stand-in for what the audience knows is really happening, thanks to the soundtrack (Figure 2.3). The audiovisual relationship grows more ambiguous as the scene continues, however. Lys declares, "What joy! What joy in having killed our children!" Modot's face is seen in close-up, and now his left eye is bleeding profusely, as he, overdramatically, declares "Mon amour! Mon amour! Mon amour!" The surrealists singled out this scene in their manifesto (signed by Louis Aragon, André Breton, Dalí, Paul Éluard, and others), printed in the film's program:

> Buñuel has formulated a theory of revolution and love which goes to the very core of human nature; that most tragic of all debates, galvanized by well-meaning

Figure 2.3: The Visual Stand-In for a Bedroom Scene, *L'Age d'or* (1930)

cruelty, finds its ultimate expression in that unique instant when a distant yet
wholly present voice, so slowly yet so urgently, yells through compressed lips so
loudly that it can scarcely be heard:

LOVE . . . LOVE . . . Love . . . Love.[40]

The voice that seems to come from Modot, though through his mind and not
his lips, was actually provided by the surrealist poet Paul Éluard, providing
yet another level of disjunction between sound, image, and meaning. These
scenes reveal how different kinds of asynchronous sounds were some of
Buñuel's most crucial devices for distorting reality in an audiovisual medium.
By violating expectations of the diegesis in a range of ways, Buñuel intentionally revealed the multitude of options for sound, image, their combination,
and the various permutations of truth and its subversion that they offered.

L'Age d'or's Musical Soundtrack: Music as a (De-)structuring Device

Buñuel's musical choices also reinforce the film's unusual and imbalanced
structure, another means of unsettling the spectator. Buñuel opted against
collaborating with a composer for an original score and instead drew almost
entirely from preexisting classical works. The only exceptions occur at the end

of the film: repetitive drumming played by the Republican Guard, imitating the drums of Calanda, that were customarily beaten in Aragonian villages (such as the town where he was born), from noon on Good Friday until noon the next day;[41] and the incredibly brief "Gallito" by Van Parys at the end, accompanying an image of several women's scalps hanging on a cross.

Rather than using existing recordings of classical works as he did with *Un Chien andalou*, Buñuel had an orchestra record each piece he wished to incorporate into the soundtrack.[42] Perhaps more surprising than the fact that he chose to rerecord each work, however, was that the full orchestra was used. As I argued in chapter 1, critics and composers expressed broad concerns about what kinds of musical sounds would record well on the soundtrack. It was widely held that a full orchestra would not record well with primitive sound technology. These concerns were at least partly justified, as microphone fidelity improved markedly within just a few years. However, Buñuel included some of the most lushly orchestrated musical works available—Mendelssohn, Schubert, Beethoven, and Wagner. This fact is particularly striking, and the irony even greater, considering Lys's monologue about six musicians and the microphone: Buñuel did nothing to reduce the number of musicians playing on his soundtrack.

Table 2.1, which lists each musical occurrence in *L'Age d'or*, its timing, its relationship to the visual narrative, and its relationship to other sounds, illuminates several points.[43] First of all, classical music accompanies a very large percentage of the film, some pieces playing continuously for minutes at a time. Schubert's "Unfinished Symphony," for example, is heard almost continuously for close to ten minutes in the middle of the film. Second, it becomes clear why Buñuel did not use preexisting recordings for the film: these versions are manipulated, with measures and other transitions added. For instance, the film opens with Mendelssohn's *Hebrides Overture*, but with a two-measure transition directly into Mozart's *Ave verum corpus*. Later, Schubert's "Unfinished Symphony" is interrupted by a theme from *Tristan und Isolde*. Buñuel did not just cut and paste to compile the soundtrack. He timed each scene and manipulated the music intentionally, a fact backed up by his own words in his shooting script in reference to the "Liebestod" from *Tristan und Isolde*: "The orchestra must constantly repeat this part of the musical score, in case the previous love scene takes on more importance than the shots used to show the playing of *Tristan and Isolde*."[44]

In addition to the manipulation and placement of the music in the film, the table makes the structural oddity of the film clear, revealing the musical soundtrack's purpose as a (de-)structuring device. The experimental nature of the film's structure is significant but often overlooked: the narrative of the couple is not even introduced in the film until about a third of the way through, it is constantly interrupted, and it is bookended with unrelated material. The musical soundtrack reinforces these structural stylistic oddities, and further enhances them by constantly shifting the musical accompaniment's function.

Table 2.1 MUSIC IN *L'AGE D'OR* (1930)

Timing (Kino DVD)	Composer	Musical Work	Action	Comments/Other Sounds
0:59–3:23	Mendelssohn	*Hebrides Overture* (1832), m. 1–75 (with two-measure transition at end)	Scorpion documentary, with intertitles	
3:24–4:38	Mozart	*Ave verum corpus* (orchestral arrangement), m. 1–21 (ritardando added at end)	Bandit walks on rocky cliffs, bishops chant on the rocks	Sounds of waves crashing on the shore, sounds of chanting
5:24–7:35	Beethoven	Symphony No. 5, Mvt. III, m. 1–132 (with measures 96–132 repeated)	The bandits' hideaway	Brief synchronized dialogue over music (mostly unintelligible)
9:32–11:51	Debussy	"La Mer est plus belle" (orchestral arrangement) (entire song)	Bandits walk up the rocky cliffs back to the bishops	Diegetic sounds of waves crashing
11:52–14:15	Mozart	*Ave verum corpus* (orchestral arrangement), m. 1–36 (with cadence in D major added at end)	Boats arrive; passengers come ashore and walk up cliffs; they see bishops' corpses	Diegetic sounds of passengers arriving; waves crashing
14:42–17:50 (interrupted 15:25–15:33)	Wagner	Prelude to *Tristan und Isolde*, m. 25–90	The couple is interrupted; Modot's visions of toilet; Modot dragged away; Modot kicks a dog and crushes a beetle	Music interrupted by toilet flushing; man's speech over music (postsynced); dog bark; crowd noises; sound of beetle crushed
17:53–20:34	Mendelssohn	Symphony No. 4, "Italian," Mvt. III, m. 1–92	Founding of Rome (1930); shots of Imperial Rome (punctuated by intertitles), in the style of city symphonies	Exploding building (20:06–20:18)
20:35–20:53	Beethoven	Violin Concerto, Mvt. I, mm. 511–14 (only solo violin part)	Man kicks a violin down the street, steps on it	Sound of violin being crushed

(continued)

Table 2.1 CONTINUED

Timing (Kino DVD)	Composer	Musical Work	Action	Comments/Other Sounds
20:54–22:35	Mendelssohn	Symphony No. 4, "Italian," Mvt. III, m. 80–92 (2x); silence; m. 36–76	Continuation of city symphony montage; Modot is led down the street; poster/vision of female masturbation	None; music interrupted by silence (21:35–21:40)
22:57–23:20	Wagner	Prelude to *Tristan und Isolde*, m. 16–17 (2x)	Lys sprawled on couch; Modot continues to be led away	
26:09–27:20	Wagner	Forest Murmurs from *Siegfried*, repeated ostinato (does not align with score)	Cross-cuts between Lys at mirror and Modot being led down the street	Sounds of cow's bell, dog barking, wind
28:23–28:53	Mendelssohn	*Hebrides Overture*, m. 244–260 (first beat)	Flashback to Modot at the International Goodwill Society	
30:11–34:27 35:07–39:48	Schubert	Symphony No. 8 "Unfinished," Mvt. I —exposition, truncated repetition of exposition —silence/gunshots —resumes m. 114–329 —seamlessly transitions into next excerpt	Guests' arrival at the Marquis de X; guests socializing at party; groundskeeper greets his young son; maid faints at fire in kitchen; groundskeeper shoots son; guests look out the window then resume the party; Lys and Modot gaze at each other across the room; Modot angry with Marquise who spills drink, slaps her	Car engines and horns; bell; horse/cart; maid's shriek and percussion indicating fire; silence; groundskeeper's gun shots; sounds of guests; Modot's slap

Timecode	Composer	Music	Action	Sound
39:48–41:41	Wagner	"Love Music" from *Tristan und Isolde* Act II (seamless transition from Schubert)	Woman recovers from slap; Lys and Modot find each other and sneak out to be together	
43:45–47:38 (interrupted by phone conversation)	Wagner	"Liebestod" from *Tristan und Isolde*	Lys and Modot embrace; guests listen to concert; Modot looks at statue's foot; servant announces phone call; Lys sucks on statue's toe; phone call; Lys/Modot reunite	None; servant announces phone call; interruption by telephone call; voice-over conversation
48:45–52:45				
54:20–55:13	Twelve Drummers of the Republican Guard	Drums of Calanda	Modot storms away and walks inside	
55:13–55:52	Wagner	"Liebestod" from *Tristan und Isolde*	Modot throws himself on the bed in despair, pulls apart down pillow	
55:52–1:02:19	Twelve Drummers of the Republican Guard	Drums of Calanda [two different rhythms]	Modot defenestrates objects; 120 Days of Sodom scene (Château de Selliny); orgy survivors emerge from castle	Crash of falling objects; shriek of woman inside Château
1:02:19–1:02:28	X [Georges Van Parys]	"Gallito," *paso doble*	Image of women's scalps hanging off a crucifix	

Large sections of the score behave almost as silent film accompaniment: in the opening sequence, for instance, we hear Mendelssohn's *Hebrides Overture* while we see images of scorpions, explicated through intertitles. The music transitions to Mozart's *Ave verum corpus* just in the manner that a silent compilation score might. Up until this moment, nothing indicates that the film will be anything but a silent film with a postsynchronized score. Diegetic sounds begin to enter, with the sounds of waves crashing on the shore and the bishops chanting. Still, most potential diegetic sounds in the first fourteen minutes of the film are drowned out by loud music, bringing into focus the expansiveness of the hills and the barrenness of the landscape. The diegetic sounds that we do hear (the dialogue of the bandits, the chanting of the bishops) are mostly semantically obscured.

The next long section of the film focuses on the couple's attempts to be together, and features a range of music, sounds, and dialogue, including the orchestra concert, the only instance of diegetic music in the film. When the couple's lovemaking is permanently thwarted, the Calanda drumming begins, signaling the third section of the film. The drumming, in its incessant repetition, acts as an auditory equivalent to the resolution or consummation that never arrives for the couple. It also serves as a bridge into the final section of the film: the 120 days of Sodom.

L'Age d'or then ends with the shortest musical statement in the entire film: a mere few seconds of a conventional *paso doble* to finish off the film (Example 2.1). This musical tag is in a completely different style from anything that came before it, a deliberately jarring auditory experience before the film ends. It is a musical resolution detached from any kind of related exposition or development. Though the melody itself was newly composed, the popular style is utterly conventional, almost comically commonplace. Its upbeat style in juxtaposition with such grotesque sexual violence is disturbing, especially considering the weighty musical works that preceded it. *Paso*

Example 2.1: "Gallito," *Paso doble, L'Age d'or* (1930)

doble means "two-step" in Spanish, and in this musical gesture, Buñuel, as a Spaniard working in France, puts his personal signature on the film. It also signals the story has come to a close. Musical closing gestures are common at the end of films, but here it makes no narrative or musical sense, and artificially resolves the disjointed narrative. Its tacked-on nature makes the film's ending as unsettling as the hour that preceded it.

L'Age d'or's Musical Soundtrack: Music as a (De-)familiarizing Device

Buñuel chose the musical excerpts he did for two additional reasons: their associations with elite culture, and their extramusical signification. Unlike an original score, Buñuel's compilation score of preexisting classical works could offer a dimension of intertexuality not present in the images alone. Pairing the beloved works of Mozart, Beethoven, Wagner, Mendelssohn, Schubert, and Debussy with graphic and offensive images not only added a layer of audiovisual irony to the film but also attempted to do violence to the cultural status of these musical works.[45] Priscilla Barlow argues, "[b]ecause he aimed to shock the bourgeoisie, he used the most shocking music possible, which was the most familiar and irreproachably bourgeois music one can imagine."[46] Indeed, Buñuel chose standards of the classical music repertoire, pieces that his audience would have been familiar with. By juxtaposing them with grotesque imagery, Buñuel drew attention to the incongruity of sound and image. But, perhaps more disturbingly, by placing them together, he drew connections between the images and the musical works that accompanied them by highlighting their similarities, defamiliarizing them, and making them complicit in the film's call to revolution.

In case his message of musical violence was not clear, Buñuel brings it into the visual iconography of the film itself. In the scene where the city of Rome is introduced, we see a "highly respectable-looking gentleman" kicking a violin down the street, in a manner, Buñuel suggests, equivalent to the "way that some people avoid stepping on the lines in the pavement."[47] A musical cue provides the aural signifier of the violin: a solo phrase from Beethoven's Violin Concerto. But then the man steps on the violin to crush it; and the Beethoven melody is silenced. The crushing of the violin is symbolic of the film's attack on the bourgeoisie and its values; the casualness of his action makes it all the more shocking.

Music signifies in a number of ways in the film's soundtrack. It does so most obviously when there is explicit extramusical meaning attached to the work, through either a title or text. Mendelssohn's programmatic music was particularly suitable in this respect. The *Hebrides Overture* serves as a literal overture, accompanying the images of the scorpions at the film's opening.

His *Italian Symphony*, which was inspired by Mendelssohn's visit to Italy, accompanies images of "Imperial Rome" that are reminiscent of the city symphonies of the 1920s.[48] Beethoven's Fifth Symphony is not programmatic, but many have interpreted the opening motive to represent "knocking on death's door." Buñuel uses the third movement to depict the bandits as they themselves seem to be at death's door; to top it off, there is a knock on the door (death, perhaps?), which the bandits choose to ignore. The first movement of Schubert's "Unfinished Symphony" is literally unfinished in the film, interrupted by music from *Tristan und Isolde*. The connections between these works and the images they accompany seem obvious, almost facile. But that was likely the point. Their associations with the visuals are exaggeratedly literal, and they stop there. For instance, the *Hebrides Overture* was a concert overture, a stand-alone piece rather than a true overture, and therefore only connected to the visual overture in name.

Other works added meaning through their texts, which, while absent from the instrumental arrangements on screen, would have been known to the audience if they recognized the piece. Mozart's *Ave verum corpus* accompanies the bishops as they chant on the rocky cliffs, and again when we see their skeletons. The Latin religious text focuses on Christ and his bodily suffering:

> Hail, true body of Christ,
> born of the Virgin Mary,
> having suffered, sacrificed
> on the Cross for mankind,
> From whose pierced side
> flow water and blood,
> Be unto us a foretaste,
> in the trial of death.

When associated with this text, the musical excerpt seems benign in its first occurrence, appropriately paired with the visuals of the bishops as they chant. But in its second appearance, it becomes chilling: the decayed bodies of the religious figures become too literally aligned with the text (Figures 2.4a–b). This moment pointedly underlines one of the film's broader messages: its critique of the church and equation of religious martyrdom with violence (seen most explicitly at the end of the film).

These two occurrences are separated by an instrumental arrangement of Debussy's "La Mer est plus belle," as the bandits make their way from their hideaway to the top of the cliffs. Debussy was the only French composer featured in the soundtrack, and Debussy's song sets the text of symbolist poet Paul Verlaine, whom the surrealists admired. Again, the title seems apt for the visual imagery at hand, as the bandits walk up the cliffs by the ocean. But the text itself, even in its quintessentially symbolist ambiguity, offers an added

Figures 2.4a–b: The Bishops, First and Second Appearance, *L'Age d'or* (1930)

layer of meaning. In addition to antireligious undertones ("The sea is more lovely / Than the cathedrals"), the text references dying without suffering ("A friendly breeze frequents / The wave, and sings to us: / 'You without hope, / May you die without suffering!'").[49] This act of violence in the imagery of the text set by Debussy foreshadows the violence to come in the film's own imagery.

Finally, the parallel between the onscreen couple's unfulfilled desire and Wagner's *Tristan und Isolde* is one of the most striking musical choices in the film. The couple is introduced by the sounds of the opera's Prelude. The love theme from Act II accompanies their discovery of each other from afar at the Marquis's party. And their final attempt at consummation of their love occurs while the orchestra plays the "Liebestod." Predictably, perhaps, their love becomes permanently thwarted during this scene. Wagner's endless melodies and unresolved harmonies aptly musicalize the couple's continuous frustration. The requisite death of the operatic couple also parallels the violence and death throughout the film.

Incorporating Wagner into the musical soundtrack was a common convention in silent film scores. Silent film accompaniment frequently drew on Wagner, and his musical style had already substantially shaped film-scoring practices.[50] *L'Age d'or*, with respect to its music, was as much an extension of conventional practices as it was a violation. But Wagner's music is also subjected to the most violence of perhaps any musical excerpt in the film. In one of the most famously shocking audiovisual moments, as the couple gets separated at the height of their passion, Lya Lys sucks on a statue's toe just as Wagner's music swells (Figure 2.5). What else could have been the intent of this scene than to shock the bourgeoisie by knocking their sacred Wagner off a pedestal and equating sublime love with plain old sexual desire? This kind of shock was surely just what the surrealists were hoping for.

While this was undeniably part of Buñuel's intent, an additional factor further complicates his treatment of the soundtrack: he loved the very music he used to signify all that he hated about the bourgeoisie. The shock of hearing

Figure 2.5: Lya Lys Awaits Her Lover to the Sounds of Wagner's "Liebestod," *L'Age d'or* (1930)

Mozart, Wagner, and Mendelssohn while seeing scorpions, rotting corpses, and a couple making love is merely one layer of meaning. Buñuel loved classical music. In his memoirs, he describes his childhood experience anticipating for months in advance the Madrid Symphony's visit to Saragossa, his hometown.[51] He loved Beethoven, Franck, Schumann, and Debussy, and, in particular, Wagner: he was a self-proclaimed "incorrigible Wagnerian."[52] In other words, Buñuel loved these composers and their works too much to mock them wholesale. While he may have been aware of the potential shock value of his unexpected juxtapositions, an earnest reading of his musical choices is worthwhile.

If we consider the scene from this perspective, Buñuel's pairing of the "Liebestod" with the couple's profession of desire legitimates the actions of the couple. Instead of mocking Wagner, it makes their lust for each other sublime, almost mythicizes it.[53] In the moments immediately following, when the conductor stops playing, he is overcome with emotion, and he grips his head in pain. The emotion wrought by the music becomes too much for him to bear. When the music stops this time, the couple's lovemaking is permanently thwarted (at least within the confines of the film). The woman, also overcome with musical emotion, transfers her lust for Modot to the conductor, and, by extension, the music he makes.

Perhaps that is part of what makes its soundtrack so unsettling: Buñuel both brings the music down into the realm of the mundane by juxtaposing it with the film's images, and elevates the images and narrative through the musical works. The music serves to *familiarize* the otherwise alienating images. Buñuel shows how irony alone is not as disturbing as an audiovisual aesthetic that simultaneously, and contradictorily, embraces *and* critiques musical meaning. The revolutionary politics of surrealism found in this film are thus not just enhanced by the score, but shaped by the manner in which it interacts with the image.

LE SANG D'UN POÈTE

Unlike Buñuel, Cocteau was not part of the formal surrealist movement. In fact, he was perhaps the French artist and writer most hated by the surrealists. And Cocteau vehemently denied any association between his film and the surrealist movement: in 1946, he claimed, "surrealism did not exist when I first thought of [the film]."[54] Yet, his works were aesthetically connected to a number of surrealist artistic ideals, including dream logic, unexpected juxtapositions, semantic dissonance between media and incongruence between the arts, and the exploration of inner desires.[55] It is therefore not surprising that his first film would contain many of the surrealist markers of his earlier multimedia works.

Prolific in a number of media—poetry, theater, and illustration—Cocteau had been the creative motivator behind several modernist musical projects throughout the 1920s, including writing the famous 1918 manifesto *The Cock and the Harlequin* and the scenarios for the ballets *Parade*, *Les Mariés de la tour Eiffel*, and *Le Bœuf sur le toit*. Although he had no filmmaking experience, many of his multimedia collaborations contained intertextual references to cinema, most notably *Parade* (incidentally the ballet that prompted Apollinaire to coin the term "surrealism"), and cinema was the logical extension of these experiments. He was also very fond of cinema and wrote about it in his journal the same year.[56] He singled out Buster Keaton's *Sherlock Holmes Junior*, Chaplin's *Gold Rush*, Eisenstein's *Battleship Potemkin*, and Buñuel's *Un Chien andalou* as "great" films, and he wrote about attending *L'Age d'or*, calling it a "revealing film."[57] He was eager to work with the medium, declaring in his journal that his next work would be a film.

In January 1930, while Buñuel was shooting *L'Age d'or*, the Vicomte and Vicomtesse de Noailles gave Cocteau and composer Georges Auric one million francs to make an animated sound film.[58] Auric, too, had been interested in film for some time, and he and Cocteau were good friends and logical collaborators for the project. Again, Noailles initially funded the project with few restrictions. By April, Cocteau and Auric abandoned the idea of an animated film because it proved too difficult to realize at the time. The project evolved into *La Vie d'un poète*; they later changed the title to *Le Sang d'un poète*. They shot the film at Joinville-le-Pont over the summer, finishing in September.[59] Cocteau invited the Noailles and their friends to be extras in a scene, where they sat in a theater box and applauded.

Cocteau screened the film privately at the Noailles household on November 16 and 20, 1930, and again on January 3, 1931.[60] By this time, the scandal around *L'Age d'or* and its subsequent censoring made his patrons more cautious. They expressed concern about their scene—they were shocked to see Cocteau had edited the film so they and their friends were applauding a suicide—and Cocteau had to reshoot the scene with other actors. The film was not publicly released until 1932, when it was shown on January 5 at the Vieux Colombier theater, followed by a gala public opening on January 20, where Cocteau delivered an introductory address. By this time, sound film was no longer new to France, so his audacious experiments with the form did not have the kind of scandalous effect they might have had a year or two earlier.

Though the content of Cocteau's film was not nearly as political as Buñuel's, his exploration of audiovisual surrealism was just as bold. The film explores the relationship between a poet, his mind, and his poetic creations. As Francis Steegmuller has suggested, the film itself is conceived of as a poem, representing through sounds and images a few moments in a poet's life.[61] It opens and closes with a shot of a chimney being demolished, suggesting that the entire film has taken place in the blink of an eye. The rest of the film is divided into four episodes. First, an artist sketches a face, only to find the face's mouth has come to life. When he tries to smudge out the mouth, it becomes affixed to his own hand. He places the mouth onto a statue of a woman, which then becomes animated. The statue encourages the poet to pass through a mirror. He does so, and in the second section of the film, the artist walks down a hallway, peering through the keyhole into the various rooms. He sees a man in a sombrero get shot by a firing squad (only to stand back up and be shot again), Chinese opium smokers, a girl wearing bells who begins crawling onto the ceiling, and a hermaphrodite. The artist is handed a gun, and, instructed by an unidentified voice to shoot himself, he does so but does not die. He returns through the mirror and smashes the statue. In the third episode, we see a group of schoolboys having a snowball fight. One boy throws a snowball at another, but it hits him with the impact of a large marble stone, and the boy dies. The final episode features a card game with the poet and the animated statue, over the body of the dead boy, which is carried off by an angel. As the poet realizes he has lost, he commits suicide, as a theater audience looks on and applauds. The woman transforms back into the statue. The various episodes all represent different manifestations of the poet or artist's creative process. The film lasts less than an hour, but it feels as if time is suspended, unfolding in slow motion. Cocteau suggested his own interpretation of the film, that the solitude of the poet is so great, he lives out his own creations, so vividly that the mouth of one of his creations is imprinted on his hand like a wound; that he loves this mouth, that he loves himself, in other words; that he wakes up in the morning with this mouth against him like a chance acquaintance; that he tries to get rid of it, that he gets rid of it, on a dead statue—that this statue comes to life—that it takes its revenge; that it sends him off into terrible adventures. . . . that the snowball fight represents the poet's childhood and that when he plays the card game with his Glory, with his Destiny, he cheats by drawing from his childhood instead of from within himself. . . . afterward, when he has tried to create a terrestrial glory for himself, he falls into that "mortal tedium of immortality" that one always dreams of when in front of famous tombs.[62]

Yet, in the next breath, in true Cocteau fashion, he dismissed the interpretation he himself provided, instead encouraging a more open interpretation of the film from his audience: "I'd be right to tell you all that, but I'd also be wrong, for it would be a text written after the images."

Le Sang d'un poète and Synchronized Sound

Much like Buñuel with *L'Age d'or*, Cocteau did not shy away from employing sound for a range of surrealist audiovisual effects in his film. Cocteau exploited his self-professed inexperience with film to experiment with the form in a number of unconventional ways. He later said that he "didn't know anything about the art of film" and "invented it for [himself]" as he went.[63] Whether it was his outsider status, his experience with other avant-garde multimedia forms like ballet and theater, or his love of films as a spectator, he incorporated a number of audiovisual techniques that indicate that he was eager to take advantage of the form's technical possibilities. Just like Buñuel, Cocteau exploited sound film's unrealistic capabilities by avoiding most instances of perceived audiovisual unity. His varied approach to sound throughout the film serves to undermine narrative clarity and unsettle any expectations of realism, heightening the dreamlike qualities of the images through sound.

The film's visuals are stylistically diverse, with some sections that resemble animated films, allowing for a range of images beyond those grounded in cinematic realism (Figures 2.6a–b). Cocteau additionally used optical effects, such as juxtaposed images (the living mouth on the hand), reversed portions (the man shot by a firing squad who rises up again), and stop tricks—or pausing the camera and adding or removing an object while keeping its surroundings intact—to make objects seem to suddenly appear. To create an eerie, dreamlike effect in the poet's movements, Cocteau nailed the sets to the floor and filmed the scene from above, so the poet "drags himself along instead of walking, and when the scene is put right again, you see a man walking very strangely

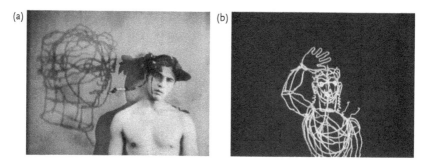

Figures 2.6a–b: Elements of Animation, *Le Sang d'un poète* (1930)

with great effort, and the movements of his muscles do not correspond to the effort of his walk."[64]

To match the strangeness and variety of the visuals, most of the sounds Cocteau incorporated into the soundtrack eschew both semantic logic and exact synchronism between sound and image. Even more so than Buñuel's film, there is little spoken dialogue: the only characters who speak onscreen are the poet, the mouth on his hand, and the statue (the last of which is an in-animate artwork turned animated), and those moments are minimal. Cocteau intentionally strips other moments with dialogue of their semantic clarity. As the poet traverses the hotel hallway and peeks inside the keyholes, for in-stance, he hears the voices of the Chinese opium smokers, speaking unintelli-gibly. These voices remain acousmatic, as we never explicitly see their sources. Instead of dialogue, Cocteau frequently employs a voice-over, which acts as a narrator throughout the film.

Instead of using realistic sound, Cocteau employed sound to create a sense of audiovisual and narrative disjointedness. There are some diegetic sound effects—the poet smudging the mouth on his drawing, the sounds of bubbles as he submerges the mouth into water, the sounds of the poet breaking the statue, and the applause of the theater-goers—but not all actions produce re-alistic sounds. On the contrary, most sounds contribute to the film's other-worldliness. A gun is fired three times in the film, and each time it receives different sonic treatment: we hear the corresponding sound of gunshots both times the firing squad shoots the man in the first room; then, when the poet shoots himself, the sound of the gun is represented by a bass drum hit; and when the poet pulls out a gun to shoot himself when he loses at cards, there is silence. When the poet jumps through the mirror, we hear the sounds of a crowd gasping in awe, and when he comes back through the mirror we hear a "[r]eligious choir of childish voices."[65] To represent the interiority of the poet's experience, Cocteau famously recorded his own heartbeat, which appears in several moments in the film.[66] He also added sounds of a tractor motor, a ticking clock, and an intermission bell, all of which are incorporated

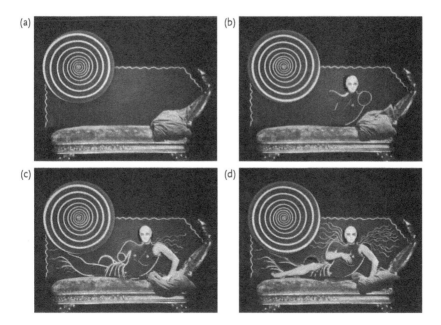

Figures 2.7a–d: Several Synch Points during the Appearance of the Hermaphrodite (Accompanied by a Drumroll), *Le Sang d'un poète* (1930)

into the soundtrack almost as musical accompaniment or drones. Many of the stop tricks are accompanied by a drumroll, which signal the appearance of each new object, such as when the "hermaphrodite" is presented, the sudden appearance of each new body part accompanied by clear percussive sync points (see Figures 2.7a–d). The drumrolls add auditory emphasis and suspense that translates to a visual importance each time a new body part appears.

Cocteau also incorporated a great deal of silence, which is almost more unsettling than the range of sound effects. In the scene where the poet passes into the dream world after entering the mirror, there is no music or sound to signal his interior thoughts as the camera slowly zooms in on him, his figure surrounded by darkness. Both sound and silence heighten the unreality of scenes as they unfold. They also interact holistically with the music, to the point where some sound effects act as musical accompaniment, and vice versa.

Le Sang d'un poète's Musical Soundtrack: "Accidental" Synchronization and Music as a Device of Structural Prolongation

Auric was excited about cinema as a modern form of expression for composers, and had begun his collaboration with Cocteau enthusiastically. Sound film seemed the perfect juncture to make his first foray into cinema. As composer for the film, Auric received almost equal billing as Cocteau. But several things caused him to sour on the experience. He later expressed frustrations with early sound film technology's shortcomings, which caused constraints on the timbre and instrumentation he could use, and with the liberties Cocteau took with his music once it was completed. Despite these two significant challenges Auric experienced in composing the film's score, his music reinforces *Le Sang d'un poète*'s dream logic and audiovisual incongruities, particularly by enhancing the film's sense of prolonged time. Whether the decisions were Auric's or Cocteau's, the strangeness of the musical structure appropriately fits the strangeness of the narrative and visual structure, both on the level of individual phrases and on a broader structural level throughout the film. Through slow pacing and incongruity between sound, image, and musical style, *Le Sang d'un poète* presented a very different kind of film rhythm than *L'Age d'or*. Its rhythm creates a sense of temporal suspension, which removes narrative anticipation.

Auric felt he was a victim of crude technology. Unlike *L'Age d'or*, which was filmed and recorded with Tobis-Klangfilm equipment, *Le Sang d'un poète* was recorded using RCA Photophone technology, under the supervision of sound engineer Henri Labrély; Auric's score was recorded by the Flament Orchestra, conducted by Édouard Flament. Auric was warned against full orchestrations (despite the fact that Buñuel's film had been scored for full orchestra). The sound engineer cautioned Auric about "unphonogenic" instruments and registers, placing a number of constraints on the kind of music the composer could write. Later recalling his experience composing for the film, Auric claimed,

> The "sound engineer," an essential figure, always seemed to us much more formidable than he was in reality. Before I could even begin my work, I was convinced that all kinds of constraints must be observed: this instrument recorded badly, this other, quite the opposite, should be chosen without hesitation; some "high pitched" sounds would never "come out" and some "bass" notes would have to be sacrificed, if we rigorously took into account the instructions of our technicians. So that's why I decided to do away with the "strings" in my orchestra and create a sort of village band: the epitome (I was convinced of it!) of what was imposed on me by film and that famous "mic."[67]

As a result, Auric opted for a chamber orchestra consisting of woodwinds, percussion, and piano. Though he was frustrated by this constraint, it was actually aesthetically consistent with the instrumentation of many of his compositions of the period.[68] Furthermore, within the timbral restrictions he felt were placed on him by the infamous microphone, Auric nevertheless composed a score with a wide range of musical themes, moods, and textures.

More so than the mic's effect on his music, Auric was frustrated with what Cocteau did with his music once he composed it. Auric recalled that he attended almost all of the projections of the rough cut of the film, and he wrote his music during the course of these projections.[69] He took care in composing music specifically for each scene. Auric approached his scoring task fairly traditionally, producing, in the words of Ned Rorem, "what is commonly known as love music for love scenes, game music for game scenes, funeral music for funeral scenes. Cocteau had the bright idea of replacing the love music with the funeral, game music with love, funeral with game."[70] Cocteau experimented with what he called "accidental synchronization" (*synchronisme accidentel*), and, much to Auric's displeasure, rearranged Auric's musical cues to avoid any audiovisual relationships he deemed to be too related or redundant. Cocteau's idea of accidental synchronization is similar to the surrealist "exquisite corpse" (*corps exquis*), a collaborative means of writing poetry or drawing images where only the last part of the previous contributor's text or image is visible: they both detach elements intended to be joined together and rejoin them in unexpected ways, therefore defamiliarizing them. Though Cocteau may have overstated the extent of "accident" in his manipulation of the soundtrack, it remains the most frequently discussed feature of the score. If we are to believe Cocteau and Auric, though the musical notes may have been Auric's, true artistic control over the soundtrack was taken out of his hands.

The extent to which Cocteau actually left the musical cues up to chance has been debated.[71] Cocteau likely wanted to exert authority over one of the aspects of the film over which he had less control, claiming his own hand in the construction of the musical score. But regardless of the extent of accidental synchronization present in the score, both Auric and Cocteau in fact had a similar set of goals: to move away from what they perceived to be musical-cinematic clichés, or musical redundancy with the image, and create a soundtrack that was capable of enhancing meaning and the audiovisual experience in unexpected ways. And they accomplished this goal, both through Auric's compositional language, and through unexpected audiovisual pacing caused by Cocteau's editing. Both techniques serve to reinforce the strangeness—surrealness—of the artist's self-journey, the unexpectedness of the onscreen occurrences.

If Auric went about composing traditional film cues, he certainly did not approach them conventionally. Much in line with his *esprit nouveau* style he had developed through the 1920s, the score is characterized by clarity, simplicity, and emphasis on melodic line over harmonic motion. At the same time, the "anti-teleological" nature of Auric's score, to borrow Daniel Albright's description of Erik Satie's music, "takes up time without seeming to move forward in time."[72] The melodies are often simple and diatonic; themes are paired with darker, contrasting accompaniments and textures, and moods change abruptly.

Because of its shifting musical style, Auric's score most often does not signal to the viewer when to be tense or which moments are important, as a traditional film score might. Some of Auric's most energetic themes occur when nothing significant happens on screen, elevating in importance seemingly mundane moments through musical emphasis. For example, near the end of the film, a group of spectators watches a card game between the poet and the statue that has come to life. The energetic music is at odds with the stasis of the shot, and emphasizes the slow deliberateness of the statue's gestures. In contrast with the upbeat music, there is little movement, and Auric's score gives the viewer few emotional or narrative indications.

Conversely, the lack of clear sync points between the score and some of the more dramatic moments of the film renders important or odd events normal or unremarkable. As the unnerving scene where the poet first discovers the living mouth on his hand unfolds, the upbeat music, which James Deaville and Simon Wood have characterized as "carnivalesque,"[73] switches between dissonant, minor, major, and augmented chords, making the accompaniment's mood intentionally undecipherable. The texture then reduces to a solo flute, then unsettling silence, as the poet discovers the mouth. The scene's meaning is further obscured by the poet's blank expression on his face as he stares at his hand. Only after the music cuts out does he register any kind of concern. The music is typical of Auric's compositional style during this period, but it was also quite effective in removing clear musical meaning that could help guide the viewer.

The few exceptions to this rule, therefore, call attention to themselves, but even then, only fleetingly and inconsistently. For instance, as the poet angrily approaches the statue after returning from his trip through the mirror, a relentless musical repetition of B-flat in the trumpets mimics his unwavering resolve. As he destroys the statue with a hammer, the music suddenly becomes frantic, corresponding with the emotional nature of the scene, and then triumphant, at his successful destruction of the statue. But then the musical gesture ends, and the poet's own frightening transformation into a statue receives no musical accompaniment. Similarly, the angel's musical theme is slow, diatonic, and lyrical, featuring a solo saxophone melody (Example 2.2). The gentle nature of this lyrical theme, corresponding with the calm presence of the angel as he places a blanket over the dead boy, stands out in contrast to the boy's death, especially the unsympathetic nature with which the statue and the poet play cards right next to him and the audience looks on. But even this musical gesture is interrupted, with the sound of an airplane engine, as the angel's image transforms into its photo negative (Figures 2.8a–b).[74] Potential moments of clear audiovisual correspondence, therefore, are ultimately thwarted.

The film's larger-scale musical structure also intentionally obscures emotion and meaning. The repetition of certain themes bears no obvious narrative significance. Most notably, a slow minor contrapuntal theme (Example 2.3)

Example 2.2: Angel's Theme, *Le Sang d'un poète* (1930)

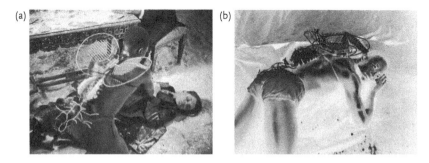

(a)   (b)

Figures 2.8a–b: Angel, *Le Sang d'un poète* (1930)

is repeated almost every time the poet walks down the hallway to approach another door (except for the second time, for no apparent reason). The music stops for us to see and hear the action in each room as he peers through the keyhole. The resulting effect is much like a rondo, as Colin Roust suggests, though each iteration of the theme is slightly different.[75] This theme reappears in the third episode, when the boy has fallen down from the impact of the snowball and is seen bleeding to death. There is no clear connection between these moments in the film. Similarly, the carnivalesque theme from the opening is repeated as the boy lies dead on the ground, and again as the audience watches the card game. The trumpet fanfare also becomes a repeated musical gesture; yet, it is repeated frequently and in a number of different contexts, which means the extent of its semantic function is turning our attention to whatever happens next in the film, and nothing more. Whether or not these thematic repetitions were intended to connect scenes or actions, the seeming arbitrariness of their repetition works to strip the musical themes of any potential for clear signification.

Auric's score, therefore, though it may have been traditionally conceived, does not provide the emotional commentary typically found in a film score. His music does not indicate what the listener is supposed to feel from the

Example 2.3: Rondo Theme, *Le Sang d'un poète* (1930)

musical cues alone. With a few notable exceptions, the music operates on a different plane from the images: not contradictory, but incongruous. The music works against the action, not in a sense of irony or subversion, but in terms of the visual pacing of the scenes. The lack of sync points deemphasizes important events; likewise, seemingly mundane moments are elevated in importance through musical emphasis. Each track—sound and image—serves to undermine the pace of the other.

Because sound and image seem to work against each other in this way, the film's unusual narrative mode is placed in further relief. Just as music underlined the structural oddities of Buñuel's film, Auric's music for *Le Sang d'un poète* shapes and helps outline the film's unusual structure. But whereas Buñuel's film is bursting with energy and anger, Cocteau's film is slower and contemplative. *L'Age d'or* looks from the inside outward—at the external forces that work against one's inner desires—and *Le Sang d'un poète* looks inward, by expressing the poet's most personal memories and emotions. The film's pace is much slower, more careful; Auric's music, and Cocteau's reordering of the score, contributes to this notably expansive pace.

It may seem that Cocteau attempted to undermine music's importance by intentionally stripping it of its ability to signify. But using pacing, disjunction between mood of sound and image, and a musical style that evades obvious emotional cues, Cocteau and Auric experimented with a different kind of role for music in the audiovisual cinematic experience. Their approach removes directionality, prolongs the film's presentation of time, and plays with the subjective quality of duration.[76] The film becomes a kind of dream-image, as described by Gilles Deleuze—an abstraction of narration that plays with actual and virtual images—or a recollection-image, a cinematic image that brings the past into the present.[77] The music enacts this play with structural prolongation, through Auric's musical language and through Cocteau's structural manipulation of the score. Instead of undermining music's importance, this kind of audiovisual treatment depends on its score. The film's connection with Cocteau's experiments on the stage, including ballet and opera, is clear. But at the same time, in this way, Cocteau's and Auric's approach was specifically cinematic. Though it was more subtly shocking than *L'Age d'or*, the final result is just as disorienting.

CONCLUSION

Much like many of the multimedia avant-garde spectacles of 1920s Paris, *L'Age d'or* and *Le Sang d'un poète* each provoked a veritable *succès de scandale*. But neither Buñuel's nor Cocteau's film had a widespread enough distribution to prompt a full-fledged cinematic artistic movement during France's transition years: Buñuel's film was banned too quickly, and Cocteau's was screened too late. Buñuel abandoned the surrealist group in 1932 in favor of the Communist party; he also left France, working in Spain, America, and Mexico, before returning to direct his next French film in 1956. Cocteau would not direct another film until 1946: in the later 1940s and 1950s he picked up many of his own experiments where he left off, continuing what was to become known as the *Orpheus* trilogy, of which *Le Sang d'un poète* marked the first. But the audacious experimentation found in these directors' first sound films was short-lived. The scandal surrounding both films caused the Vicomte and Vicomtesse de Noailles to stop funding film projects. The patronage of individuals such as Noailles did not prove sustainable in the era of sound, as it became increasingly costly to produce films.

Yet, instead of demonstrating that there was no place for music in surrealist cinema, Cocteau and Buñuel's experiments reveal in different ways just how crucial music was for a surrealist audiovisual cinematic conception. Both films de-emphasized the importance of synchronized dialogue, a key component of cinematic realism and one of the most important features in the early years of sound film. Instead, they explored the range of meanings that sound *juxtaposed with* image could create in different combinations. More than the random joining of unrelated audio and visual components, juxtaposition was an active manipulation of both to create audiovisual incongruence and ambiguity, through new kinds of film rhythm, pacing, and the negation or purposeful avoidance of the extramusical associations of musical works or styles. Both films avoided realism, and by extension synchronized spoken dialogue. Synced dialogue, in fact, was the least important element of the soundtrack in their films. Their approaches to the soundtrack eschew realist audiovisual possibilities of sound film.

The soundtracks of *L'Age d'or* and *Le Sang d'un poète*, when considered side-by-side, offer a different model of what surrealist music might be. Most definitions of surrealist music focus on written or choreographic works, leaning on the seeming nonrelationship or detachment between the music and the visuals or text. These films offer a different model of surrealist music, one that does not merely pair images with anempathetic musical styles or accompaniment. This form of audiovisual surrealism requires a self-conscious manipulation of the sound and image to actively work together to create disjunctions. This revised definition of surrealist music gives both sound and image greater agency when brought in interaction with each other.

Buñuel's and Cocteau's films epitomized several key aesthetic priorities regarding the relationship between sound and image that many French critics and filmmakers expressed in their early writings about sound film (analyzed in chapter 1). With its reliance on audiovisual counterpoint and de-emphasis on spoken dialogue, surrealist sound was one of the most successful ways to enact the elusive musical analogy in an audiovisual cinema. Surrealism and French musical modernism interacted most closely and, perhaps, most successfully, through the conduit of surrealist sound cinema, providing a model for a different kind of treatment of sound than was found in the imported films from Hollywood. Although a "pure" surrealist sound cinema did not advance much beyond *L'Age d'or* and *Le Sang d'un poète* immediately following their release, surrealist audiovisual principles much like those found in these two films ended up having a profound effect on the French film industry. Audiovisual surrealism was folded into mainstream French cinema in the years following 1930. Directors like René Clair, whom I discuss in chapter 4, and Jean Vigo, the subject of chapter 6, employed some of the audiovisual devices of surrealism within a much more varied aesthetic toolbox, using music as a structural tool and juxtaposing it against unexpected images within more traditional narrative frameworks.[78] Clair, Vigo, and other directors pulled these principles out of the surrealist social and artistic context, incorporating the same set of aesthetic priorities and practices in less radical ways. Surrealist moments in more traditional narrative films most often center on dreams or flashback sequences, and music plays a crucial role in mediating the temporal discontinuity of these scenes. Some of Cocteau's and Buñuel's bold experiments evolved into techniques that became convention, even cliché, in later decades.

Lastly, my analysis of these two films highlights the inherently surreal characteristics of the sound film medium itself. Michel Chion points out that, in mainstream cinema, the "physical nature of film necessarily makes an incision or cut between the body and the voice. Then the cinema does its best to restitch the two together at the seam."[79] Though our expectations of sound film today typically take for granted the binding of sound and image into an organic unity as an accurate representation of reality, sound and image are actually recorded through separate apparatuses, edited, and only reunited after the fact. In other words, through its material heterogeneity, the very ontology of sound film carries the potential for surrealist incongruities between sound and image, a fact not lost on Cocteau and Buñuel. Furthermore, because of this process, any perceived representation of reality in film is in its own way already a distorted, manipulated reality. Mainstream filmmakers, even in the earliest talkies, have typically attempted to erase this aspect of sound film's ontology, aiming to maintain the illusion of unity between voices and bodies. But Buñuel and Cocteau rejected realist audiovisual possibilities of sound film, instead *highlighting* the material heterogeneity of the form. These experiments in early surrealist sound cinema remind us that, in some respects, all sound film is fundamentally surreal.

CHAPTER 3

"An achievement that reflects its native soil"

Songs, Stages, Cameras, and the Opérette filmée

"And now, enough with opening credits. Since we're in a talking film, it would be best to start by talking." Thus opens the 1930 musical film *Chacun sa chance*, the line uttered by an emcee standing on a stage in front of a curtain. Indeed, beginning in 1930, French audiences experienced a rush of French-language sound films, and the talking did not stop. But importantly, now talking films were talking in French.

But just because the actors spoke French did not mean the films were French productions. In fact, French producers struggled to assert themselves and play a role in defining filmmaking practices in France. Because American and German companies controlled important sound film patents, many French-language films were first produced outside of the French industry. To reach the French market, German companies brought French actors and creative teams to Germany to shoot sound films in French. Meanwhile, the Hollywood company Paramount Pictures opened a studio in Joinville, outside of Paris, and produced sound films in multiple languages, including French, for international distribution. During the few years when the French industry lagged behind and strove to play catch-up, countless French actors, directors, and composers got their start in sound films not with French companies, but with American and German ones.

Within this context of international production, the genre of the film operetta, or *opérette filmée*, became quite popular with French audiences. The film operetta, the European equivalent of the American film musical, drew influence from diverse stage genres and national contexts. But, much in the same way that early Hollywood film musicals confronted the tension be-tween "notions of artifice and reality," in the words of Richard Barrios,[1] film operettas raised important new questions for filmmakers: how should song and dance factor into a naturalistic medium like sound cinema? Should sound film model itself on stage genres or on silent cinema? In what ways could a film operetta differentiate itself aesthetically from its stage counterpart? The *opérette filmée* became an important genre for audiovisual experimentation as directors attempted to answer these questions. Although heavily reliant on stage traditions, the *opérette filmée* also provided filmmakers the opportu-nity to de-emphasize talking and bring the focus back to what French critics thought was quintessentially cinematic about film: visual rhythm and camera movement.

This chapter examines the *opérette filmée* genre, focusing on how directors and performers navigated the tension between theatrical and cinematic aes-thetics, and between realism and fantasy, while drawing on modern themes and popular musical styles that appealed to French audiences and critics. I focus on three successful French-language film operettas that appeared during the first years of European sound film production: *Chacun sa chance* (1930), *Le Chemin du paradis* (1930), and *Il est charmant* (1932). Each was written specifically for the screen, and attempted to depart from stage-bound aesthetics and push the boundaries of the cinematic, though some more forcefully than others. In different ways, each also maintained debts to stage traditions (particularly operetta and music-hall). With up-to-date mu-sical styles to match their contemporary plots and characters, each film in-cluded songs that became popular outside of their original contexts within the films, generating phonograph and sheet music sales, and extending each film's influence beyond the bounds of the screen. Although these films seem stylistically distant from the surrealist experiments seen in chapter 2, many of the underlying preoccupations were actually quite similar. The blatant arti-ficiality of the musical spectacle in the *opérette filmée*, just like the audiovisual pastiche of surrealist sound cinema, offered a profoundly different aesthetic from the perceived audiovisual realism of spoken dialogue. Just like the sur-realist sound films of Buñuel and Cocteau, the *opérette filmée* was defiantly antirealist, but unlike surrealist cinema, it was unabashedly commercial.

All three films came from international production contexts. *Chacun sa chance* was a Franco-German joint production, which featured the screen debut of well-known French music-hall performers. *Le Chemin du paradis*, the French-language version of the German company UFA's *Die Drei von der Tankstelle*, directed by Wilhelm Thiele, is a quintessential example of in-ternational collaboration that was typical of what was called the MLV, or multiple-language version. An MLV was a film shot in multiple languages for different international audiences. Each version would use the same sets and songs and reshoot the film with different actors and a translated screenplay.[2]

Il est charmant, produced by Paramount Pictures at its studio in Joinville, was praised as the first noteworthy film operetta to be shot in France with an almost entirely French creative team. Though many of the first French-language *opérettes filmées* came from German or American companies (a fact of great concern for many filmmakers in France), these international productions contributed substantially to a broader critical embrace of sound cinema in France.[3]

I focus on these three films in particular because of their contemporary take on the operetta. There were many approaches to the operetta on screen during the transition era, emerging out of different national practices. Many popular film operettas were adapted from stage works: *L'Opéra de quat'sous*, for instance, the French version of G. W. Pabst's adaptation of Brecht and Weill's *Die Dreigroschenoper* (produced by Tobis-Klangfilm in 1930), was critically and commercially successful in France. Others showed clear debts to Viennese and American conceptions of the operetta, with restrained, highbrow musical styles, lavish costumes and sets, and stories set in faraway times and places. The successful UFA film *Le Congrès s'amuse* (the 1932 French-language version of *Der Kongress Tanzt*) is one such example. But the films examined in this chapter were not only written specifically for the screen, but were also set in the present-day and were sleekly modern in their subject matter, characters, and music. Their contemporary plots, settings, and songs seemed to correspond to the novelty and excitement of sound film technology. Furthermore, fantasy was created not through the representation of a far-away time and place, but exclusively through the songs and the use of the camera.

Over the course of this chapter, I discuss some lesser-known figures of French film music history. Many of the personnel involved, including directors, composers, librettists, and stars, were big names from the operetta or music-hall stage, but have been more or less forgotten today. Nevertheless, they were key to the films' success, and were crucial players in the mediation between the theatrical and the cinematic. Individuals like Henri Garat, the music-hall performer with magnetic star-power in front of the camera, Albert Willemetz and Raoul Moretti, a composer-librettist team that made the successful shift from stage to screen, and Louis Mercanton, a director who took a playful approach to cinematography, were influential in the development of a style that critics generally agreed brought a lightness and freedom back to French film, not long after sound had threatened to destroy it.

SOLVING THE "LANGUAGE PROBLEM": INTERNATIONAL FILMMAKING

The first years of sound film proved a challenging time for the international distribution of films. Silent films could be easily distributed internationally: all that was required was changing the intertitles, a cheap and straightforward process. Spoken language was much more difficult. At first, international audiences were willing to accept sound films in other languages—*The Jazz Singer*, which was shown in Paris with a separate screen projecting a translation of the lyrics, was a hit with French audiences—but as the novelty of sound wore off, production companies realized that a longer-term solution was needed. Both subtitling and dubbing were attempted, but given the state of the technology at the time, neither solution was deemed to be very successful. Both techniques detracted from what was thought to be the most attractive feature of spoken dialogue: audiovisual realism. As Ginette Vincendeau points out, the "new sense of completeness" offered by sound film in "reconciling body and voice" was "immediately upset" by dubbing's lack of credibility and by the dislocation of sound and image caused by subtitles.[4] Furthermore, French audiences resented the foreign incursion of talkies onto their screens. There were even reports of riots, when the American film *Fox Movietone Follies of 1929* was shown with subtitles in France without any warning in the advertising.[5] Therefore, producers felt the need to reach international audiences through other means.

Filmmakers attempted a range of strategies to break national language barriers and make their films accessible to wider audiences. A few directors attempted polyglot films. French director Julien Duvivier's 1931 film *Allô Berlin, Ici Paris*, produced by the German company Tobis, focuses on a French telephone operator who falls in love with a German operator. One protagonist speaks primarily in French and the other in German, and the challenge of communicating with each other in their different languages is a major feature of the plot. Similarly, Austrian director G. W. Pabst's 1931 film *Kameradschaft* (*La Tragédie de la mine*), coproduced by the French company Gaumont-Franco-Film-Aubert and the German Nero Film, focuses on a real-life rescue from a collapsed mine on the border between France and Germany, where communication between francophone and German-speaking characters is central to the story's unfolding. But these solutions only somewhat widened distribution. Other films were released internationally with an added prologue or new characters who would periodically offer commentary, in order to provide a local audience with just enough context to follow along with the plot.[6] This technique was a relatively easy fix but still risked quite a bit of the film's narrative becoming lost in translation.

One of the most common strategies for global distribution of sound films was the MLV. With the same sets and songs reshot with different actors in different languages, the MLV's editing was often identical between different versions, with only dialogue and actors differing. Several American companies produced MLVs, first on American soil and then in Europe, and many European producers followed suit, particularly Tobis and UFA in Germany. Although MLVs solved the language problem of international distribution, they frequently posed a problem because, according to Vincendeau, they were "on the whole, too standardized to satisfy the cultural diversity of their target audience, but too expensively differentiated to be profitable."[7] Intertwined with these economic problems were issues of national pride, and French critics continued to desire films made by filmmakers and actors from their own country. Indeed, French audiences were initially resistant to foreign attempts at francophone cinema; newspaper critic Maurice Mairgance wrote in August 1930, "After 18 months of effort, it is truly regrettable that the two best productions on our screens at present are American films in French."[8] Although a large number of French-language films were created within a context of international collaboration between German and French, or American and French, production companies and creative teams, it was not a given that French audiences would accept MLVs as truly "French" films.

Musical films were extravagant and expensive productions. But the musical film could, more easily than a dialogue-heavy film, strike the balance of appealing to both local and global audiences. Because of its reliance on audiovisual spectacle over dialogue, it simultaneously and paradoxically allowed for easier international distribution while highlighting and embracing the particulars of national popular music and its stars. Perhaps this is why American musicals like *The Jazz Singer* and *The Broadway Melody* were popular with French audiences. But French audiences also liked seeing and hearing French stars sing on screen. The first French-language talkie filmed in France, *Chiqué* (1930, dir. Colombier), took place in a French cabaret and featured several song and dance numbers. Though short and fairly crudely edited, *Chiqué*'s musical and choreographic spectacle, and focus on French musical performance (using a pair of American tourist characters who are interested in soaking up real French entertainment in order to highlight its Frenchness), whetted audiences' appetites for more. Both within France and abroad, song and dance spectacles soon abounded.

THE FILM OPERETTA

The *opérette filmée* was a particularly important subgenre of the musical film in the transition era (although the genre remained popular through the 1950s). The *stage* operetta had been a key fixture of the Parisian musical-theatrical scene since Offenbach. It began as a lighter alternative to the increasingly serious fare of the *opéra comique*.[9] At theaters like Les Bouffes Parisiens, audiences were exposed to upbeat, comical theatrical spectacles with song, dance, and dialogue; the light, fantastical genre seemed to capture the French musical spirit. Beginning in the 1910s and continuing through the 1920s, operetta composers began to move away from older musical styles (like waltzes) and incorporate contemporary popular musical and dance styles into operettas, folding jazz, music-hall, and the foxtrot into their scores. Operettas like the 1918 production *Phi-Phi* (by composer

Henri Christiné and librettist Albert Willemetz) blurred the line between operetta, *café-concert*, and music-hall stage genres.[10] Soon, major stars from all three contexts—including Dranem, Maurice Chevalier, Georges Milton, Michel Simon, Fernandel, and Jean Gabin—appeared on the operetta stage. Musical scores began to include more syncopation, and operetta librettists increasingly got their start with music-hall revues. Conversely, in the revues of the Casino de Paris, the Moulin-Rouge, and the Folies Bergères, operetta authors like Willemetz would write parody sketches of current events, and stars would premiere new songs by operetta composers.[11] By the end of the 1920s, the operetta had in many ways become inseparable from the more popular-style music-hall. Although nostalgic Viennese-influenced operettas continued to thrive, this more contemporary operetta subgenre, called the *comédie musicale*, was fresh and modern, the French answer to the Broadway musical.[12]

Furthermore, although the operetta in France had always had international influences, particularly Viennese and German, the 1920s saw an increase in transnational productions on the operetta stage, when a number of Broadway successes made their way to France in French translations. The term "operetta" in America held somewhat more specific connotations in the 1920s than in France in terms of subject matter, singing style, and cultural prestige. But both operettas and musicals crossed the Atlantic to reach French audiences. In 1926, the musical comedy *No, No, Nanette* became a huge success in France; in 1929, *Show Boat*, which was renamed *Mississippi* and adapted by Lucien Boyer, premiered at the Châtelet Theater. Gershwin's *Tip-Toes*, with French lyrics by André Mauprey, premiered at the Folies-Wagram the same year.[13] French audiences appreciated these Broadway operettas and musicals, much in the same way that film musicals from Hollywood and Germany became successful with French audiences in the years following. In other words, although French critics were resistant to the idea of foreign incursion on French filmmaking in the late 1920s, audiences and critics were quite accustomed to cosmopolitan productions when it came to the *stage* operetta. The *opérette filmée*, growing out of the stage operetta, became a product of this transnational cinematic exchange within the context of French cultural institutions.

When stage musicals were translated to the stage, then, why were they called *opérettes filmées*, and not *comédies musicales filmées*, *music-hall filmé*, or simply *films musicaux*? Early Hollywood operettas, such as *The Desert Song* (1929), *Show Boat* (1929), and particularly Ernst Lubitsch's film operettas *The Love Parade* (1929), *Monte Carlo* (1930), and *The Smiling Lieutenant* (1931), were typically distinguished by their exotic or fantastical settings, their extravagant costumes and sets, and their more elevated singing style. Musical comedies, by contrast, were film musicals with modern-day settings and popular-style songs. In France, the lines differentiating the categories of films with popular songs, *comédies musicales*, and *opérettes filmées* were not as distinct. But films that featured songs integrated into the narrative (as opposed to backstage musicals) were most often labeled *opérettes filmées*, regardless of musical style. The word *opérette* may have also provided just the right amount of cultural cachet, symbolically distinguishing it from its American counterparts that were deemed too light and inconsequential, while also nodding to the stage genre's preoccupations with witty, satirical, upbeat crowd-pleasing entertainment. The term "operetta" perfectly encapsulated what French producers and critics hoped would emerge from the French film industry: films that were fantastical, culturally acceptable, and highly entertaining.

The first *opérettes filmées* negotiated expectations of stage and screen aesthetics in a myriad of ways, often resulting in a tension between stage-bound and more distinctly cinematic approaches. Whether they were filmed in Germany or Paris, with Tobis-Klangfilm, Paramount, or Pathé, the *opérettes filmées* were strongly indebted to the stage. Many well-known stage performers became the first musical screen stars, including Henri Garat, Jean Gabin, Florelle, and Meg Lemonnier. Likewise, following the transition to sound, a number of composers for the stage—including Maurice Yvain, Raoul Moretti, and Georges Van Parys—turned to the screen. Songs were frequently performed as if the singers were on a proscenium stage, the camera remaining static, with long takes and infrequent edits, so as not to distract the viewer from the illusion that the onscreen performance was unfolding in real time. There were technical reasons for filming songs in this manner, because at the time, the practice of playback (recording a song in advance in the studio and playing it back while shooting the scene, to be lip-synced by the actors) had not yet been widely adopted.[14] Instead, this "stagey" approach approximated live performance, and was often filmed using direct recording, which also served to emphasize the synchronization of the voice and onscreen body.

As some filmmakers became concerned with approaching sound film as its own medium with distinct aesthetic priorities, they adopted what critics identified as a more "cinematic" approach to the genre. The operetta, a stage genre that was already fantastical and artificial at its core, was easily adaptable on the screen to allow for experimentation with the camera and with music's role in shaping film rhythm. Music could, instead of being a hindrance to camera movement, become a structuring device in and of itself. In "cinematic" *opérettes filmées*, optical special effects and brisk editing pace, techniques that had abounded in French silent film, were right at home. These kinds of deliberately unrealistic effects made the prospect of a character spontaneously bursting into song more plausible within an already fantastical cinematic world. Additionally, exterior settings could distinguish a cinematic song from a stagey song. For all of these reasons, directors soon relied on postsynchronized musical numbers or shooting to playback to achieve their desired effects. French critics preferred this approach to the genre, much in the same way that musical films from other national contexts (perhaps most notably, Hollywood) were increasingly striving for greater camera movement.

Of course, the terms "stagey" and "cinematic" are not absolute, and there is a give and take, and even a fluidity, with how they can be interpreted. For instance, a song could be shot on location but with "stagey" editing and framing. A more complicated example is the use of direct address in early film musicals, where actors would speak directly to the audience, or even encourage audience participation. This kind of reflexivity was common in early sound film in the United States, particularly in short films, where stage acts from vaudeville would be transposed for the screen with little change.[15] While it was a practice borrowed from the stage, this kind of overt reflexivity could also call attention to the act of viewing a film, and the technology of sound film in particular. It could familiarize the still novel experience of sound film for spectators, while simultaneously highlighting the difference between live theater and cinematic operetta. It could also function as a transitional device, to draw audiences from the real world into the world of cinematic entertainment (using the stage as a familiar conduit), then the narrative world of the film, and back out again. Additionally, performers who got their start in live stage genres might initially align a film more closely to the stage; but if they successfully translated their performance style for the screen, their presence could become a marker of the cinematic.

It is important to emphasize that there was not a clear trajectory from the stagey to the cinematic as filmmaking practices became more sophisticated. In fact, the interplay between the two approaches has continued to mark the musical film genre. Though the particulars may have changed, the two aesthetics have always existed in combination and in tension. French critics, however, strongly valued the cinematic over the stagey, and evaluated films accordingly. The following case studies—*Chacun sa chance*, *Le Chemin du paradis*, and *Il est charmant*—reveal the different manners in which individual films, originating from different transnational production contexts, navigated the tension between the theatrical and the cinematic, each contributing to a French conception of the musical film.

CHACUN SA CHANCE: THE JOINT PRODUCTION

Chacun sa chance is one of the many early musical films that were heavily indebted to live stage genres; and despite attempts to straddle theatrical and cinematic aesthetics, the film overall remains more firmly rooted in theatrical traditions. At the same time, its incorporation of popular songs, modern urban setting and story, and French stars provided a new cinematic experience for French audiences. Although it was advertised as a "film parlé et chanté français," *Chacun sa chance* was a Franco-German collaboration. Coproduced by the French company Pathé-Natan and the Romanian-born independent film producer Marcel Hellman, who worked in both Germany and England, it was filmed in Joinville-le-Pont outside of Paris at the Pathé-Natan studios.[16] Although Pathé was a coproducer, the creative team hailed primarily from Germany and the film seems to have been initially conceived of in German. Written by German librettist Bruno Hardt-Warden, with music by German operetta composer Walter Kollo, it was adapted into French by René Pujol and codirected by Pujol and German director Hans Steinhoff. (Pujol, who got his start writing for the stage, would become a key figure adapting a number of the French versions of MLVs for French audiences.) The film premiered in December 1930 at the Max-Linder Pathé Theater.[17] Steinhoff also directed the German-language version (*Kopfüber ins Glück*), which opened the following month in Germany.

The film is proudly marketed as an "Opérette Filmée," which is announced just below the title in the opening credits. Its story blends ingredients of traditional operettas (nobility, mistaken identity) with modern musical comedy (the modernity of Paris and the popular musical styles). It follows a department store salesman, Marcel Grivot (Jean Gabin), who dreams of living an upper-class lifestyle. One evening, he borrows a tuxedo from one of the store mannequins and goes out on the town, where he is mistaken for the wealthy Baron de Monteuil. He attends the theater, and meets a beautiful young woman, Simone (Gaby Basset), a young chocolatière who is also posing as a wealthy socialite. The case of mistaken identity leads to a comedy of errors involving Marcel, Simone, and the real baron and his wife. Much of the story takes place in the lobby and behind the scenes of a theater, allowing for several diegetic music and dance performances. Despite the film's relatively cohesive plot, the diegetic numbers give it a variety show flavor, highlighting the influence of vaudeville and music-hall.

The film's stars, Jean Gabin and Gaby Basset, were well-known stage performers. Gabin is today best remembered for his brooding, serious roles in a number of poetic realist films from later in the 1930s, but his career began on the music-hall stage as a comic singer.[18] Basset also began her career in cabaret and music-hall before starring in the film. The two were married from 1925 to 1930, but had divorced shortly before costarring in *Chacun sa chance*. The other stars, including André Urban (the baron) and Renée Héribel (the baroness), were also well-known stage actors.

It is therefore not surprising that from the very opening, the film displays clear debts to the theater. In fact, these debts are highlighted in an explicitly reflexive gesture. The opening credits, which run silent, feature a stage curtain in the backdrop. Charles O'Brien suggests that the silence of the credits allowed theater orchestras to play live music at the start of the film, an element that would have been a staple of both silent film screenings and live stage performances.[19] Next, an emcee steps out from behind the curtain, announcing the beginning of the film (Figure 3.1). He introduces the lead actors, then signals to the maestro, located in the pit below the stage, to begin playing the overture. The diegetic screen orchestra plays, and the camera cuts and pans among the various musicians as they play. At the end of the overture, a musical underscore picks up immediately as the image cuts to the exterior of a theater, literally setting the stage for the opening of the film's story. The

Figure 3.1: The Emcee, *Chacun sa chance* (1930)

direct address of the emcee to the cinematic audience is reminiscent of the first Warner Bros. Vitaphone shorts from 1926 to 1927, and even some feature films like *The Jazz Singer*, where actors would speak directly to their audience as if they were copresent, cracking jokes and mentioning the presumed applause or laughter of the audience. As Charles O'Brien suggests, the opening performance "occur[s] less on the screen itself than in the space between screen and audience."[20] Indeed, this opening serves as a framing device, a transitional space to bring spectators from theatrical expectations of live theater (of both music-hall and the live performances expected in a silent movie theater) into the narrative world of the film. It gives spectators permission to "step into" the cinematic world through the intermediary of the emcee and the maestro's orchestra. But by calling attention to the medium itself ("Since we're in a talking film, it would be best to start by talking"), the emcee signals the start of the cinematic spectacle by suggesting the synchronized sound technology is a crucial part of the audiovisual entertainment to come. In other words, sound cinema will be essential to the spectacle in the same way as singing and dancing.

Gabin's opening song, "La Chance de Marcel," exemplifies the film's negotiation of the theatrical and the cinematic. It remains grounded in theatrical convention with modest attempts at developing a cinematic operetta style, most notably with camera movement. In this slow, rubato waltz, Marcel sings about how he is prone to bad luck and unhappiness, never having had much money, many friends, or true love. The song reappears in the underscoring throughout the film to represent Marcel's character. The chorus begins and ends with the lyrics: "Depuis l'enfance, la chance me fuit" (since childhood, luck has escaped me) (Example 3.1). Marcel sings of his relatively humorous misfortunes: it rains on his vacation, and when he boards the city bus it is always already full. Gabin's performance style is reminiscent of Maurice Chevalier, although more subdued in his gestures and facial expressions, matching the understated melodic and lyrical content of the song. He begins behind the store counter where he works, singing directly to the camera, which frames him in medium close-up (Figure 3.2a). As he sings, he walks around to the front of the counter and to the other side of the room, and ends facing the opposite direction from where he began the song. The camera follows him with a long tracking shot, then remains static as soon as he arrives on the other side of the room (Figures 3.2b–c), only briefly cutting away toward the end of the song for a close-up, and cutting back to a medium close-up as the song ends. Gabin's direct address to the camera and the camera's static framing of his song are indicative of recorded theater: the editing and performance style mimic a performance on a proscenium stage. At the same time, the tracking shot violates the spatial layout of a proscenium stage, breaking theatrical expectations about audience point of view, and moving a small step toward a cinematic approach to musical performance.

The leading couple's duet, "Au Clair de Lune," again mediates the space between the theatrical and the cinematic, while remaining primarily rooted in theatrical aesthetics. The song is an upbeat foxtrot, jazzy and modern like much of the rest

Example 3.1: "La Chance de Marcel," *Chacun sa chance* (1930)

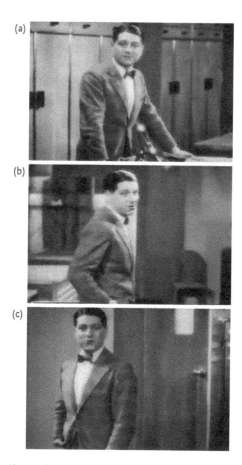

(a)

(b)

(c)

Figures 3.2a–c: "La Chance de Marcel," *Chacun sa chance* (1930)

of the score. The couple sings it toward the end of the film, after they enter the baron's house. As they sing the chorus, a long tracking shot follows them as they walk around various parts of the house and wander through doors and around furniture. This blocking would have been difficult on a proscenium stage, and was intended specifically for the point of view of the camera (Figure 3.3a). As the chorus ends, they sit down on a chair, and the camera cuts to a medium close-up. A few moments later, the camera follows them as they stand back up and walk to the salon. The second time they sing the chorus, edits occur with greater frequency, but the sense of a proscenium stage is preserved more closely, as each camera shot is from the same general perspective. From this point on the couple performs the song more clearly toward the camera, though not directly at it (Figure 3.3b).

The song reprises at the very end. The couple has just discovered each other's true identities and they happily embrace. The shot of the couple in the salon is replaced by a shot of the couple in the same position, but now on a stage (Figure 3.4). Gabin sings the song's chorus once more, as the camera very slowly zooms

Figures 3.3a–b: "Au Clair de Lune," *Chacun sa chance* (1930)

out so more of the stage is visible. The chorus ends, and the curtain closes. Just like the opening, the return of the characters to the stage serves as a framing or transitional device, this time to bring the spectators back out of the narrative, with an explicit reminder of the spectacle they just observed.

Despite *Chacun sa chance*'s star-studded cast, it received lukewarm reception in the press. For critics, the *opérette filmée* had not yet proven itself to be a cinematic genre. They found the film entertaining but too derivative of live theater, designed for an uncritical public eager to see and hear talking films but unconcerned about their cinematic merit. The cast was highly praised: Jean Prudhomme wrote in *Le Matin* that the songs "enliven the well-directed, upbeat, and cheerful scenes, that are performed skillfully by such performers as André Urban, Renée Héribel, Gaby Basset, and Jean Gabin."[21] A reviewer in *L'Ami du peuple* also found the acting to be of high quality and the music to be lively and entertaining, but for him it was despite the film's status as a filmed operetta:

> It's a filmed operetta (a subtitle informs us) and therefore it's necessary to take precautions.
>
> But we wouldn't want to give the director, Hans Steinhoff, or the adaptor, Mr. René Pujol, any grief about that. Once we admit that it's an operetta, we can complain instead that they did not dare to approach the domain of outrageous fantasy that permits us to more easily accept the simplicity of the plot.[22]

For this reviewer, a film "operetta" was by its very nature theatrical, but he also believed that a good operetta film required a greater degree of fantasy to enliven an otherwise banal plot. A reviewer in *Echo* agreed that the actors' performances were strong, but critiqued the very genre of the "filmed operetta" as overly reliant on theatrical convention:

> The filmed operetta currently holds a very important place in the productions being offered to us. . . .
>
> We have deliberately used the term "filmed operetta" because this description seems to make clear the concern that film directors will relegate cinematic elements to a position to which they don't belong: second place.

Figure 3.4: "Au Clair de Lune" reprise, *Chacun sa chance* (1930)

> Is it such a delicate task to agree on essential laws without which cinema is no longer cinema, regardless of the subject?
>
> And is it so difficult to make a film that, while conserving its character and inspiration from operetta, is instead a cinematic operetta?
>
> It's worth stating this hypothesis, and *Chacun sa chance* isn't the only film that persuades us to think in this way.
>
> In *Chacun sa chance*, which, incidentally, one has to admit, is not half bad, the director wasn't looking to reside in the cinematic domain but was more interested in merely removing purely stagey effects.[23]

This reviewer believed the *opérette filmée* was by its nature uncinematic, owing to its overreliance on the stage, and that *Chacun sa chance* did nothing to challenge the dominance of theatrical elements found in the genre. Indeed, *Chacun sa chance* mostly preserved unity of time and place, editing and cutting to maintain a semblance of a proscenium stage. Perhaps the close-ups and occasional violations of this spatialization was what the reviewer suggested as "removing purely stagey effects," but in this reviewer's opinion it did not go far enough toward creating a "cinematic operetta," which would not relegate cinematic elements to second place.

As these reviews suggest, though the film successfully brought French musical performers to the screen, critics viewed its status as an *opérette filmée* with more disdain than enthusiasm, and the genre was viewed with skepticism. With other films, however, the genre took on more positive connotations, becoming closer to the "cinematic operetta" that *Echo*'s reviewer had hoped for. *Le Chemin du paradis* marked an important contribution.

LE CHEMIN DU PARADIS: THE MULTIPLE-LANGUAGE VERSION

Just months before the release of *Chacun sa chance*, the highly successful *Le Chemin du paradis* arrived on the Parisian screen, to the enthusiasm of both audiences and critics. Although produced in Germany, the film was received as a French success. The German company UFA produced the film, simultaneously releasing a German version (*Die Drei von der Tankstelle*) and a French version. Wilhelm Thiele directed both versions, with help from Max de Vaucorbeil for the French version, and Werner Heymann composed the music. As with many other MLVs, the exact same sets and costumes were used in each scene, and the German and French versions are almost identical shot-for-shot.[24] Programs for the film advertised it as an international "super-production," distributed by the "Alliance Cinématographique Européenne," while also emphasizing that it was the "First Film Operetta completely spoken and sung in French" and "directed with the participation of a troupe of French artists."[25] For French critics, *Le Chemin du paradis* represented a significant aesthetic step forward for French sound cinema.

The film follows three male friends—Willy, Jean, and Guy—who, after finding out they are completely broke, decide to open up a gas station. They each separately meet Lilian, a frequent customer who is the daughter of a wealthy businessman, and they each fall in love with her, unbeknownst to the others. The absurd plot is punctuated by a number of upbeat and playful songs, many of which became highly popular in both their German and French versions. The biggest hits in France were "Avoir un bon copain," "Tout est permis quand on rêve," and "Le Chemin du paradis." Many of the songs remain closely connected to the story, at the same time as they were easily excerptable for consumption as popular songs.

English-German actress Lilian Harvey played Lilian in both the German and French versions. Born in London and raised in Berlin, Harvey had experience in both theater and silent cinema before becoming a star in numerous German film operettas of the 1930s.[26] Henri Garat acted alongside Harvey for the French version. Garat was a well-known music-hall performer, who frequently performed alongside Mistinguett at the Casino de Paris and Moulin Rouge.[27] *Le Chemin du paradis* launched his film career: he went on to star in countless musical films in the 1930s, and was even voted the "most photogenic French male star" in a survey for *Pour Vous* in 1931.[28] Garat and Harvey costarred in several other MLVs after *Le Chemin du paradis*, including *Le Congrès s'amuse* and *Princesse, à vos ordres*. René Lefèvre, a stage and silent screen actor, who later became best known for his starring roles in René Clair's 1931 film *Le Million* and Jean Renoir's 1936 film *Le Crime de Monsieur Lange*, played Jean. Despite the two separate casts and language barriers, the French cast developed a tight rapport, made all the more remarkable by the fact that Harvey needed to develop this rapport with two entirely different sets of actors.

The film's story was suited for the technological modernity of the cinema.[29] The centrality of the automobile not only highlights the contemporary setting of the plot; it also emphasizes the mobility of its characters, its musical numbers, and the camera. The film opens with a simple leitmotif, which imitates a car horn (Example 3.2). The car horn leitmotif returns frequently throughout the film, often signaling the arrival of the character Lilian but also appearing at other moments, including once as a diegetic song in a nightclub. The ubiquity of the leitmotif provides unity to the soundtrack and also highlights the soundtrack as a tool for storytelling within its modern operetta context.

Much like *Chacun sa chance*, the film's editing style reveals an attempt to negotiate theatrical and cinematic conventions; but *Le Chemin du paradis* features a much broader range of approaches to both editing and cinematography. During dialogue scenes, the camera framing remains relatively static, in order to keep the focus on the spoken word. But the song sequences allow for more fantastical cinematic experiments. The songs are choreographic in nature, clearly influenced by early sound animation as much as by the theater, and the camera plays a substantial role in this choreography, creating scenes that would be impossible on the stage. The song "Fauché," for instance, sung by the three friends right after they find out they are completely broke, explores different points of view that break with proscenium framing. They sit down, disappointed with their fate, and start singing, all facing the camera. As the song continues, they stand up, and walk and dance around the room, leaning on a desk and moving their feet in rhythm in a decidedly artificial manner. When a creditor comes to seize their furniture, the moving men dance toward them from the opposite side of the room. Then, the furniture begins to fly out of the house and into the moving truck of its own volition—first a sofa,

Example 3.2: Leitmotif, *Le Chemin du paradis* (1930)

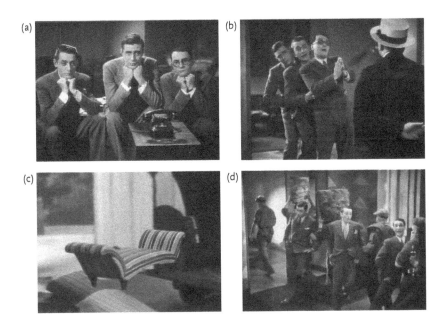

Figures 3.5a–d: "Fauché," *Le Chemin du paradis* (1930)

then a cabinet, next a rug. A slide whistle punctuates the movement of each piece of furniture. The three friends continue to dance, weaving in and out between the moving men as they work, the camera now at a different angle from the start of the song (Figures 3.5a–d). Though the camera still tends to capture moments of singing and dancing head-on, the framing is not an approximation of a proscenium stage. In fact, the frequent change in camera angle breaks theatrical expectations about audience point of view, moving the film more squarely into the realm of the cinematic.

The first full performance of the title song demonstrates a similar kind of style. The song appears at multiple times throughout the film, but is first sung in its entirety by Lilian and Willy at the gas station (Example 3.3). The staging of the song begins with a clear "front," and as Willy and Lilian trade off lines of the song, the camera alternates between a medium close-up of each character and a medium shot of the two of them together. After the chorus, the couple dances a shuffle together in front of Lilian's car. Here, the camera remains static as the couple performs the dance directly to the camera. The space in front of the car serves as a stage for their dance, and the choreography is camera-facing (Figure 3.6a). Next, however, Lilian dances around to the other side of the car, and Willy jumps through the car to the other side. The film cuts to the exact opposite point of view as the couple finishes its shuffle on the other side of the car (Figure 3.6b). Throughout, the dance is playfully energetic, conveyed through the couple's genuine smiles, the seeming spontaneous quality to the choreography, and the couple's switch to the other side of the car halfway through their performance.[30] The music continues after Lilian

Example 3.3: "Le Chemin du paradis," *Le Chemin du paradis* (1930)

De la grand-e dame au p'tit trot - tin qu'el-le soit bru - ne rousse ou bien châ - tain,

La femm' n'a plus qu'un rêve au - jour-d'hui a - voir une au-to et un per - mis.

(a) (b)

Figures 3.6a–b: "Le Chemin du paradis," *Le Chemin du paradis* (1930)

drives away, seamlessly transforming its function to musical underscoring during the next brief dialogue scene at her house. The audiovisual style of the song suggests a negotiation between theatrical and cinematic expectations for an operetta on film: the stasis of the camera for certain aspects of performance combined with its 360-degree play with camera placement, the popular song's transformation into underscoring for a scene in a new location, and the playfulness of the song and dance performance.

The very end of *Le Chemin du paradis*, just like the opening of *Chacun sa chance*, shifts significantly to a self-reflexive, theatrical mode. The story ends happily with the union of Lilian and Willy, all three friends working together in harmony again. As the ensemble finishes its final song, Lilian and Willy embrace, and a curtain closes behind them. Lilian looks at the camera, and addresses the spectator directly: "Look, Willy!" "What?" he asks. "All these people." "All these people?" "The public!" "Where?" "There." The shot changes slightly, now peering up at them from the point of view of the front row of a theater. Willy notices and says "Oh, yes!" "But what should we do? The film is over," Lilian inquires. Willy: "I'll ask them. Ladies and Gentlemen . . ." But before he can finish asking his question, Lilian interrupts: "Willy, wait. [Whispering] The finale. There's always a finale in a grand operetta." Willy agrees: "Oh yes! One moment, please . . ." (Figure 3.7a). They disappear behind the curtain, and the curtain reopens a few seconds later, showing Jean and Guy sitting on what was their office desk in the previous scene, now serving as a dancing platform on a stage. This time, a backdrop decorates the back of the set, and musicians sit in various positions along the back wall. A kick-line of women enters the frame. The spectacle becomes increasingly over-the-top, as more women appear to dance onstage, while the camera slowly zooms out to catch all of the action. Characters from the film enter and dance in front of the kick-line, and Willy and Lilian reappear and dance another soft-shoe (Figure 3.7b). The dance ends, the curtain closes, and the film is over. This ending suggests that the entire story, no matter how fantastical, could have all unfolded within the confines of a stage.

The finale scene in *Le Chemin du paradis* packs a complex punch: it playfully draws on both the anxieties and excitement of sound film. This overtly theatrical ending, this shift in mode from narrative absorption to spectacle, is in some ways at odds with the rest of the film. But, in the same playful manner as the rest of its songs, it parades the artifice of the operetta in full splendor. It lightheartedly mocks, while also acknowledging, the film operetta's reliance on theatrical conventions. The closing curtain, much like *Chacun sa chance*'s opening curtain, serves as a transitional device back into the space of the theater. Willy's direct address promises a back-and-forth engagement with the audience, but the film humorously acknowledges the impossibility of this kind of real-time interaction between actors and audience when Lilian cuts him off before the audience can respond. In this way, spectators are also briefly

Figures 3.7a–b: Ending, *Le Chemin du paradis* (1930)

reminded of their displacement in time and space from the actors, a crucial difference between a theatrical and a cinematic experience.

For a genre that most critics wrote off when discussing *Chacun sa chance*, the French press was overwhelmingly positive about *Le Chemin du paradis*. Many admitted that their preconceived expectations for *opérettes filmées* were twofold: that operetta itself was a stale, dated genre, and that the talking film was decidedly uninteresting from an artistic standpoint. But critics almost unanimously expressed their amazement at what could be accomplished in the film operetta. For instance, Gaston Thierry wrote in *Paris Midi* that the

> French talking film—100 percent—directed in Germany, is a complete success. It's an operetta, merely an operetta, but directed with endless taste, played to perfection and accompanied by a more than enjoyable score. Add to it the spectacle, which is "a spectacle" in all meanings of the word, . . . and you'll understand my indulgence for a genre that I've condemned many times; only exceptions of this quality will contribute to the genre's rehabilitation.[31]

Others took the idea even further, using the film as the evidence that the film operetta could become, surprisingly, the very genre that would offer a much-needed breath of fresh air to save the talking film. The film operetta might even become something new: a distinctly cinematic musical fantasy genre. Critic P. D. wrote,

> Once and for all, operetta seems to have found in the talking film a freshness, and new possibilities. . . .
> Finally, operetta has found, in the juxtaposition of the unreal, of the arbitrary nature of "sung" theater with natural settings (a real sky, real trees . . .), a particular atmosphere that, for my part, I find quite agreeable in the way it's presented in the film *Le Chemin du paradis*.[32]

J.-M. Aimot claimed that the film was "the road to liberation. . . . This time, even if the inspiration was found outside of cinema [through its use of the operetta format], the cinema was used without being suppressed. . . . A filmed operetta can be a film."[33] Critic Alexandre Arnoux implied that the film would not have been of such significance if the future of talking films did not seem so bleak, but he still conceded that it seemed an important path to sound cinema's salvation: "I don't want you to think I've attached too much undeserved importance to *Le Chemin du paradis*. A humble work, I'll repeat, but a happy, vivacious one, and one that shows that the cinema, after a dark cloud that threatened to destroy it, recaptures on the screens what had threatened to be chased and usurped."[34]

Émile Vuillermoz was particularly effusive, and wrote in no uncertain terms how important the film's aesthetic was for the future of sound film, particularly French sound film. He credited the music in particular with helping to shape this new audiovisual style:

The libretto and the score aren't extraordinarily original, but the merit of this work is that it gives us, for the first time, a true "operetta of the screen." Here, the director didn't give up . . . the cinematic richness that we see sacrificed all the time by the obsession with the microphone. Here, the scenery maintains its flexibility, its mobility, its ubiquity. But the real treasure was how it guaranteed the same privileges to the music.

Until now, the screen, like in the theater, has made music the slave to the idea of unity of place. From this point forward it will be freed from this servitude. A rhythm can freely take off as a point of departure, attain in the distance another objective, without slowing down or rushing its momentum and imposing its discipline on other images and actions. An operetta couplet begun outdoors can be followed by one in a salon, continued in an automobile and completed in a factory. A refrain can simultaneously galvanize a range of beings; pass from one to another with a tremendous rapidity and set in motion an element of cheerfulness in the most diverse settings, conserving the discipline of the unity of time.

The music, therefore, becomes a miraculous animator that flows through all of the cells of the film. . . . Its role has become radically magnified and extensive. This conquest . . . opens for us unforeseen horizons for the future of the lyrical screen.[35]

Though his praise for the film may appear hyperbolic today, Vuillermoz sensed that a reliance on fantasy, which used music as a unifier of diverse places and times and allowed the camera a range of powers and functions, would become truly important for the film musical genre, both in France and abroad. Jean Fayard expressed a similar sentiment, claiming that Thiele found a solution to the previously static use of song in film:

The thing that motivates my enthusiasm, besides the pleasure of one evening, is that I have found in it, just as in the golden age of silent film, real *cinema*, completely unlike in the theater, consisting of visual ideas.

It's also *talking* cinema, thanks to the rhythm that makes the fantastical plausible, and thanks to the charming music.[36]

The music, in other words, was used to its full potential as a structuring device to bring the cinematic back to sound film. The overwhelmingly enthusiastic sentiments of the critics made *Le Chemin du paradis* one of the most influential films to be released in France in the first years of synchronized sound.

IL EST CHARMANT: PARAMOUNT IN PARIS

As German-directed French-language *opérettes filmées* became increasingly successful, French composers, librettists, and directors began to have the opportunity to try their hand at the genre at home. One studio that welcomed French personnel was the Paramount studio in Joinville. From 1930 until 1933, Joinville was known as "Babel on the Seine," a studio where crews and actors worked in numerous languages producing films for distribution around the world. Paramount produced one hundred features and fifty shorts in fourteen different languages.[37] Paramount's Joinville studios gave the American production company a huge influence over film production in France during a time when French studios were still playing catch-up. But Paramount also gave French filmmakers, actors, and composers an opportunity to create sound films for French audiences on French soil. One such film was *Il est charmant* (1932). Though *Il est charmant* was produced by an American company, the writer, composer, director, and actors were all French, and the film was produced specifically with the French filmgoing public in mind.

Albert Willemetz wrote the screenplay and libretto. Willemetz was a well-established librettist who had been writing successful stage operettas since 1918. Raoul Moretti composed the music. Moretti, who was born in Marseille, wrote music for a number of stage operettas, music-hall productions, and popular songs; he wrote songs for Maurice Chevalier and was credited as the author of the first "fox-trot."[38] Swiss-born Louis Mercanton, the director, began his career with His Majesty's Theatre in London, where he also directed a few silent films. He directed *Le Mystère de la villa rose* (1930), one of the first French talking films. His experience directing in both English and French made him a useful asset at the Paramount in Paris studios. *Il est charmant* was his first film for Paramount, but he directed several others, and was on his way to becoming one of France's most promising directors before he died suddenly of an embolism in 1932.[39] Though Willemetz, Moretti, and Mercanton were new to sound film, they all were very invested in the new audiovisual possibilities in the *opérette filmée*, shaping their approach to the form through their experience with French musical, stage, and silent cinematic traditions.

The film's stars, too, showcased French talent. Henri Garat, after his success in *Le Chemin du paradis*, returned to France and entered under contract with Paramount. Garat played Jacques Dombreval, a failed law student who inherits his uncle's notary office. His costar was Meg Lemonnier, who played Jacqueline, a successful law student who ends up being hired at Jacques's notary office. A stage performer born in London to French parents, Lemonnier began as a dancer and a chorus girl at age fifteen, performing in vaudeville revues in England and touring in Canada with an English company before coming to Paris in 1927 to star in a stage production called *Broadway*. From that point on, she was an important fixture on the Parisian stage, particularly the operetta company the Théâtre des Bouffes Parisiens (the film even announces her affiliation with this company in the opening credits). Though she had a slight English accent, French critics identified her as a French actress owing to her parents' origin.[40] Garat and Lemonnier would costar in several Paramount operettas following *Il est charmant*. The film also starred Dranem, a slightly older comic singer who performed with les Bouffes Parisiens and was also known for his performance of classical repertoire.

The song "Histoire de voir" is a quintessential example of Moretti and Willemetz's compositional style—playful and modern in its content and delivery—as well as Garat's star persona, and exemplifies the manner in which the music shapes the audiovisual aesthetic of the film more generally. The entirety of the song takes place on a streetcar. Jacques meets Jacqueline on the street and jumps onto the streetcar to talk to her. The song is jaunty and upbeat, and Garat accentuates each quarter note to emphasize the rhyme scheme of the lyrics in the chorus (Example 3.4). Jacques tries to woo Jacqueline, who

Example 3.4: "Histoire de voir," *Il est charmant* (1932)

only playfully resists, but smiles as he sings to her, which is reflected in the song's lyrics:

Histoir' de voir ce que ça donnera,	Let's just see what will happen
Histoir' de voir si ça rendra,	Let's just see what will unfold
Suivons de loin, ma foi, nous verrons bien	Let's follow it from afar, by golly, we'll see
Car, qui ne risque rien,	Because, if we don't risk anything
N'a rien	We won't gain anything
Deux seul's chos's peuvent se produire:	Only two things could happen:
Ell' rira, ou n'voudra pas rire,	She'll laugh, or she won't laugh.
Histoir' de voir ce que ça donnera!	Let's just see what will happen
Vous avez ri, alors ça va!	You laughed, so it's all good!

The camera remains fixed on the couple (Figure 3.8), only once cutting to a close-up of the two, where we see Jacques subtly try to slip his hand around Jacqueline's waist and Jacqueline quickly slap his hand away. Throughout, the

Figure 3.8: "Histoire de voir," *Il est charmant* (1932)

city streets whir past behind them. When the conductor walks by to demand payment, Jacques turns around briefly, giving Jacqueline just enough time to run away. An older woman moves to Jacqueline's place, and Garat turns around and grabs her hand, only noticing that it is not his love interest a few moments later. The song ends, he exits the streetcar, and the older woman beams, saying "What a charming young man!" ("Il est charmant, ce jeune homme!"). The song reprises a few moments later, as Jacques and Jacqueline coincidentally arrive at the same place to take their law school exams. The musical style of the song calls for a playfulness of delivery, and Garat performs the song with a smile, as Lemonnier hardly contains her own smile in response. Their gestures are flirty but subtle, intended for a screen and not a stage audience. Meanwhile, the constantly shifting scenery of Parisian city streets in the background serves as a reminder to the viewer that they are viewing a film, not a play.

Unlike many musical films of the era, *Il est charmant* featured a complete, newly composed operetta score that was conceived of holistically just like its stage counterparts. In contrast to *Chacun sa chance* and *Le Chemin du paradis*, *Il est charmant* has a more traditional operetta structure, with more singing and frequent ensemble numbers. The sheer number of songs in the film is impressive—thirteen songs (nearly twice as many as *Chacun sa chance* and *Le Chemin du paradis*) and multiple reprises—as is the number of ensemble numbers. Almost all the songs are nondiegetic, with the exception of a couple of diegetic songs performed during a ball toward the end of the film. Moreover, the boundaries between dialogue scenes and musical numbers are fluid, with almost continuous underscoring during dialogue scenes to integrate the songs more closely with the rest of the film. Because of this fact, the pace of the entire film is shaped by the way the musical numbers are shot.

The opening scene makes it apparent how *Il est charmant* negotiates its debts to the stage within the realm of the cinematic, particularly with respect to the staging of the ensemble. The film opens with an ensemble number that also introduces Jacques as a fun-loving, carefree, and playful character who does not take life too seriously. We are presented with an empty city square. A chorus sings in unison from off screen and soon after we see a crowd enter, Jacques carried on two men's shoulders. The crowd has been out celebrating all night. As they enter the city square, they stop to sing together. Jacques sings a line and several soloists follow, ending with the entire group (Figure 3.9a). The song ends suddenly, when a policeman appears. As a musical underscore plays underneath, he yells at them about the time and tells them to go to bed. They agree and sing the chorus once more, much more quietly.

This ensemble number features a range of camera positions, but the city street setting is still configured much like a proscenium stage, and the ensemble's blocking and choreography could have easily been transposed to a stage. The over-the-top playfulness of the performance style is borrowed from the stage; but it is also perfectly suited to a style of cinematic fantasy where

Figures 3.9a–b: Opening, *Il est charmant* (1932)

singing on screen must be somehow made plausible within the world of the film. The ensemble remains jocular, as a few minutes later the policeman seems to "conduct" them as they encourage Jacques to run off and study for his exams (Figure 3.9b). Again, this kind of lightheartedness could be equally effective on a stage, but also helps to establish the kind of musical fantasy world of the film.

Throughout, the ensemble also offers plenty of opportunities for optical effects, such as dissolves and superimpositions, establishing a style of musical fantasy that is distinctly cinematic. In one scene, Jacques is at home trying to study, singing about how he would prefer to be at the Folies Bergères. He falls asleep in his chair, and suddenly we see his dream become animated: a group of chorus girls (listed in the opening credits as "Les 24 Mangan Tillerettes Girls") dressed in Roman-inspired costumes emerge from his Roman law book on his desk. They sing and dance in miniature, while we see him asleep next to them (Figure 3.10a). The desk provides a perfect stagelike platform for their dance, but the humor of the number is based on the novelty of this composite shot. In another scene, after Jacques and Jacqueline take their exam, Jacques sings to her in the hallway of the law school building in front of several imposing statues. Suddenly, the statues begin to sing to Jacques and Jacqueline (Figure 3.10b). Later in the film, as the chorus sings a reprise of the title song, a woman in a painting sings the final line. These special effects match the playful, fantastical operetta world, the kind of world where characters spontaneously burst into song. They also differentiate the film operetta from the stage operetta, where these kinds of effects would be impossible.

The lead actors' songs also feature optical effects, which are mostly used to represent a visual manifestation of their imaginations. Later in the film, when the two are at the notary's office far from Paris, Jacques sings a song to Jacqueline called "En parlant un peu de Paris" (While Speaking of Paris). They sit in front of a wide window, and suddenly the window becomes a screen, where we see a montage of scenes from Parisian city streets. Even more striking is Jacqueline's solo number, "Il est charmant," which relies heavily on superimpositions and clever edits. Before the song begins, Jacqueline talks

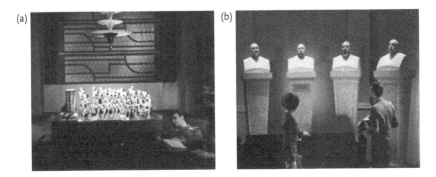

Figures 3.10a–b: Optical Effects in *Il est charmant* (1932)

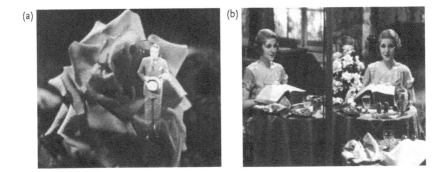

Figures 3.11a–b: "Il est charmant," *Il est charmant* (1932)

to her doubled reflection in the mirror, discussing the man she just met, and, unexpectedly, her reflection responds. She holds a conversation with herself, the camera adopting a shot/reverse shot pattern to make it appear as if her reflection is speaking to her. She opens up a book as she begins to sing, but she sees Jacques's face superimposed on the pages. She sees his image again as she looks at a flower on her table (Figure 3.11a). As she begins to sing the chorus, her reflection listens to her (Figure 3.11b), then harmonizes in a descant part (Example 3.5). The camera continues to alternate between her and her reflection. The scene experiments with voice-over, mirror reflections behaving differently than their source, and superimposition of images; moreover, these effects are built into the compositional structure of the song itself.

The very end of the film, much like *Chacun sa chance* and *Le Chemin du paradis*, engages directly with the audience. In this case, the film seems to break with stage operetta conventions and move more squarely into the realm of the music hall or silent cinema theater. After the finale, the music continues to play as the end credits roll. The music continues and the lyrics to the song "En parlant un peu de Paris" begin to scroll across the screen. The orchestra plays an instrumental version of the song, and the text changes

Example 3.5: "Il est charmant," *Il est charmant* (1932)

in appropriate timing with the music, intended to encourage a sing-along. This kind of sing-along was a holdover from the illustrated song, a silent film practice that began at the turn of the century, which would feature a solo performance of a song while pictorial slides illustrated the text. The last slide usually contained the words to the chorus and encouraged the audience to join in.[41] This kind of call to participation occurred in other early sound films in France as well: Pière Colombier's 1930 film *Le Roi des resquilleurs*, for instance, which starred the famous comedian and singer Georges Milton, ends with a song and dance performed directly to the camera. Then Milton acknowledges the "cher public" directly, invites everyone to sing together, and sings the song once again; this time the lyrics are projected across the screen to encourage audience participation. In *Il est charmant*, audience members are simultaneously drawn into the film through their encouraged participation and brought out of the narrative world of the film and back into the communal space of the movie theater audience. Much in the same manner as *Chacun sa chance* and *Le Chemin du paradis*, the final song offers a transitional space between stage and screen, theater and narrative. The music ends as we see a final credit, the Paramount logo with the text "C'est un film Paramount."

Critics praised the film, both for its aesthetic contributions to sound film and also, importantly, for its Frenchness. L.-P. Coutisson called the film "pure fantasy from the first to the last image," which is "what makes the charm of this film."[42] C. Tony was particularly excited that such a successful film should come from within France:

> Here's an operetta that will put at ease those who are detractors of cinema. . . .
> Because whether they like it or not, this time they will have to admit that here's
> a film that approaches a masterpiece with its humor, liveliness, and joy. . . .
> Everything in this film contributes to unleashing a "truly French" joy. . . . *Il est
> charmant* is a model of the genre and Paramount, the responsible party for this
> delicious cinematographic operetta, brought a huge triumph to French cinema-
> tography . . . since the artists, director, *ideas* are all French in *Il est charmant*.
> The music is French. A bit more than French . . . since it was written by the
> Marseillaise composer Raoul Moretti, and those from Marseille are doubly
> French.[43]

Paul Gordeaux suggested the creative team had developed a whole new, uniquely French operetta style, explaining that in 1918, "Mr. Albert Willemetz discovered with *Phi-Phi* the formula for a new genre of French operetta, which, for twelve years, would give the lyric stage a whole repertoire of nimble, ele- gant, light works. In 1932, Mr. Albert Willemetz gives us, with *Il est charmant*, the formula for cinematic French operetta. It's a good formula."[44] He remarked that it went far beyond "the comedies that we've been saturated with for two years where, suddenly, the action and the rhythm are interrupted to arbi- trarily make space for a song plastered onto the film," and he found it "one of the most agreeable spectacles that the screen has offered us this year."[45]

Vuillermoz, in his typical fashion, contemplated extensively on the film's contribution to French filmmaking, praising it as "an important evolution in taste in the history of cinematographic entertainment."[46] He saw the playful style as unique to the French spirit of music and theater. He la- mented that this lightness had been lost with the advent of sound film, and praised *Il est charmant* for restoring this quintessentially French aesthetic to cinema.

> Since the dawn of time, our authors, our actors, and our musicians have excelled
> in enjoyable fantasies where good humor and irony mix together, whose effer-
> vescence irresistibly evokes the frothy lightness of our national wines. This is
> the reason why for a long time I have deplored the slowness that film directors
> have shown in welcoming in their studios this Parisian spirit that has made, up
> to now, the fortune of a good part of our theater and our song traditions. . . .

The new Paramount operetta seems to indicate a happy reversal on the part of our film editors. . . . The result is excellent. . . . [I]t's an achievement that reflects its native soil.

What's particularly happy about this technique is the timely return of a certain richness of cinematographic style that had been completely given up for a while. The professionals of photographed theater, who ignore the technical virtuosity of silent film, had discredited superimposition and diverse methods of visual counterpoint that we called, a little frivolously, "tricks." Louis Mercanton had the intelligence and the courage to restore these precious privileges to the moving image. . . .

Personally, I would have wished to see this collaboration completed by a composer more individualistic than Mr. Moretti. . . . But even if they lack originality, the refrains by Mr. Moretti are at least written in a serious and solid way and are popular and earnest, which will assure their immediate success.[47]

Though Vuillermoz found the music to be slightly generic, Paul Granet praised Moretti's score. He mentioned that the film's music was already playing on phonographs throughout France, signaling its success and popularity with French audiences: "It's charming, this light, fanciful, very, very crazy film, but always cheerful and always in a good style. The elegant music by Moretti is also charming. As expected, the airs are already being heard on the phonograph."[48] Moretti's melodies were not only suitable for the character of the film but also held up on their own, as indicated by Granet's observation of the popularity of phonograph records and sheet music sales.

CONCLUSION

The operetta film provided a unique format for experimenting with cinematic fantasy, creative editing, and other optical effects during a time when French critics felt they were most lacking. Not all operetta films of the era exhibited such an approach to the genre: films like *Mam'zelle Nitouche*, *Nuits de Venise*, and others maintained a more static camera and staging during songs, which were set apart from the rest of the dialogue aesthetically and narratively. Nevertheless, it is interesting that French critics and filmmakers celebrated the return of cinematic experimentation in the era of sound within a commercial, internationally produced genre. The differing approaches to the form found in *Chacun sa chance*, *Le Chemin du paradis*, and *Il est charmant* reveal that the genre was flexible enough to accommodate a range of aesthetics. Popular songs appearing in films that were not explicitly labeled *opérettes filmées* could adopt a number of these approaches as well, with respect to the narrative and the song's relationship with the image.

The phase of international collaboration for musical films was short-lived: MLVs became too costly to continue, the Joinville studio shut down production in 1932, and companies reverted to dubbing around the same time, once technological means of doing so had improved. By the mid-1930s, French production companies had caught up with their American and German counterparts. But companies like UFA, Tobis, and Paramount left an indelible mark on French filmmaking in the early sound era, giving French directors, composers, and actors the freedom to experiment and develop new sound film practices when French production companies would have slowed the process down.

The *opérette filmée* was far from the only screen genre indebted to stage traditions. As we shall see in the following chapter, theatrical adaptations of straight plays were abundant in the early sound era in France, more so than in most other countries. However, the *opérette filmée* offered a unique set of audiovisual possibilities determined and structured by its music. Songs gave filmmakers permission to delve into the realm of fantasy, something that had been an important value for many avant-garde practitioners of silent cinema. The fantasy was simultaneously adopted *from* the stage and employed as an attempt to *differentiate* cinema from theater. The similarities, tensions, and seemingly irreconcilable differences between theater and cinema also profoundly shaped the experiments of two of the most influential—and diametrically opposed—filmmakers of the early sound era: René Clair and Marcel Pagnol.

CHAPTER 4

Théâtre filmé, Opera, and Cinematic Poetry

The Clair/Pagnol Debate

Ascreening of an American film in London would become the turning point in the careers of two pioneers of French sound cinema. In 1929, when the opportunities to encounter sound film technology in France were still slim, a number of French artists and filmmakers made the pilgrimage to attend MGM's backstage musical film *The Broadway Melody*.[1] Playwright Marcel Pagnol and silent film director René Clair both left the film with clear ideas about what they believed the future of sound cinema should look and sound like. They both articulated these theories in writing over the following years. And they both enacted them in a series of films in the early 1930s. But their visions for sound film were diametrically opposed, and they fought about their opposing conceptions of sound film's ontology openly and passionately in the press. The 1929 screening of *The Broadway Melody* in London inspired Clair and Pagnol to develop further their existing aesthetic preoccupations, becoming a springboard for a lively and very public debate between two major artistic forces in France fighting to define cinema's future.

Pagnol, who grew up in Marseille, had become one of Paris's most popular playwrights. He was catapulted to fame with his play *Marius* (1929), which was praised for its authentic portrayal of Provençal life. He was previously uninterested in cinema, and he might have returned home from London with concern about live theater's future and the new medium's encroachment on its domain. Instead, he interpreted *The Broadway Melody* as a theatrical production, translated to the screen. He became fascinated by sound film's potential to record and disseminate theater and become a vehicle for the spoken word.

He was also intrigued by sound film's ability to transport a play to more natural locales, serving to enhance its realism while maintaining its theatrical integrity. Pagnol gained success by writing screenplays, and later, directing and producing films, which emphasized spoken dialogue and on-location shooting as the medium's most salient elements. His *Fanny* trilogy epitomized this particular *théâtre filmé* approach to sound cinema. But this emphasis on audiovisual realism and the spoken word left seemingly little place for music in the soundtrack. His films nevertheless possess their own form of musicality, enacted not by a musical score, but by the rhythm of spoken dialogue.

Clair was an avant-garde silent film director associated with the surrealist movement. He feared realistic sound would threaten cinema's poetic potential. He believed cinema was a predominantly visual medium, and was adamantly opposed to bringing theater—particularly the spoken word—into the realm of film. Clair's very resistance prompted a creative aesthetic response to synchronized sound.[2] He praised *The Broadway Melody*'s technical innovations, claiming that its camera movement and innovative use of sound made it "neither theatre nor cinema, but something altogether new."[3] He sought to accomplish this same feat in his own sound films. Aiming to establish a fantastical screen poetry that maintained the cinematic abstraction found in silent film and avoided an overemphasis on spoken language, he incorporated music into his stories and soundtracks in unusual, provocative ways that created something that was neither silent cinema nor recorded theater. He explored this kind of audiovisual cinematic fantasy in his first three sound films, *Sous les toits de Paris* (1930), *Le Million* (1931), and *À nous la liberté* (1931). To accomplish this style, Clair's films drew heavily from a different kind of live theatrical model than Pagnol's: opera and operetta.

This chapter focuses on the famous debate between Pagnol and Clair, both in the press and through their films, on the very ontology of sound cinema. I first analyze Pagnol's approach to sound and music in *Marius* (1931), a film based on his stage play of the same name. Although music was sparse in his films, it nevertheless served an important (if subtle) function in establishing setting, producing meaning, and revealing the unexpressed motivations of Pagnol's characters. Still, music's role in the soundtrack remained contained, in order to make space for what was most important: the rhythmic cadence of the spoken word. Pagnol's reliance on live theatrical aesthetics exemplified an approach to sound cinema that became ubiquitous in the French film industry well into the 1930s.

Next, I turn to *Le Million*, Clair's well-received second sound film and a film whose musical treatment merits in-depth analysis. Particularly in *Le Million*, Clair's attempt to avoid overreliance on the spoken word led him to draw instead from musical-theatrical genres, specifically operetta and opera, as a tool for cinematic fantasy. His approach to the musical film was influenced by the *opérette filmée* as discussed in chapter 3, but distinctive to Clair's own aesthetic preoccupations. For one thing, he took particular advantage of the "recorded" nature of cinema to accomplish relationships between sound and image not possible in a live setting. Though Pagnol did not publicly write about the role of music in his cinematic aesthetic, Clair did frequently, and the accounts of his collaborators further provide a window into his working process and the ways in which he put his theories into practice.

The debate had much symbolic importance during the transition years, both men tremendously successful in presenting diverging paths for sound cinema's future. Pagnol's approach was more widely adopted in the French film industry, but Clair's early audiovisual cinema style is today remembered as one of the most innovative of the early sound era. Although seemingly on opposite ends of the "cinema as theater" spectrum, a side-by-side analysis of *Marius* and *Le Million* reveal that they were perhaps not as diametrically opposed as their creators may have thought: they both used music to explore the relationship between the live and the mediated, the theatrical and the cinematic. The debate between Pagnol and Clair, and the films where they enacted their theories of sound cinema, reveals the aesthetic connections and tensions between live theater (both straight and musical) and cinema, and music's importance in articulating those tensions.

MARCEL PAGNOL: SOUND CINEMA AS RECORDED THEATER

Pagnol approached sound cinema as a proud outsider. He first gained success as a playwright with the Parisian premiere of his satire *Topaze* (1928). Even more successful was his realist play that followed, *Marius*. *Marius* is about the romance between the title character and his childhood friend Fanny. Marius finds himself increasingly drawn to the sea and wishes to travel to exotic places, and he ultimately must choose between his love, familial obligation, and the seafaring life he desires. Included in the story is a cast of colorful local characters, such as César, a bar owner and Marius's father, and Panisse, a rich older man who proposes to Fanny. The play drew on the local culture and language of Marseille, where Pagnol grew up. It was an instant hit and a critical success, running for over two years.[4] Its sequel, *Fanny*, debuted in 1932 and was just as successful.

Pagnol had very little interest in silent film. Before he attended *The Broadway Melody* he wrote only one article about cinema, in 1923, about Abel Gance's film *La Roue* (published under the name J.-H. Roche). There, he wrote, somewhat disparagingly, "it is certain that the seventh art has a potential equal to that of theatre, if I may compare the two; and intellectuals worldwide are still anxiously awaiting the ingenious *cinégraphiste* who will produce the first work of art worthy of that name."[5] Pagnol's naturalist aesthetic was at odds with the predominant silent film artistic movements in France, particularly the impressionist and surrealist silent filmmakers who valued cinema's unreality.

When sound film came to France, however, Pagnol was in a position to renegotiate his relationship to cinema. He diverged from many French filmmakers reluctant to adapt to sound; instead, he saw sound film as a valuable tool for playwrights. Over the following years, he wrote, often polemically, about the ontology of sound film and its relationship to live theater. He quickly realized the possibilities of sound film as a tool for adaptation—a mode for recording and disseminating preconceived works—and eagerly encouraged playwrights to exploit sound film for the theater. For Pagnol, sound cinema was a means of expanding audiences and making certain that every word playwrights had written could be heard clearly. Cinema did not replace theater; it simply relocated it to the movie theater, improving the spectator's viewing experience in the process. He wrote in 1930:

> And that's the miracle of the camera: *every spectator sees the image exactly as the lens saw it, at the same distance and from the same angle. . . .*
>
> The microphone has the same property: every spectator would hear the actor's words just as the little round box hears them when they are recorded; in a cinema hall there aren't a thousand spectators, there is only one.
>
> The consequences of this property are immense.[6]

Less than a month later, he spoke critically of the French film industry's reaction to synchronized sound, claiming, "The talking film has most of the producers of talking film against it. Almost everyone who works for the New Art do all they can to turn us off it." Theater practitioners, on the other hand, "will understand soon that the 'talkies,' far from being a rival, are only a broadening of their art."[7] Pagnol strongly emphasized sound film and live theater's close relationship, imagining sound film as a new context for theatrical productions that had until then been bound to the stage and to a much more limited distribution. He continued to articulate this idea in the press, still writing in 1933 that film was "the art of imprinting, fixing, and diffusing theater."[8] (This conception of sound cinema, of course, also held the promise of great personal gain for Pagnol.)

Pagnol believed the talking film could not just emulate live theater, but improve upon it in two important ways: in its capacity for realism and in its ability to transmit spoken dialogue more clearly and comprehensibly than in an auditorium. For the former, on-location shooting could provide a greater degree of realism than was possible on a stage. But the latter was even more significant for his conception of sound film. Language was an important component of his theatrical realism, and he naturally found it to be crucial to sound film's ontology. In *Marius* and *Fanny*, his actors all spoke with a distinct Marseillaise accent, and speech was one of his most potent tools for delivering the local flavor of his dramas. The microphone offered a point-of-audition that was more or less the same for each spectator, and actors would no longer have to be concerned about whether their words were projected to the back row of the theater. The microphone would guarantee the primacy of the voice of the soundtrack, as speech would take absolute priority over anything else in a film. In 1933, Pagnol declared that a "talking film which can be shown silent, and remain comprehensible, is a very bad talking film."[9]

Pagnol had the opportunity to enact his theories of sound cinema when a scout at Paramount in Paris approached him and expressed interest in adapting *Marius* for the screen. *Marius* was part of a larger effort on the part of Paramount to move away from multiple-language versions and appeal to the French public with specifically French stories, dialogue, and actors. To prepare, Pagnol spent a few months studying various aspects of production at the Joinville studios.[10] The Hungarian-born director Alexander Korda, a seasoned director with experience in sound film and a reputation for a talent with adaptation, was signed on to direct. *Marius*'s style emphasized dialogue, naturalistic acting, and on-location shooting, and featured the same troupe of actors that had performed the stage version the year prior. The tremendous success of *Marius* inspired Pagnol to continue working in sound film.[11] He eventually tried his hand at directing, and in 1932 founded his own production studio in Marseille, the only real rival to Paris in terms of French film production.

MARIUS (1931), FANNY (1932), AND MUSIC IN THÉÂTRE FILMÉ

Although Pagnol emphatically insisted that sound cinema was at its best as recorded theater, his films contain more cinematic elements than he would have perhaps liked to admit. In the 1950s, André Bazin asserted,

> Looked at from [Pagnol's] point of view, his work is indefensible. It constitutes in effect an example of what should not be done in the adaptation of theater to the screen. . . . Even if *Marius* was a success at the Theater of Paris before Alexander Korda directed the screen version, it is clear that this work's basic form is, and will continue to be, cinematic. . . . Pagnol's cinema is quite the contrary of theatrical, then: it immerses itself, through the intermediary of language, in the realistic specificity of film.[12]

Pagnol's visual style has been criticized for being static, with a mise-en-scène that prioritizes intelligibility of dialogue over camera movement. And Pagnol's approach was indeed quite different from Buñuel's, Cocteau's, and even the directors of *opérettes filmées* who drew heavily from stage genres. Yet, as Bazin suggests, the predominance of spoken language, paired with the realism of on-location shooting, could be used for distinctly cinematic purposes.

Because Pagnol's early soundtracks placed such a high priority on speech, and because of his emphasis on realism, music in Pagnol's films is sparse.

Music serves important but limited functions. In both *Marius* and its sequel *Fanny*, music mostly takes the backseat to spoken dialogue; but occasionally, the hierarchy between dialogue and music is inverted, revealing how music can serve an important function even in a dialogue-heavy film. These musical moments are often the films' most visually "cinematic" moments as well, where the camera is used most freely.

Francis Gromon, a studio composer and arranger at the Paramount studios in Paris, composed the music for *Marius*.[13] There are fewer than twenty minutes of music in the two-hour film, and its role is mostly unobtrusive and decorative, meant to highlight the emotions that are already present in Pagnol's dialogue. Music is first heard during the opening credits, which present three distinct musical themes. These same themes are heard again in the middle of the film, when Marius and Fanny first embrace (which marks the end of what would be Act II in the stage version and the transition into Act III), again right before they go to bed together (between Acts III and IV of the stage version), and once more at the end of the film, as Marius leaves on the ship. In these four instances, music highlights important structural moments in the narrative and bookends acts of the play. The reuse of the musical themes for this kind of decorative function might have been a practical and cost-saving decision, since it almost does not matter what music plays to highlight these moments, as long as there is *some* music present. Music appears briefly only a few other times throughout the film. In one case, it indicates movement between locations: when César humorously rushes to a romantic rendezvous, dialogue is absent, and the music underscores his rapid movement through the city streets. Diegetic music also appears briefly a couple of times, in the bar where Marius meets the ship captain, and when drunken sailors sing and play guitar in the street.

A closer examination of the music of the opening credits reveals that the score does provide subtle narrative information, albeit in very prescribed ways. The score also helps signal to the audience the characters' wishes and motivations, which are not immediately expressed in the dialogue. The brief audiovisual introduction to the main characters and the setting uses music, combined with image, to foreshadow much of what comes later in the film. It opens with a shot of the sails of an impressive-looking ship in the Marseille harbor. The credits are overlaid over a panning shot of the ship, as the music begins with a triumphant theme that includes trumpet fanfares, introducing the setting and the start of the story. The opening theme gives way to a second distinct theme, which is dramatic and restless, with a soaring melody, constantly shifting tonal center, and full orchestration. This second theme will come to represent Fanny and Marius's relationship (Example 4.1). The third musical theme is a more playful upbeat pastoral theme, which represents Marseille, played as we see an establishing shot of the city and a bell is heard sounding in the background. The camera lands on a street corner, and the

Example 4.1: Dramatic Musical Theme, Opening Credits, *Marius* (1931)

music briefly cuts out. Then we see Panisse sitting outside his sail shop, asleep with his hat over his face, accompanied by humorous music, a brief musical detour from the three main themes. The humorous music continues as we see César asleep at his bar. This music signals that the two older men will provide much of the film's comic relief. Then the music returns to the first theme, as we see Marius tidying up the bar. As he walks outside, where Fanny is sitting, the second theme returns, and we see him gazing longingly at the ship—the shot pans from his face to the ship, and back to his face (Figures 4.1a-b). As the music fades out with a harp arpeggio, we hear Fanny's voice calling his name, and the camera cuts to a medium close-up of her face (Figure 4.1c).

The importance of the Marseille setting, the comic relief provided by Panisse and César, and, most important, the internal conflict Marius feels between his love for Fanny and his attraction to the sea are all introduced musically in the opening credits. Fanny's interruption of the music breaks Marius's daydream, launching the beginning of the near nonstop dialogue to come. But an astute listener can detect from the very beginning that Marius will end up boarding the ship instead of staying with Fanny, all from the way in which the music of the opening credits combines with the image.

The repetition (with slight variation) of the opening credits music later in the film reinforces this interpretation: the music reenters as the couple embraces for the very first time. The camera pans to an image of a boat hanging on the wall, then cuts to the harbor, to a lighthouse at night, to waves breaking on the shore, then once more to the harbor, where a title reads "One month later." The music serves as a bridge between Acts II and III and signals the passing of time. The panning shot to the painting of the boat serves

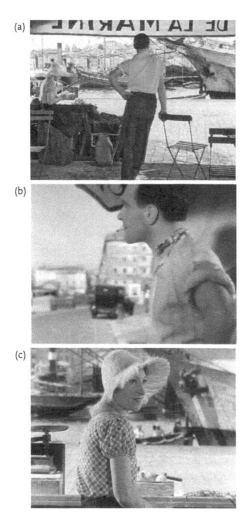

Figures 4.1a–c: Opening of *Marius* (1931)

to avert the camera's eye from the couple's embrace. But the fact that the romantic musical theme reappears paired with the image of a painting of a ship and a montage of the ocean indicates again, even at the height of Marius and Fanny's passion, that the title character's wanderlust is stronger than his bond with Fanny. This occurs once more before the couple sleeps together for the first time, with the same melody and the same lighthouse as the visual stand-in for the lovemaking act. The same music plays again (in slight variation, and with more repetition) under the last ten minutes of the film's dialogue, when Fanny, teary-eyed, encourages Marius to go on the ship before it departs and distracts his father César as it leaves the port. Though the reuse of these themes during structurally important moments might have been expedient, their placement alongside the images imbued additional meaning into the characters' wishes, desires, and relationships and prompted a freedom of the camera not found in other, more dialogue-focused parts of the film. These moments briefly shift the burden of meaning off dialogue and allow the music to express the otherwise inexpressible, which would become an important function of musical underscoring in classical French cinema of the later 1930s.

These musical moments are few and far between in Pagnol's films, however. *Fanny*, the sequel to *Marius*, was directed by Marc Allégret and produced by the French producer Braunberger-Richebé. In many ways, it picks up where *Marius* left off, both narratively and aesthetically, and even featured the same cast members; but in this film, music takes more of a backseat to the dialogue and action. This film marked the beginning of a long-term collaboration between Pagnol and the composer Vincent Scotto. Scotto was a Marseille-born operetta and song composer, who perhaps became best known for his song "J'ai deux amours" (1930), which was made famous by Josephine Baker.[14] He became a frequent collaborator with Pagnol, and even starred in Pagnol's 1934 film *Jofroi* (although he had no prior acting experience). Scotto's score for *Fanny* was even sparser than the score for *Marius*, and, apart from the opening credits, the first forty minutes of the film contain no musical cues. Again, music's primary functions are to demonstrate movement from one locale to another, to illustrate the passing of time, and to indicate structurally important moments in the film (the beginning, the wedding between Fanny and Panisse, and the end). *Fanny*, more than *Marius*, epitomized an approach to sound film that prioritized dialogue and diegetic sound, leaving a very limited role for music.

Pagnol became the poster boy for a much broader trend in early French sound film, but theatrical adaptations of boulevard comedies and serious dramas predated Pagnol's involvement in cinema. *Théâtre filmé* was ubiquitous from the moment sound arrived in France. This trend was not unique to France, but it was particularly robust there and the approach outlasted the reliance on theatrical adaptation in Hollywood in the early sound years. According to Ginette Vincendeau, "the ability to hear [their] own language spoken . . . proved a source of unending pleasure for French audiences."[15] The very first French-language feature-film, *Les Trois Masques* (1929), was a theatrical adaptation, with a mise-en-scène that mimics a proscenium stage and very little camera movement or editing. Because Paris served as France's theatrical and cinematic capital, famous stage actors like Raimu, Harry Baur, Michel Simon, Fernandel, and others easily made the transition to the screen in films like *Jean de la Lune* (1931), *La Petite Chocolatière* (1931), *Les Gaîtés de l'escadron* (1932), *Ces Messieurs de la santé* (1933), *Le Coq du regiment* (1933), and *Théodore et Cie* (1933), to name only a few. These actors became a big draw, and, as Dudley Andrew has ruefully noted, the theatrical model in France was so successful in part thanks to "the particularly powerful entente between actor and audience that claims precedence there over all other considerations, outweighing obligations to the film as a well-made object or work of art."[16] Countless films from 1929 through the 1930s highlighted famous actors' performances—using close-ups to emphasize their facial expressions and gestures, and using direct sound to pick up the actors' witty dialogue and well-known vocal inflections.

Just like the adaptations of Pagnol's plays, the music of these highly successful theatrical adaptations was extremely limited. In many films, music was restricted to opening and ending credits. For instance, Jean Renoir's first sound film, *On purge bébé* (1931), which was based on a play by Georges Feydeau and starred Michel Simon, features music only during the opening credits and the closing of the film. This is also the case with *La Petite Chocolatière* (1932), adapted from a play by Paul Gavault, directed by Marc Allégret, and starring Raimu; in fact, the closing credits music for *La Petite Chocolatière* reused the exact same credits music from *On purge bébé* (both films were produced by Braunberger-Richebé). In both cases, no composer is credited. Music was an afterthought, not considered an important aesthetic element of the film. The appearance of nondiegetic music in other moments of theatrical adaptations was almost always brief and during transitions between scenes, just as in *Marius*. Other films additionally featured diegetic music, giving music a greater role within the narrative. Diegetic music offered a narrative excuse for playing music during an otherwise naturalistic scene; although, as we shall see in chapter 5, some directors played with the possibilities of diegetic music in creative and unexpected ways that were not necessarily entirely grounded in audiovisual realism. On the whole, however, music in theatrical adaptations of straight plays was a low priority, as it took attention away from the spoken word and the performances of the stars reciting those words. This would change as the decade continued, and musical underscoring gradually increased even in theatrical adaptations, though their soundtracks remained vococentric, never sacrificing the intelligibility of dialogue.

Nevertheless, the spoken word produced a different kind of musicality in these theatrical adaptations. In Pagnol's films especially, the rapid-fire dialogue is frequently presented in a manner that accentuates the rhythmic, musical qualities of the spoken word. The passing of dialogue back and forth between characters becomes the aural equivalent of montage, structuring a scene sonically instead of visually. Music may not have played a significant role in Pagnol's films, but his soundtracks are still rife with phrasing, rising and falling in pitch and volume, contrasting timbres, cadences, and rhythmic variety, all contained within speech. The emphasis on regional accents in his films further exploited the variety of sounds possible in the French language.

The humorous and fast-paced verbal exchanges between César and Panisse in the café in *Marius* serve as particularly apt examples of the musicality of the spoken word, and reveal how dialogue structures the visuals in Pagnol's films. In one scene, the two men argue about whether or not Marius has been rude to Panisse. César invites Panisse to the bar for a glass of champagne, and Panisse agrees out of politesse, even though he swore he would never set foot in the bar again after Marius's rudeness. He threatens to kick Marius in the backside next time he sees him. César refuses to believe that his son has been rude, and threatens to kick Panisse if he lays a hand on Marius. Their dialogue begins rather slowly, as Panisse enters the bar dramatically and speaks with slow deliberateness to take his stand. As they begin to argue, the dialogue increases in rapidity, and the men's lines begin to overlap. A young boy whom César employs as a messenger observes the argument, and he occasionally interjects, interrupting the rhythmic cadence of the men's duet by attempting to stop the impending violence between César and Panisse. Throughout, the image is structured around their verbal exchange, as the camera alternates between a medium close-up of each man and a medium shot of all three characters standing at the bar. Their voices increase in volume, pitch, and intensity until their argument comes to a head, César grabs Panisse's neck, and Panisse lets out a yell. A moment later, the champagne cork pops, startling them. Panisse screams, "Le bouchon! Le bouchon!" (The cork! The cork!), the aural climax of their skirmish. Momentary silence—a brief caesura—follows as they both run over to the bar to pour the overflowing champagne into two glasses and drink it so as not to waste it. Their argument reaches a humorous resolution as they agree, now in voices that are more subdued in pitch, volume, and tempo, that the champagne is a bit too warm.

As is apparent in this scene and many others, Pagnol's films, and *théâtre filmé* more broadly, presented an ontology of sound cinema where language, in all its nuances, dictated both the image and the other elements of the soundtrack. That does not mean that the other elements were absent or completely ignored, but rather that they were relegated to a supporting role.

CLAIR: SOUND CINEMA AS POETRY

René Clair reacted quite differently from Pagnol to the arrival of synchronized sound film. He was an established silent film director, who directed his first film, *Paris qui dort*, in 1923, and soon gained recognition from the French avant-garde literary and musical communities with his 1924 short film *Entr'acte*, featuring a scenario by Francis Picabia and a musical score by Erik Satie. Part of the *cinéma pur* movement, which focused on visual elements of film like motion, rhythm, and composition of the shot, Clair enthusiastically embraced the medium's surrealist potential and was deeply interested in the "visual poetry" of the cinematic image that could be created through fantastical elements and experimental optical effects. He believed this approach to cinema provided a richer palette for filmmakers than written or spoken language.[17]

But sound film threatened to destroy his visual aesthetic. Clair, who had been a journalist before turning to directing, writing about his philosophies on cinema through the 1920s, articulated his opposition to the arrival of sound film in Europe through a number of articles published between 1929 and 1931.[18] After seeing *The Broadway Melody* in London, he wrote about his initial reaction in what has come to be called "Three Letters from London," and went on to publish several articles over the next few years. He feared that decisions were being made for financial rather than artistic gain, but his concerns soon developed into a strong stance over the technology's proposed applications, and, ultimately, over the very essence of cinema.

Clair, unlike Pagnol, was adamantly opposed to bringing live theater into the realm of film, believing it would destroy the expressive power of the cinematic image. Unlike silent cinema, which he believed had the potential to transcend everyday life, synchronous sound threatened to reduce film to a recording medium. In a 1929 article, Clair wrote:

> The cinema must remain visual at all costs: the advent of theatrical dialogue in the cinema will irreparably destroy everything I had hoped for it. . . . In the theater, what is seen exists only to serve what the actors say, their words; in the talking cinema, it's the opposite: the word gains its power only in relation to the image. We have to avoid what could be a great catastrophe for the talking cinema: its incapacity to reach the level of poetry.[19]

Grieving the destruction of cinematic poetry he had so deeply valued in his silent films, he lamented, the screen "has conquered the world of voices, but it has lost the world of dreams. I have observed people leaving the cinema after seeing a talking film. . . . *They had not lost their sense of reality.*"[20] It was not sound per se, but rather spoken language that he thought should have no important place in cinema.

Clair recognized that sound could indeed be used effectively in film, but he critiqued the practices that had developed to that point and proposed different solutions to combining sound and image. He took offense at Pagnol's suggestion that cinema "needed" theatrical personnel to help it realize its full potential. In a July 1930 article titled "Film Authors Don't Need You," he called Pagnol's May 1930 article "particularly shocking."[21] He wrote, the "talking picture will survive only if the formula suitable to it is found, only if it can break loose from the influence of the theater and fiction, only if people make of it something other than an *art of imitation*."[22]

A few months prior, he had already proposed one means of avoiding an "art of imitation." He praised *The Broadway Melody* not for its musical spectacles but for its soundtrack, which at times conveyed information different from that of the image. He singled out a scene where "we hear the noise of a door being slammed and a car driving off while we are shown Bessie Love's anguished face watching from a window, the departure which we do not see."[23] Instead of employing exact synchronism, which he found to be redundant and uninteresting, Clair suggested audiovisual counterpoint: "if *imitation* of real noises seems limited and disappointing, it is possible that an *interpretation* of noises may have more of a future in it. . . . We do not need to *hear* the sound of clapping if we can *see* the clapping hands."[24] Rather than using sound to create an illusion of organic audiovisual unity, Clair proposed a number of experimental relationships between image and sound that were unique to cinema. He aimed to use the microphone and camera as separate entities with separate storytelling capabilities.

Clair's debate with Pagnol, and his concerns about cinema as theater, informed his own work as he put his philosophies into practice, and his first sound films served as exemplars of his proposed form. In 1929, Tobis-Klangfilm established a studio at Épinay near Paris, so they could begin producing French-language films in France. The company had been importing French-language versions of German films into the French market; but Tobis hired Clair to direct its first homegrown French films. Within two years, Clair had directed *Sous les toits de Paris* (1930), *Le Million* (1931), and *À nous la liberté* (1931), all filmed at the Tobis studios in France. In all three of these films, music proved an indispensable tool for maintaining a poetic, distinctly cinematic, audiovisual style.

LE MILLION (1931), OPERA, AND MUSICAL FANTASY AS CINEMATIC POETRY

Though he was adamantly opposed to live theater's encroachment on cinema, Clair's approach to sound in film ended up relying on live performance aesthetics, albeit in a very different way from Pagnol. Instead of turning to straight theater, where the spoken word reigned supreme, Clair drew on musical stage genres—operetta and opera—to develop his aesthetic of cinematic fantasy. In *Le Million* (1931) in particular, Clair explored the tension between live and mediated genres. Inspired by the *opérettes filmées*, particularly the French-language versions of *Le Chemin du paradis* and *L'Opéra de quat'sous*, Clair used song as an important vehicle for narrative delivery and as a means of freeing the camera from expectations of realism. But even more importantly, Clair drew on the unnaturalness and artificiality of opera as a mode of storytelling and to comment on his own approach to sound cinema, a tactic unique to Clair's film.

Le Million as Theatrical Adaptation

Rather than writing his own scenario as he usually did, Clair adapted a 1913 theatrical comedy, a French-style vaudeville farce, by playwrights Georges Berr and Marcel Guillemaud.[25] Given Clair's resistance to the importation of live theater into sound film, it is surprising that he chose to adapt a stage work. The story, however, shared many commonalities with his silent film *Le Chapeau de paille d'Italie* (1928), whose fast-paced action featured a number of comical chase scenes, and perhaps he saw promise in *Le Million*'s story for a similar brand of visual comedy. Or perhaps he saw an opportunity to completely transform the work into something uniquely cinematic.

Yet, he encountered difficulties adapting the comedy's scenario for the screen, and he began to worry about the project. In an interview years later, Clair said:

> To conserve [the vaudeville] rhythm on the screen, it would have needed far too much dialogue. Frightened, I asked Tobis to stop the negotiations with the playwrights. They told me: "Too late. As of yesterday we paid eighty thousand francs." I was forced to continue. In the face of this necessity, I imagined that it might be possible to regain the unreal nature of vaudeville by replacing the words with music and songs. From that moment on my work began to interest me. I was delighted to have discovered this operetta formula where everyone sings except the main characters. . . . Now I would go and conceive of musical elements directly inspired by the action, and that posed a number of fascinating problems.[26]

He adapted the live theatrical comedy into a sung cinematic form, which allowed him to eschew spoken dialogue. However, a film operetta did not necessarily guarantee camera movement and avoidance of a theatrical mise-en-scène, as is apparent from the films discussed in chapter 3. It would require a concerted effort on Clair's part to adapt the *opérette filmée* form for his own aesthetic purposes.

To find composers to help him write his film operetta, Clair turned to Armand Bernard, the music director at the Tobis studios at Épinay who had worked with him on *Sous les toits de Paris*. Bernard enlisted the seasoned operetta-writing duo Georges Van Parys and Philippe Parès into the project. Parès and Van Parys had collaborated together on numerous operettas for the stage, including the successful *Louis XIV* (1929). But they also had some screen experience: they had written music for the film *La Route est belle*, a 1929 French *film sonore* filmed in Great Britain with a musical score added in postsynchronization.[27] The pair knew Bernard because he had been conductor for performances of their operetta *Lulu* at the Danou Theater. For *Le Million*, the composers were faced with a different task, closer to what they were accustomed to in their stage works: to write a number of songs that were directly integrated into the film's narrative.

The film's story is framed through one long flashback to a pair of passersby who overhear a group of revelers and ask why they are celebrating (Figure 4.2). From there, the plot centers on a poor artist, Michel (played by René Lefèvre), who owes money to many creditors. He discovers he has won the lottery, but he left the winning ticket in his jacket, which his fiancée Béatrice (Annabella), a dancer at the opera, had unknowingly given to a criminal, Père la Tulipe (Paul Ollivier), fleeing the police, who sold it to an opera singer looking for

Figure 4.2: Opening Scene, *Le Million* (1931)

a costume for his performance that evening at the Opéra Lyrique. The majority of the film revolves around a snowballing chase to find the lottery ticket, which culminates at the opera house during the singer's performance, when the film's story becomes comically intertwined with the on-stage events.[28] While Clair remained mostly faithful to the original play, the opera house scene was his own invention.

By incorporating song into the formal design, Clair managed to retain most of the original play's plot while experimenting with an approach that did not rely on the spoken word. But the use of song in the film also allowed him to explore the tension between live stage genres and mediated recorded ones. In some instances, this tension is intentionally highlighted—the story unfolds in such a way to draw attention to it, as live sung performance becomes directly implicated in the plot—but it also plays out, perhaps unintentionally, in the filming process and technique. Opera ultimately becomes the locus of this live-mediated tension.

Operetta and Fantasy

Clair experimented with a variety of relationships between sound and image in *Le Million*. A prime example of audiovisual counterpoint occurs during a struggle for the jacket: Clair superimposes the sound of a crowd cheering at a rugby match, allowing the artificial addition of sound to comment on the on-screen events. In other scenes, a character's subconscious is articulated through a sung chorus, while the character appears mute onscreen, such as in the songs "Michel, Michel, que vas-tu faire?" and "Prosper, que fais-tu?"[29] Sometimes the music underscores the dialogue or action, using musical themes to connect characters or events; other times, the instrumental music seems to silence the possibility for dialogue, accompanying pantomimed action (as in a silent film). In the moments where there is spoken dialogue, Clair had the actors improvise so as to create a feeling of spontaneity.

But the majority of *Le Million* unfolds, both in narrative form and musical style, as a comic operetta, where all of the actors except the main characters sing. (Having the main characters refrain from singing was a significant departure from the *opérettes filmées*, where the leading actors were often known especially for their singing voices.) Clair had this idea planned out from the start, and he played a large role in the development of *Le Million*'s songs. He wrote all of the couplets to be set to music, and articulated strong ideas for how musical numbers would tie together. In his first meeting with the composers, he handed them a copy of the shooting script, which was already meticulously constructed. Parès recounted in his memoire:

> In getting to know the shooting script, I remember our surprise. From the beginning to the end, everything was planned from a musical perspective, up to the precise timing of each musical occurrence and the indication of even the smallest effect. The choruses were written and we didn't need to change a single comma: it was the first time that I had seen that in the cinema. I haven't seen it again.[30]

Clair's shooting script, housed at the Bibliothèque Nationale in Paris, confirms this account.[31] He wrote it with scrupulous detail and precision, making preparations in advance to an extent quite unusual for the period, particularly when it comes to indications of the soundtrack.[32] He noted when he wanted musical numbers to connect and when text should be spoken in rhythm with the orchestra. And he had written all of the couplets by the time the composers started their work. From there, the composers divided the scoring duties: Parès wrote most of the choruses, Van Parys wrote a waltz sung by the opera stars, and Bernard wrote the "opera" scene that occurs as the site of the culminating chase for the jacket, a deliberate parody called *Les Bohémiens*.[33]

Clair articulated his approach to the film operetta in an article for the journal *Cinémonde* in 1931, a few weeks before the film premiered in April, discussing his own film as a means of critiquing existing methods in sound cinema. There, he pointed out new possibilities for the medium.

I wanted to sustain, rather than slow down, the pace of the scenes and the links between them. Song and music appeared in the cinema even before speech and have been the worst enemies of cinematic movement. Ordinarily, during sung verses, the action either stops completely or kicks up its heels, and the subject is frittered away. In *Le Million* . . . you will never see the plot sacrificed to the demands of the songs.[34]

Clair was clear that the mere existence of songs in a film did not guarantee a cinematic aesthetic. In fact, music could cause the very same problems as spoken dialogue—a static camera and loss of visual interest. He wanted neither the plot nor the "cinematic movement" to be lost with the addition of songs to the story. In other words, he did not want the inclusion of songs to make his film any less cinematic.

To prevent an overreliance on theatrical conventions, Clair went to great lengths to avoid a static camera, taking the experiments found in *opérettes filmées* like *Le Chemin du paradis* even further. One of the biggest technical and musical challenges came with filming songs that occurred in multiple locations—for instance, the song "Millionaire," when the various creditors share the news that Michel has won the lottery. Because the practice of playback had not yet become widespread, most songs had to be recorded as *son direct* (direct sound), essentially live during filming.[35] Many filmmakers of the period kept the camera static as a result of these technological restrictions, which often led to a more "stagey" theatrical effect. By freeing up the movement of the camera, Clair decidedly does not resort to static cinematic framing, but it was a challenge to realize his cinematic ideas: variable tempos and dynamics in the live orchestra would have made smooth editing impossible. Clair insisted the composers attend each day of shooting to ensure the music's tempo remained consistent in each shot, a method of making up for a technology not yet equipped to create the cinematic effects Clair desired.[36] He also relied on René le Hénaff, the film editor, to help smooth out the transitions. Van Parys remarked, after shooting and recording all of the music, that he "was helped a lot by the editor René Le Hénaff, who is a true musician, and who put together all of the fragments of the small ensemble numbers with a surprising precision."[37] Therefore, while Clair incorporated and adapted some techniques borrowed from live theater, such as an orchestra hidden just behind the scenes, he ultimately created scenes that would be impossible on a live stage.

Instead of freezing narrative time for musical performances to occur within the story, *Le Million*'s songs *propel* time and action forward. Clair elaborated further on his aesthetic motivations in his *Cinémonde* article, writing:

It's only in the theater that people open their mouths, one after another . . . in order to be clearly heard by the spectators at the back of the hall. Obviously, it would be ridiculous to begin a scene as a talkie and suddenly turn it into a silent one. But when the same scene changes in framing (camera distance and angle), when a bit of music or a noise happens to replace a speech, the latter is no longer necessary and should, consequently, be suppressed. For the cinema, it seems to me, instead of copying life, interprets it.[38]

This statement suggests that for Clair, song could become a crucial element distinguishing cinema ontologically from live theater. Of course, song alone did not distinguish a cinematic work from a theatrical one. But in Clair's view, the function of *recorded* song alongside the visual possibilities of cinema provided another layer of the fantastical, contributing to his desired "world of dreams."

Clair did not seem to care so much what exactly the music sounded like, but more when and how it was deployed. For instance, it is striking that most of the actors in Clair's film were not trained singers. The actors' voices are sometimes strained, often slightly out of tune. Vocal quality was not the point: the mere fact that they were singing was most important to Clair. The songs are simple— mostly diatonic, with a limited range, and fairly repetitive, as seen in the melody for the opening song "Ils ne savent pas cette histoire," sung by the entire cast— and, as sung by actors without trained voices, the songs seem to invite participation (see Example 4.2).[39] But throughout, the songs are paired with actors' movements that are playful and choreographic, and there is overall a more fluid relationship between the songs and the events unfolding on the screen.

Indeed, at times, it even seems as if the characters are playfully aware of the fact that they are singing. For instance, in one scene Père la Tulipe pretends to be a conductor for the criminals as they sing the "Chanson des criminels." In the "Chœur des créanciers au commissariat" the entire group of creditors sings as they bail Michel out of prison, carrying him away on their shoulders (Figure 4.3). This gives the characters a decidedly unrealistic mode of communication within the cinematic world. Clair played off the artificiality of both

Example 4.2: "Ils ne savent pas cette histoire," *Le Million* (1931)

Ils ne sa - vent pas cette his - toi - re, Nous all - ons vous la ra - con - ter

Mais vous re - fu - se - rez d'y croi - re, Si nous di - sons la vé - ri - té

Mais vous re - fu - se - rez d'y croi - re, Si nous di - sons la vé - ri - té !

Figure 4.3: "Chœur des créanciers au commissariat," *Le Million* (1931)

mediums: the songs of live operetta and the visual poetry of cinema. Dialogue, a conveyer of information, is replaced by a form of artistic abstraction; and song, rather than "copying" human interaction, "interprets" it.

Opera and Artificiality

In addition to Clair's reliance on operetta for *Le Million*'s form, he folded opera directly into the film's narrative and aesthetic framework in a profound way.[40] While the majority of *Le Million* unfolds as a comic operetta, the film's story culminates at the opera house, and the film and its musical forms take a self-reflexive turn. By this point, the jacket, with the lottery ticket in the pocket, has passed through several hands and has fallen into possession of the opera star Sopranelli; and Michel, his friend Prosper, and a gang of thieves are all separately trying to get their hands on it, while the backstage crew desperately tries to keep everyone from disturbing the performance. Béatrice is angry with Michel because of his flirtation with the beautiful American woman Vanda, but they get trapped onstage when the curtain goes up, and must stay there until the song, Van Parys's waltz ("Nous sommes seuls") is over (Figures 4.4a–b). As the operatic couple walks onstage, Michel and Béatrice hide behind the

Figures 4.4a–b: "Nous sommes seuls," *Le Million* (1931)

scenery and sit on a bench underneath a fake tree, as the opera singers begin to sing the lyrics (written by Clair):

Nous sommes seuls enfin ce soir	We are alone, at last, tonight
Tout dort, à present sur la terre	Everyone else has gone to sleep
Nous sommes seuls sous le ciel noir,	We are alone under the dark sky
Assis sur le vieux banc de pierre.	Sitting on the old stone bench.
Nous pouvons enfin nous parler librement,	We can finally speak to each other freely
Loin des hommes fous, loin du bruit des cités	Far from the crowds, far from the noise of the city
Loin du monde et de ses tourments,	Far from the world and its agonies.
Nous retrouvons la verité.	We will find the truth.

We see the film's leading couple react to the lyrics of the song, as they realize that the singers are describing the silent couple's own predicament. Yet, Michel and Béatrice are neither alone nor able to actually speak freely: the shot of the diegetic audience watching the opera serves as a reminder that people are watching and listening to the film as well. And yet, in a sense, the operatic world of the romantic song is more effective than the cinematic world's "reality," allowing the leading couple to finally be honest with each other. As the song continues, the inaudible conversation between Michel and Béatrice seems, through their gestures and expressions, to parallel the text of the song, as an even further abstraction of dialogue. The song successfully encourages them to make up, and they embrace to the scene of a two-dimensional paper moon, a fake forest, and falling petals thrown by a stagehand. The song's sentiment and the artificially romantic setting bring about their reconciliation. By pointing out the mechanics involved in creating the stage effects, Clair points to the deeper truth of the emotions represented. Meanwhile, the over-the-top operatic couple has been faking their romance for the audience, and the minute the curtain goes down they begin to bicker again.

In this scene, Clair forces opera and film, live and mediated, to confront each other, highlighting the artificiality of both. By drawing attention to its status as both opera and film, the opera scene reveals how the artificiality and unreality of Clair's cinematic world is, in a sense, borrowed from the artificiality and unreality of opera, where music structures action and suspension of disbelief is required. Furthermore, by providing a marked visual contrast between his on-screen protagonists and the opera's leading couple (Figure 4.5), Clair also seems to call into question the standard cinematic relationship between image and soundtrack. The artificiality and over-the-top nature of opera is emphasized, but Michel and Béatrice are ultimately moved by its artifice.[41]

By highlighting the visual ridiculousness of the operatic couple and pairing their beautiful voices with the images of Michel and Béatrice, more aesthetically pleasing for the screen (the fact that they are an artist and a dancer underscores their visual importance), Clair also challenges the talkies' value of the flawless illusion of unity, or "match," between voices and on-screen bodies.[42] Because neither Michel nor Béatrice sings in the film, the opera singers' voices can attach themselves to these characters more freely, even if they are never intended to depict a realistically unified body–voice pairing in a single person or character. Clair takes advantage of cinema's unique ability to pair beautiful voices with attractive bodies, even if they do not seem to "match" or belong together; and by questioning these conventions and exposing these workings of the cinematic apparatus, he begins to show his solution for cinematic specificity.

Figure 4.5: The Two Couples, *Le Million* (1931)

Yet the process undergone to shoot the opera scene suggests an interesting tension. In his diary, Van Parys expressed concern about the vocal abilities of one of the actors. Constantin Stroesco, a singer who had performed in *Pelléas et Mélisande* at the Opéra-Comique, played the tenor Sopranelli, and Odette Talazac, the daughter of the *pensionnaire* of the Opéra, was slated to play the female opera star. Van Parys believed that although Stroesco was apparently unaware of the fact that he was playing a caricature, his voice and conviction were perfect for the role.[43] Talazac, however, was another story. According to Van Parys, although she only had the waltz to sing, "the poor one has only a wisp of a voice. . . . The timbre of the soprano, with age, has fallen to a sort of hoarse baritone. How will it work out, with Stroesco who himself is a tenor? The waltz is written in a rather high tessitura, and I deeply fear that she will not manage to sing it."[44] Van Parys continued to worry about Talazac. On February 4, 1931, the day they were supposed to work on "Nous sommes seuls," Van Parys recounted, "She lost her voice and absolutely cannot let out a single note." Surprised at Clair's indifference, Van Parys asked, "I thought that you hired her because she was a singer?"[45] Clair responded: "Wrong, my friend. Completely wrong. I hired her because she has the ideal silhouette for the role. The fat opera singer whom I will flank with braids and who is going to be pushed around like a wagon. Her voice, if you think that I don't care. . . . We will . . . find a real singer who will dub it. The primary thing for me is that we SEE Talazac, not that we HEAR her."[46]

No other indication exists anywhere to suggest that Talazac's voice was dubbed. Yet if we believe Van Parys's account, there is a further irony to the scene: even though Clair was representing the "live" world of opera in contrast with his cinematic world, he used cinematic tricks (dubbing) to obtain the effect, making the live "better" than it could have been in reality. He provides the visually ridiculous female lead a beautiful voice to complete the audiovisual "mismatch" necessary for the scene (Figure 4.6). Therefore, while Clair's cinematic world of *Le Million* highlights the artificiality of opera, it also requires the perceived authenticity of the operatic unity of voice and body—if only to critique its absurdity.

Yet the manner in which opera is mocked comes across as playful, and, in some ways, even serves as an homage to the genre, which ultimately shares many of the same fantastical qualities of Clair's cinematic style, and perhaps even (as Clair might have argued) of cinema more generally. *Les Bohémiens*, the opera that follows the waltz, is the site of a dramatic struggle for the jacket between Michel and his friend Prosper. While the two friends each try to grab the jacket on stage, the gravity of their battle is rendered absurd through the opera's parallel story, as two men fight to the death (Figure 4.7). The scene lightheartedly pokes fun at opera's lack of subtlety, through over-the-top gestures, excessively dramatic musical phrasing, and ad nauseam repetition of text, turning the opera's tragedy into comedy. As the antagonist is dying,

Figure 4.6: The Visually Ridiculous Operatic Couple, *Le Million* (1931)

Figure 4.7: The Opera Scene, *Le Million* (1931)

he announces, "Je meurs," which is echoed by his mother, holding him in his arms: "Tu meurs." The sentiment is repeated one last time by the entire chorus onstage: "Il meurt." This representation of opera as over-the-top is a source of humor, and it highlights the very redundancy between sound and image that Clair aimed to avoid in cinema. But by paralleling the film's plot with the opera's, it seems to imply that Michel and Prosper's conflict is inexpressible in words. Only through the vicarious experience of the opera's characters can their emotions be truly represented. In this way, and in the way that Michel and Béatrice's reconciliation could only be brought about on stage while listening to a love song, Clair uses opera to further his commentary on film. Opera is shown with respect, as a form that, in all its unnaturalness, sound film might emulate.

CONCLUSION

Pagnol and Clair's debate was in many ways more symbolic than anything else: though their stances on sound film differed substantially, the filmmakers respected each other in real life, and later even became friends.[47] But they became symbolically important as high-profile, diametrically opposed figures during the transition to sound. And their approach to music in their films epitomizes their overall aesthetic priorities. Pagnol used sound film as a recording device, maintaining in many respects the theatrical integrity of his adaptations, while incorporating cinematic elements to provide further depth to characters' emotions and highlight the particularities of local culture of Marseille. As a result, music was never included at the expense of realism, or of the poetic cadence of the spoken word. Clair, on the other hand, expanded his "poetry of the image" to encompass "poetry of sound and image." By having characters sing rather than speak, and by creating a cinematic world whose logic is as much driven by musical structure and devices as by narrative, Clair's cinema maintained the fantastical, surrealist, and humorous qualities that characterized his unique version of cinematic poetry in his silent films. But his cinematic approach was, ironically, dependent on live musical-theatrical genres. Music's role in cinema for Clair and Pagnol was rooted in each man's understanding of the most aesthetically significant applications of the microphone and the camera, and their films of the early 1930s reflect their experimentations with testing the limits of both human performance and sound film technology, and how live performance and technology can relate and interact.

Pagnol's model for sound film was quite influential. Throughout the 1930s, filmed theater persisted as a prominent genre in mainstream French cinema. But Pagnol's own films belie his insistence that sound film was nothing more than a recording device for theatrical productions. His emphasis on realism, particularly through on-location shooting, was an approach that appealed to other filmmakers of the later 1930s, especially poetic realist directors like Jean Renoir and Marcel Carné. And, as we shall see in the next chapter, they would take the *théâtre filmé*'s approach to music as a starting point, while expanding considerably on the manners in which music, particularly diegetic music, could affect a film's narrative and overall aesthetic.

Although *Le Million* was an immediate success with audiences and critics, both in France and abroad,[48] Clair's musical films did not ignite a new sound cinema aesthetic movement as he might have hoped. In many ways, Clair's style was seen as inimitable, perhaps even anomalous. In 1934, he left France for England and then the United States, not to return until after World War II. Although he remained an influential director throughout his lifetime, over the course of a long career, he modified his thoughts on film sound, generally leaving his early sound film aesthetic behind.[49] While we might find traces of Clair's musical fantasies in contemporary surrealist comedies, and perhaps in the Hollywood film musical, more than anything, *Le Million* points to an alternative path that sound cinema might have taken. Nevertheless, his humorous brand of audiovisual surrealism had a subtler influence on poetic realist directors, particularly filmmakers like Jean Vigo, the subject of chapter 6.

A close examination of Pagnol and Clair side by side brings the live (straight theater as well as opera) and the mediated (cinema) closer together, forcing them to confront each other in both their similarities and differences. It is the very tension between the live and the mediated that drives *Le Million*, that explains the success of *Marius* on the screen, and that points to the fluidity of these boundaries. Music's role in each of these films serves to remind us of this fluidity.

CHAPTER 5

Source Music and Cinematic Realism

Jean Renoir and the Early Poetic Realists

In 1932, filmmaker Marcel Carné lamented that cinema was overrun with "flat vaudeville entertainments, so-called 'fantasy films' grinding out the same pretty stories, incessantly repeating the same tired effects. . . . The cinema lacks freshness, scope, commitment."[1] He went on, claiming the cinema was "ignoring the profound unrest of our time, the urgent problems at hand," and should focus on "subjects of real substance." While debates about cinema's proximity to theater waged on, figures like Carné hoped to see filmmakers exploit sound cinema's capabilities as a tool for reflecting reality, particularly the social realities that were emerging as the effects of the Great Depression began to hit France. Although cinematic realism had already been a topic of debate in the silent era, calls like Carné's for realism in film, especially as a tool for portraying contemporary social and political situations in France, were renewed in the early sound era. Recorded sound and music offered new tools and new challenges for filmmakers who sought to use cinema to represent reality.

By the end of the 1930s, Carné would become one of the most prominent directors of French poetic realism. Poetic realism, which grew out of the political climate that saw the rise of the Popular Front in the mid-1930s and was connected to the politico-artistic Groupe Octobre, reestablished France's international cinematic reputation and has since come to be considered the cornerstone of French Golden Age cinema. Poetic realist films focused on characters living at the margins of society, often presenting a cynical, fatalistic outlook on life, while commenting on contemporary social issues. Alongside these narrative elements, directors employed a heightened aestheticism that involved a strong emphasis on mise-en-scène, décor, and lighting, a lyrical form of cinematic representation that Dudley Andrew has described as embodying a mixture of "sophisticated and popular" motivations.[2] The group of screenwriters and directors loosely associated with the "poetic realist school" included Carné, Yves Allégret, Julien Duvivier, Jacques Feyder, Jean Grémillon, Jacques Prévert, and Jean Renoir.[3] The most famous examples of the style appeared in the mid- to late-1930s, with films like *Pépé le Moko* (1937, dir. Duvivier), *La Bête humaine* (1938, dir. Renoir), and *Le Quai des brumes* (1938, dir. Carné); however, many filmmakers began experimenting with the aesthetic and narrative preoccupations that would come to define poetic realism as early as 1930, in the first years of synchronized sound.

Although poetic realism has been the subject of much scholarly writing, the focus has mainly been on the visual and narrative markers of the style. For instance, Dudley Andrew labels poetic realism not a genre or a style but an *optique*, using "the ocular and ideological mechanisms of 'perspective'" to understand what ties poetic realist films together.[4] Very little has been written on the role of music in poetic realist cinema.[5] Nevertheless, even before poetic realism's artistic and narrative principles had fully solidified, directors used a set of relatively cohesive musical strategies in their films that contributed substantially to poetic realism's overall audiovisual aesthetic. Perhaps most notably, diegetic music played an important role in early experiments with the style.

Though some early poetic realist films had nondiegetic scores, music that was realistically motivated by the narrative was particularly prominent. The pervasive use of diegetic music was connected to broader approaches to the soundtrack, namely the widespread preference in France for *son direct*—direct sound—over rerecording. Direct sound was, according to Charles O'Brien, one of the defining features of a French national sound cinema style that differentiated it from Hollywood practices of the era.[6] Within the ideology of direct sound, filmmakers believed direct recording could create a more realist atmosphere and highlight the unfiltered sounds of an environment that would not be captured in the same way if manipulated in postproduction. Under the guise of realism, directors typically recorded ambient sounds at the same time as dialogue, sometimes at the expense of intelligibility. But, as O'Brien has pointed out, "the attempt to meet the imperative of fidelity to an original sound," instead of enhancing realism, "can serve to foreground the scene's artifice, by revealing the technology's role in mediating the viewer's perception of the image."[7]

Much in the same way, source music, whether or not it was directly recorded, seemed to offer the same promise of naturalism in a film. Poetic realist films frequently featured popular songs and street musicians that were seemingly appropriate for the film's setting, for instance. However, much like direct sound more broadly, diegetic music often ended up calling more attention to itself in the process. Even when music was purportedly connected to the narrative world of an early poetic realist film, it often packed a powerful punch, helping establish the film's milieu by incorporating musical styles associated with the French working class in social spaces where these styles would be heard, revealing the emotions or thoughts of characters, and providing commentary on the narrative at crucial moments. At times, diegetic music also worked in contradiction or conflict with the narrative, which created a range of aesthetic and emotional effects. Within the parameters of realism, music played a complex role, exemplifying the ways in which realism and stylization worked hand in hand in poetic realism's soundtrack, and in its audiovisual aesthetic more broadly.

This chapter focuses on the role of diegetic music in proto–poetic realist films of the early 1930s. The films I analyze are diverse in their subject matter and aesthetic. Nevertheless, they all contain a number of common attributes central to poetic realism: they address contemporary social issues, particularly class, and they use music to blend realism and lyricism. They often treat diegetic music pointedly: to lend authenticity to their working-class or bourgeois settings, to develop atmosphere, to create irony or humor, to universalize the plight or conflicts of individual characters, to illustrate a character's subjectivity, or even to change the course of a narrative. I analyze the role of diegetic music in a range of early poetic realist sound films by multiple directors, including Jean Grémillon's *La Petite Lise* (1930), Anatole Litvak's *Cœur de Lilas* (1931), Augusto Genina's *Paris-Béguin* (1931), and Julien Duvivier's *La Tête d'un homme* (1933).

In the second half of the chapter, I turn my attention to Jean Renoir, perhaps the most famous proponent of diegetic music in 1930s French film. Renoir is best known for his late-1930s masterpieces, including *La Grande Illusion* (1937), *La Bête humaine* (1938), and *La Règle du jeu* (1939), films that later cemented Renoir's reputation as one of the most influential French directors of sound films before World War II and an early example of an *auteur* director. Although Renoir's aesthetic and narrative preoccupations were diverse, a few of his films later in the decade were associated with poetic realism, particularly his 1938 film *La Bête humaine*. More broadly, his representations of working-class culture and incisive dissection of class tension display a deftness for social commentary that was an important feature of poetic realist cinema. His treatment of sound and music further connects his films to early poetic realist style. He was outspoken about his preference for direct sound—in his memoirs he later claimed that the "addition of sound after the picture has been shot [is] an outrage"[8]—and he frequently avoided nondiegetic music altogether. His nuanced and multivalent incorporation of diegetic music played an important role in shaping meaning in his early sound films.

I analyze Renoir's use of source music in two of his early sound films—*La Chienne* (1931) and *Boudu sauvé des eaux* (1932)—in depth. In these two films, Renoir used diegetic music for atmosphere, commentary, and contrast. But his treatment of diegetic music also differed from early poetic realist directors, particularly the extent to which he used music to point to the artifice of cinematic storytelling as a means of critiquing French society and the bourgeoisie. Renoir's approach to music remained remarkably consistent throughout the 1930s, even as other poetic realist filmmakers increasingly relied on nondiegetic underscoring. Examining Renoir's films alongside other early examples of poetic realism shows the ways in which his distinctive aesthetic of the later 1930s grew from this broader artistic milieu in the early years of synchronized sound. It also highlights the manner in which a varied but consistent treatment of sound and music diverged into quite diverse approaches by the end of the decade. The multivalent, yet cohesive incorporation of diegetic music in early poetic realist sound films by a range of directors and composers, within a broader context of direct recording, reveals how music could play an important role in balancing audiovisual realism with stylized aestheticization of social and political subjects.

EARLY POETIC REALISM AND SYNCHRONIZED SOUND

Poetic realism captured a broader political and aesthetic spirit of the times. The movement is difficult to define, in part because it was never codified in the same ways that cinematic impressionism or surrealism had been in the 1920s. Alan Williams claims it is neither a school of filmmaking nor a genre but nevertheless constitutes "something more than a style."[9] The term was first coined by Jean Paulhan, editor of La Nouvelle Revue française, to describe Marcel Aymé's 1929 novel La Rue sans nom, and was later applied to cinema by a reviewer of the novel's 1934 film adaptation by Pierre Chenal.[10] It remained closely connected to literature and literary ideals, which allowed directors to create ways of portraying the world in a manner that was understood to be culturally elevated and, at the same time, to have appeal with mainstream audiences. Although the modernist avant-garde energy of the cinema had begun to dwindle in the era of sound, cinema remained a site of explicitly political art in France in the poetic realist film.

Most poetic realist directors had experience as silent filmmakers. Julien Duvivier, Jacques Feyder, and Jean Grémillon all began as silent-era directors, although with varying degrees of success and fame. Marcel Carné worked as an assistant director for Feyder's films before he began directing on his own in 1936. These directors were connected by their collaboration with screenwriters like Charles Spaak and Jacques Prévert, who wrote screenplays for a number of influential poetic realist films, and by actors like Jean Gabin and Michel Simon, who frequently starred in their films. Other directors were not as closely connected to poetic realism but directed individual films that aesthetically and narratively fit the category: Raymond Bernard, for instance, who was better known for his large-scale historical films like *Le Miracle des loups* (1924), *Les Croix de bois* (1932), and *Les Misérables* (1934), directed *Faubourg-Montmartre* in 1931. Émigré filmmakers also made important contributions to the style: Anatole Litvak (of Russian Jewish background with experience in Soviet avant-garde theater and in the German film industry before coming to France) directed *Cœur de Lilas* (1931), and Augusto Genina (an Italian silent director who briefly worked in France during the transition era) directed *Paris-Béguin* (1931).

Although filmmakers had been depicting downtrodden, working-class characters in French films in the 1920s, sound cinema added a new dimension of realism to cinematic storytelling, which required a new understanding of and approach to the medium. Between the direct recording of the *film parlant* and the postsynchronization of the *film sonore*, the *film parlant* seemed to offer more promises of realism. As Charles O'Brien notes, the preference for *son direct* was in part because of the predominance of *théâtre filmé* and connected to a desire to reproduce actors' performances with little technological interference,[11] a quality of sound cinema valued, for instance, by Marcel Pagnol. But the fidelity of *son direct* also promised to pick up all "realistic" sounds—from spoken dialogue, to the ambient sound of an environment, to any music that might happen to be playing. Diegetic music, therefore, fit closely with the purported realist priorities of direct recording, and directors of early poetic realist cinema made frequent and varied use of diegetic music as a result. In fact, directors often preserved the impression of directly recorded music even if it was postsynchronized or mixed after the fact. Though the approach to the musical soundtrack in poetic realist films was varied, certain kinds of musical occurrences appeared frequently enough within this paradigm of direct musical recording that they can be considered an important part of the early poetic realist audiovisual aesthetic.

SOURCE MUSIC FOR SETTING

Music for Setting and Atmosphere

In many poetic realist films, music provided atmosphere and conveyed setting, particularly the working-class milieus of their characters, such as neighborhood bars, restaurants, and dance halls. Musical markers of these settings included the *bal-musette*, a working-class musical and dance style that would be performed in a venue of the same name, characterizing a quintessentially French setting and thus acting as a marker of Frenchness. The *bal-musette* might be performed by live musicians (usually featured onscreen, even if briefly), or mediated through a phonograph, a player piano, or a radio. The latter devices were frequently shown onscreen before their music was heard, providing narrative justification for the presence of music, while also drawing attention to mechanically reproduced music, a cinematic element that had only recently become available and was still a novelty worthy of highlighting. Although diegetic music in these settings was not unique to poetic realism, it was an important marker of the style. Also common was the street musician, particularly an organ grinder, who would not only provide an aural symbol of working-class Parisian streets, but also often seemed to act as an omniscient character, observing the action without actively participating in it. In all of these cases, diegetic music used for atmosphere could quickly become anempathetic, even sinister, depending on the action taking place while it plays.

Cœur de Lilas (1931) includes several examples of this type of "working-class" diegetic music. Directed by Anatole Litvak, the film featured music by the popular composer Maurice Yvain with lyrics by Serge Veber. In the film, a dead body is found in the outskirts of Paris. Detective Lucot suspects Lilas, a prostitute, of committing the murder and goes undercover to investigate. He visits the neighborhood streets and venues Lilas frequents, disguised as a working-class man. While undercover, he and Lilas fall in love. But when Lilas discovers his true identity, she runs from him—and a potential life of happiness—to turn herself in for the murder.

The film opens near the fortifications of Paris, the edge of the city known to be a center of illegal activity. A marching band plays military music as it parades down the street. The camera pans to a group of children playing nearby and marching in their own make-believe band, as the real band's music gets quieter and fades into the distance. The band having disappeared, the children turn to playing cops and robbers and discover a dead body. Unaware of what is unfolding, a blind man standing nearby begins to play a hand-cranked barrel organ, which plays a quintessential "street melody," a simple song in C minor that modulates to its relative major for the chorus (Example 5.1). The music continues as people discover the scene of the murder, its presence on

Example 5.1: Chorus of Barrel Organ Melody from *Cœur de Lilas* (1931)

the soundtrack constant until police officers tell the man to stop playing. The barrel organ serves a dual purpose: as a musical depiction of working-class Paris, and as an anempathetic soundtrack, a point of musical contrast to the events onscreen.

Throughout the film, diegetic music serves to evoke the particular social spaces of the Parisian underclass. There is no music at all in scenes that take place in the police precinct, as the detectives interview suspects. But as soon as the action moves to a lower-class street and the *bal-musette* where a large portion of the film takes place, music appears with greater frequency. The blind organ grinder reappears when we are first introduced to the neighborhood, playing the same melody heard in the first scene. This time, his music becomes the accompaniment for a song. The song is performed by Fréhel, a famous singer who had begun her career as a street singer in real life and was featured in the film. When the song begins, the source of her voice is not initially clear. But the image finally cuts to her in her apartment, singing along to the organ grinder music playing outside, which provides diegetic justification for her song and connects her and her style of singing to the inhabitants of the neighborhood. Later in the film, a phonograph plays accordion music, and a live accordion band plays in several scenes in the *bal-musette* as we see couples dancing. In each instance, the music places the action unmistakably in the working-class dance hall, with music as an instantly recognizable sonic signifier of this specifically Parisian lower-class setting.

The Realist Singer as Commentator

Fréhel's appearance in *Cœur de Lilas* was not a unique occurrence. The "realist singer" was one particularly prominent character type in early poetic realist cinema. As Kelley Conway has argued, in French cinema of the 1930s, the realist singer—a performer, usually female, who would sing about social issues—became an icon of working-class femininity and a representation of the Parisian underworld.[12] The realist singer character, typically played by a well-known singer in real life, would sing about serious, often dark issues, and the songs usually provided some kind of oblique or obvious commentary on the plot, equating the performance with the plight of the characters onscreen in significant ways. Because of the presence of the voice and of lyrics, the realist singer's song takes on a greater importance than other music on the soundtrack. Countless films of the early 1930s featured singers whose careers were originally known through their stage performances and recordings. But unlike the songs and stars in the *opérettes filmées* discussed in chapter 3, songs in poetic realist films lent authenticity to the depiction of downtrodden, working-class characters.

Faubourg-Montmartre (1931) is one such example. The film focuses on the lives of two sisters, Ginette and Céline, as they struggle to support themselves. They take in a boarder, an educated man named Frédéric, who saves the younger Céline from the fate that befalls her sister—prostitution, drug addiction, and ultimately, mental breakdown. In the film, different kinds of musical performances help set the scene and establish different characters' social standings. One scene takes place at a music hall, where the well-known performer Florelle (playing the sisters' cousin Irène) sings onstage. Irène's song is cheerful and upbeat, sung to a large crowd on an impressive stage, and her performance is intended for a respectable audience. Florelle's performance is placed in stark contrast to a different scene, where Odette Barencey, a middle-aged café-concert performer, sings "Faubourg-Montmartre." The title song was written specially for the film and chronicles the plight of people of the neighborhood. Barencey's performance is wistful, accompanied by only a piano. There is an intimacy to the performance space of this song, which makes the women listening to it, and by extension the spectator, feel its emotional impact more directly. The contrast between these two songs in the film shows the realist song as more authentic to the film's setting, thereby granting it the ability to comment on the lives and plights of the characters.

Sometimes the realist singer's voice was represented as so powerful in its emotional impact that it could drive the male protagonist to either self-realization or self-destruction. Julien Duvivier's 1933 film *La Tête d'un homme* incorporated the realist singer directly into the plot in significant ways. The film was based on a detective novel by Georges Simenon, part of a serial about the character Inspector Maigret. Maigret investigates the murder of a wealthy American woman in Paris. He comes to suspect the medical student Johann Radek, who, being mortally ill and mentally unstable, plays psychological games with Maigret. The dark, mysterious setting, the focus on down-and-out criminal characters, and the psychological tension surrounding the character of Radek, all connect the film to Duvivier's later poetic realist style. A song performed by the well-known *chanteuse* Damia becomes an important element of the plot, taking on symbolic significance as Radek's perception of ideal femininity.

The song, newly composed for the film, appears several times in the narrative. Maigret, who suspects Radek of knowing something about the murder, visits him in his dingy apartment. Suddenly, we hear a melancholy song emanating through the walls of Radek's apartment, as the camera stays fixed in a close-up of him and Maigret while they listen. The singer is Damia, billed in the film's opening credits as "*une femme lasse*" (a tired or weary woman). "Doesn't she sing well?" Radek asks after a few moments. He admits that he does not want to know what the singer looks like, as he has already pictured her as resembling the woman he loves. As an acousmatic voice, the song takes on greater powers, becoming an ideal representation of femininity for Radek's twisted mind. For spectators aware of Damia's appearance in real life, the voice's source would not have been a mystery, but within the narrative it remains disembodied until the very last scene.

In the final climactic scene, Radek brings Edna, the woman he has become obsessed with over the course of the film, to his apartment. Damia's song begins again, and he tells Edna he had always imagined the voice as belonging to her. He grabs Edna by the wrist and takes her to the apartment the song is emanating from. He opens the door and sees Damia singing casually on the bed while a party goes on around her. She seems detached and jaded, not at all the ideal woman Radek had constructed in his imagination. Radek cannot control himself any longer and cracks. The song, and the last-minute revelation of its visual source, drives Radek over the edge, leading him to violence and a blind rage that results in his death a few moments later.

ANEMPATHETIC MUSIC FOR IRONY, CONTRAST, AND NARRATIVE DISRUPTION

Much like the barrel organ music in *Cœur de Lilas*, diegetic music could go against the grain of a particular scene's mood or events. This musical approach could produce different effects: it could create an ironic contrast, a disjunct between the mood of the music and that of the characters that makes an action seem poignant or tragic, or, at times, the music could even seem to aggressively intrude on the narrative, spilling over from soundtrack into storyline.

At the end of *Cœur de Lilas*, music helps depict Lilas's decision to run away from Lucot, the investigator with whom she has fallen in love, and eventually turn herself in for the murder she committed. The two are at a restaurant where a wedding celebration is taking place. Wedding guests are seen and heard singing a song—"Ne te plains pas que la mariée soit trop belle" (Don't complain that the bride is too beautiful)—led by the well-known vaudeville stage performer Fernandel. This cheerful song comes from a music-hall tradition, in contrast with the music "*du quartier*" that appears throughout the rest of the film, and it represents the happy life that momentarily seems within Lilas's reach. The music continues in the background, even as she comes to realize the truth of Lucot's identity. She runs away, the diegetic music continuing underneath as she runs farther and farther away from the wedding, its cheeriness completely at odds with her emotional state. The music then transitions from diegetic celebratory music to nondiegetic dramatic instrumental music that fluctuates between minor and major keys, better fitting her own emotion as she frantically runs away. As the scene moves away from realism and begins to represent Lilas's psychological turmoil, the music also transitions from directly recorded to postsynchronized. She sees visions of Lucot's face, of the wedding guests, then of police (all through superimposed images, intended to portray her inner thoughts). These images cut with increasing frequency as she becomes more and more distraught, until she runs head-on into a police officer and the music comes to a definitive end.

In *La Tête d'un homme*, upbeat music plays during a man's suicide. Radek has revealed he knows the role that Willy and his girlfriend Edna played in the murder. An establishing shot reveals a jazz band playing cheerfully, then pans to show a group of couples dancing together on the dance floor. The camera cuts to a seat at the bar, where Radek, who sits with Edna, Willy, and Maigret, blackmails Edna, whom he loves, into coming back up to his room with him. After they leave, Willy, who realizes that he faces jail time or worse for his role in the crime, shoots himself in the stomach as he sits at the table. The upbeat jazz playing in the background, and the jubilant people surrounding them, are depicted in stark contrast with the mood of the characters at the table and the tragic event that has just unfolded. Here, music takes on an ironic role that serves to highlight, rather than undermine, the tension of the scene.

Music That Intrudes on the Narrative

The diegetic music in some films went beyond anempathetic or ironic, and became intrusive, either actively intervening in the narrative or responding so closely to the narrative as to become indispensable to the action. René Clair's *Le Quatorze Juillet* (1932) is a prime example. With *Le Quatorze Juillet* Clair departed somewhat from the musical model he used for *Le Million* and instead closely followed the lives of several working-class characters in a more realist Parisian neighborhood setting. Nevertheless, music plays an important role in establishing the film's setting and mood, particularly with the song "À Paris, dans chaque faubourg" (In every suburb of Paris) that recurs frequently throughout the film.

Early in the film, music interrupts the narrative in a humorous way. Anna and Jean, the leading couple, are at an outdoor celebration on the eve of Bastille Day. They dance to the music of a neighborhood band. Then a bartender walks over to the stage with a tray full of drinks. The musicians repeatedly stop their music to grab drinks, much to the consternation of the conductor. We see Anna and Jean's frustration each time the music stops, as it disrupts their dancing and threatens to ruin their night. This scene establishes music's unreliability early in the film.

But music becomes even more disruptive later in the film, when a player piano interrupts a crime. Anna is working at a neighborhood bar. At the bar, music is provided by a coin-operated *piano mécanique*, which provides upbeat, cheery, percussive mechanical music. One customer, who is trying to read a book, is particularly unhappy about the music and covers his ears as it plays, which establishes the *piano mécanique* as a distraction and an aural menace.

The bar's owner introduces the machine by demonstrating how it works: by feeding it a coin and pressing a button, the music starts. It is finicky, though, and sometimes requires a jiggle to start. A would-be thief looks on at this demonstration with great interest. The thief hatches a plan, which he brings back to his partner in crime: they will return to the bar that evening and use the music from the pianola to cover up their sounds as they rob the cash register. Jean, who has become involved with this pair of criminals, will act as lookout as the robbery takes place.

The men arrive at the bar late, and Anna is working alone. They order drinks while Jean watches guard outside. The thief puts a coin in the pianola but it does not play, even after he shakes it. Anna walks outside to close up the bar, where she encounters Jean. Jean tries to warn her not to go back inside, but she does anyway, and the thieves restrain her to grab her key to the cash register. Jean runs in to try to help her, and he and the two thieves begin to fight. He pushes one of them, who falls against the pianola, and it suddenly starts playing. As the men fight, the anempathetic musical accompaniment offers an eerily cheery mechanical sound, providing a level of irony to the scene of the botched robbery, as Anna's boss wakes up and walks downstairs and the thieves scramble to run away. In addition to its incongruous mood, the musical machine seems to have its own agency, starting when it chooses and giving the robbers away in the process. Mechanical instruments like the player piano were ideal anempathetic musical sources, creating music that was uncanny in its inhumanness. Their potential for disruption made them a threatening presence on the soundtrack.

One of the most striking examples of diegetic music used for ironic effect occurs in *Paris-Béguin*. A backstage musical, the film focuses on a music-hall revue singer named Jane Diamond who is robbed by Bob (Jean Gabin), a dangerous criminal. She grows attracted to him, and the performance she is rehearsing for becomes increasingly heartfelt and convincing as she falls for him. In one particularly dramatic scene, a radio plays music as an aural stand-in for Bob's robbery and his sexual encounter with Jane that is initially coded as rape but later becomes less clear as Jane becomes enamored with Bob.

In this scene, Jane returns home after a night out on the town. She turns on her radio, and a jazzy upbeat instrumental tune plays. She dances around to the music, then turns it off and absentmindedly hums the melody as she walks around her apartment, running a bath and taking off her jewelry and setting it on the table. She notices the window is open, but thinks nothing of it. As she begins to fill the bath, she hears a noise coming from her bedroom. While she undresses, the camera cuts to her dark bedroom, where we see a light shining from one of the robber's flashlights. Suddenly, we hear the sounds of a rugby match: the radio seems to have turned on of its own accord. Two of the three thieves run away as we see Bob's hand on the dial of the radio. He tries to turn it off but instead changes the station. A jaunty instrumental song begins to play. Jane hears the music and comes out to her bedroom, asking who is there. She turns on the lights and sees Bob, who points a gun at her. The camera cuts between Jane and Bob in a series of shot/reverse shots, where we see each of them try to make sense of the other. As she backs up and he advances, the music on the radio ends and we hear applause, and an announcer speaking in English. Next, an upbeat duet, sung by two American male singers and accompanied by the piano, begins to play as he continues to pursue her with the gun. As the tension of the scene builds, the music continues along anempathetically. Bob slowly smiles, as the camera pans down to reveal Jane's exposed leg. He reaches for her jewelry on the table as the radio song ends and we hear more applause. A new song begins—a lushly orchestrated, slower instrumental piece played by a jazz band—and she begins to shout for help. Bob covers her mouth, then looks toward the radio. The camera cuts to the radio, and back to Bob, as if acknowledging that Bob is listening to the music, perhaps to consider whether it might cover up the sounds of her shouting. He embraces her roughly, and she struggles, all to the sound of the laid-back music. The two of them struggle as they move out of the frame. We hear her voice as she protests. The image cuts from the wall behind where they were standing, then to the radio again, and zooms in on the radio as the announcer ends his evening broadcast with the words "Goodnight everybody, goodnight!"

Though we cannot see *or* hear what is happening between Jane and Bob, there is no question as to what is going on outside the frame. The radio becomes a witness to the events unfolding, providing "accidental" commentary on the scene, and becoming a visual and aural stand-in for sex. Though the contrast between the music and the act of rape seems harsh and heartless, the music also offers a clue that Jane will no longer come to see their encounter in a negative light in the morning. In the following scene, we see them the next day, as Bob dresses and sneaks out of her room while Jane, looking content, sleeps in the bed. The same lazy instrumental song plays in the background, this time without an obvious diegetic source. Now serving as nondiegetic underscoring, the music highlights her satisfaction and the beginning of her sexual awakening. Though the radio music was diegetic, it was aggressively part of the narrative during a key moment in the story, adding both contrast and commentary.

DIEGETIC MUSIC AND SUBJECTIVITY

Music also played an important role in revealing the subjectivity of the protagonist. The "doomed fate" of the (usually) male protagonist was an important narrative aspect of poetic realist cinema, and diegetic music, particularly anempathetic music, was often used for dramatic irony, making the character's fate clear to the audience before the character is even aware of it, and highlighting the tragedy of the situation he finds himself in. *La Petite Lise* and *Le Grand Jeu* are two well-known examples of early poetic realist films that use music to this particular effect, in both cases at the very end of the film.

La Petite Lise, directed by Jean Grémillon in 1930, is about Berthier, a convict in a colonial prison in Cayenne. Upon release, he goes to live with his daughter, Lise, in Paris, where he discovers Lise is making her living as a prostitute. Lise and her boyfriend André, who is a penniless musician, want to escape their lives in Paris and make a fresh start by opening a roadside garage, but they need 3,000 francs to make a down payment. They devise a plan to rob a pawnbroker, but their plan goes awry and Lise ends up killing the man. When Berthier learns what has happened, he decides to turn himself in for the crime and return to a life in prison to save his daughter from the same fate. More significant than the narrative details, however, is the general atmosphere that Grémillon creates with innovative cinematography and use of sound. The music director, Roland-Manuel, explored various means of using music to represent the characters' inner thoughts and fears. The score even featured an early experiment with soundtrack manipulation: he reversed parts of the score in playback so that the sonic envelope of each note becomes unnatural and unsettling.[13]

Roland-Manuel established the strangeness and otherworldliness of the setting from the very opening of the film. The opening credits are accompanied by "exotic" sounding music: a solo female voice sings a minor-mode melody, accompanied by drums and pitched percussion. The lyrics are in French but are difficult to understand, purposely obscured by the singer's diction and accent. A male vocal ensemble enters, singing wordlessly. The wordlessness of the chorus endows the music with a general "otherness" without locating it in a specific culture or place; but as the credits end, a title card announces that we are in Cayenne, a French colony in South America, and we see an exterior shot of a colonial prison. The music continues as we see prisoners line up to reenter the prison building. The exoticist music draws the audience into the colonial setting of the first part of the film, but the lack of stylistic specificity of the music encourages an identification with the emotional experience of Berthier, who has lived for years in a foreign, utterly unfamiliar place with no real direct contact with local culture. Though not clearly emanating from a particular source, the opening credits music serves to immediately identify the spectator with Berthier.

The opening is paralleled in the very end of the film, where explicitly diegetic music is employed to express Berthier's alienation and interior emotional turmoil. He goes to the Montmartre nightclub where André, Lise's boyfriend, has been working. The bar is packed with patrons, both black and white, and jazz music plays loudly. The music has a distinct Latin rhythm, and we see a black performer in a top hat and tails perform a gyrating dance as the band plays behind him, while patrons dance inside the crowded room. Berthier enters and watches the performance, as the camera cuts back and forth between the performer and the patrons. He has initially come to confront André, but Lise tearfully asks him not to before André comes back to his dressing room. The diegetic music continues to play quietly in the background, and we see a flashback of Berthier's time in prison. The image cuts back to Berthier's anguished face, and as the music continues to play, we hear a voice-over of the prison warden's words from the beginning of the film, telling him that he is a free man, words that are painfully ironic at this moment in the story. He leaves the dressing room and joins the crowd once again. The camera pans wildly and cuts frequently to capture the reckless abandon with which the clientele are dancing to the joyful Latin-tinged music. We hear them start to sing along. The camera briefly cuts to Berthier's unhappy face, then back to the dancing crowd. The music continues as we see Berthier walk slowly into a police precinct and approach a police officer. Though we do not hear what he says, it is clear he has decided to turn himself in in Lise's place (Figures 5.1a–d). The music suddenly cuts out to the sound of the prison bell, and the film ends.

The diegetic music in the club in this scene is multivalent. It provides a point of contrast, as the happy upbeat music is anempathetic to Berthier's tragic dilemma. It also serves as a Parisian musical equivalent to prison life in Cayenne that he had so desperately hoped was behind him for good. The joyful abandon of the patrons in the bar is in stark contrast with Berthier's emotion, and his alienation and the manner in which he is physically separate

Figures 5.1a–d: Final Scene, *La Petite Lise* (1930)

from the community is highlighted in the framing of his medium close-up. Alan Williams suggests that the pairing of "native" music in the opening with the nightclub music at the end creates "an elegant, quasi-poetic structure."[14] The musical choice at the end of the film also incisively reveals the emotional bind that Berthier finds himself in, and the tragedy of his situation, as he is ultimately free in neither Cayenne nor in Paris.

In Jacques Feyder's 1934 film *Le Grand Jeu*, diegetic music announces to both the protagonist and the spectator the unhappy destiny that is in the main character's future. Feyder, who worked in Hollywood beginning in 1929, returned to France in 1932, and this was his first film after his return. Marcel Carné was assistant director. The film focuses on Pierre, a young Parisian businessman, whose extravagant lifestyle and the expensive taste of his girlfriend Florence bring him to financial ruin. He is forced join the Foreign Legion in North Africa. When they are on break from their military campaign, he frequents a seedy hotel, run by Clément and his wife Blanche. Pierre encounters Irma, who looks almost identical to his former lover Florence, working at a local bar as a singer and prostitute. He becomes obsessed with Irma, who seems not to remember her own past. The film's score was composed by Hanns Eisler, who had recently fled Nazi Germany. But diegetic music plays an equally important role in the soundscape of the film. Though the film's soundtrack is sparse for large portions of the story, diegetic music helps to illustrate military life, create the atmosphere of Morocco, and represent Pierre's demise.

Military music bookends scenes of Pierre's service in the Foreign Legion. During the first scene after he has arrived in Morocco, we see an empty, run-down bar. The scene is nearly silent. Slowly, faintly, the sound of military music (fifes, bugles, and drums) can be heard in the distance. The music becomes louder and louder, and finally, after the camera cuts to an exterior shot, the marching army comes into view. Through a slow build-up, this scene depicts the anticipation of the quiet town, as they get ready to cater to the soldiers' worldly desires during their furlough. The music establishes the setting, as the spectator is introduced to the location where Pierre's drama will soon unfold.

The effect of the military music is markedly different when we hear it again at the end of the film. Pierre has sent Irma on a boat to Marseille, telling her he will join her a couple of days later, but he has no intention of doing so. Instead, he reenlists in the Foreign Legion. He and Blanche, the hotel owner who has throughout the film acted as part mother figure and part friend, sit around the bar drinking. Blanche tells his fortune with a deck of cards, as she had once before, earlier in the film. This time, the two cards that symbolize death—the nine of spades next to the nine of diamonds—appear side by side. Blanche quickly throws the cards to the floor, and the two try to laugh it off, but then the familiar sound of military music can be heard faintly in the distance. As the sounds of his approaching unit get closer, Pierre departs to join them, leaving Blanche behind, distraught, to contemplate the future that the cards have shown for him. In this scene, the military music makes all too clear Pierre's doomed fate: he is marching to his death. The film might very well have ended with dramatic, dissonant nondiegetic underscoring, which had appeared at other moments in the film to highlight ways in which is his fortune is determined. Instead, the stripped-down aesthetic of the diegetic military music starkly evokes a sense of the harsh, unsympathetic world the characters find themselves in.

Early poetic realist films reflect a range of experiments with what music could do within a realist aesthetic, and the multivalent use of diegetic music in these films shows the flexible understanding of cinematic realism in 1930s French cinema. Nevertheless, the treatment of diegetic music across these early poetic realist films is consistent in several respects. Music helped evoke atmosphere to highlight the realism of the films' settings, at the same time that it often added commentary on the scene at hand or contrasted with unhappy events onscreen. These techniques highlighted the unsympathetic environments many of the characters found themselves in. Though seemingly encompassed within the realist priorities of direct sound, these varied examples reveal the ways in which musical realism in early sound cinema became its own stylized aesthetic.

Director Jean Renoir explored diegetic music's role in sound cinema in similar ways to these early poetic realist films, and his treatment of music in film should be understood as part of this wider network of aesthetic and narrative experiments in the early sound era. At the same time that Renoir engaged with many of these same musical techniques, he established a distinctive approach to sound and music that he would continue to use in his later films of the 1930s. In particular, he frequently incorporated music in a manner that was so assertive that it called attention to itself, highlighting the stylization of diegetic music to a degree not found in many of the films of his contemporaries. He also used music to shed light on issues of social class (beyond representation of working-class milieus) in pointed ways.

JEAN RENOIR AND SOUND FILM

Renoir's status as an *auteur* has led his work to receive a great deal of scholarly attention. The son of the impressionist painter Pierre-Auguste Renoir, he began his filmmaking career as a silent film director, although none of his silent films, which were mostly funded by his family's wealth, were commercial successes. His wife, the actress Catherine Hessling, starred in many of his first films, including *La Fille de l'eau* (1924), *Nana* (1926), and *La Petite Marchande d'allumettes* (1928). Renoir was enthusiastic about the arrival of synchronized sound, but first had to prove himself with a commercially successful sound film before producers would back his own projects. His first sound film, *On purge bébé* (1931), was a theatrical adaptation based on a play by Georges Feydeau and produced by Pierre Braunberger. The film was shot very cheaply in only a few days. According to Renoir, he shot the film to prove himself to Braunberger in order to secure backing for his own projects.

Renoir's early sound films run the gamut in terms of source material and style—from *théâtre filmé* to historical drama—but they all take advantage of direct sound. Although his early sound films are stylistically diverse, his preference for direct sound was almost dogmatic, more so than most of his contemporaries, which is why he has been considered the paradigm of such an approach. He was interested in spoken dialogue, but for Renoir dialogue was "only part of the sound-track: a sigh, the creak of a door, the sound of footsteps on the pavement, things such as these can say as much as the spoken word."[15] Renoir valued direct recording because he believed it created a more realist atmosphere than sound manipulated in postproduction, and his propensity for direct sound and dislike of rerecording prioritized sonic realism, sometimes over intelligibility.

Related to his interest in direct sound, diegetic music was an important element of Renoir's early sound aesthetic. Renoir incorporated music into his films sparsely; Charles O'Brien remarks of Renoir's films of the 1930s, "The main fact about the music is perhaps how little of it there is."[16] Renoir once said he believed "a musical score underlining the acting suggests that those actors are incapable of playing their parts with talent alone and must be helped by the musical score. . . . Good actors do not need too many props; they do not need a musical score, either."[17] But his statement about music belies the actual importance of music in his films: each musical occurrence is highly intentional and packed with meaning. In the analysis that follows, I consider music in two of Renoir's early sound films in depth to explore Renoir's approach to diegetic music, and the ways in which he heightened its purpose and meaning to intensify the tension between naturalism and cinematic stylization.

BOURGEOIS MUSIC, DIRECT SOUND, AND *LA CHIENNE* (1931)

La Chienne (1931) was Renoir's second sound film. An adaptation of a widely read novel by Fouchardière, the film, in the words of Dudley Andrew, "ushered in a type of cinematographic naturalism" that had a broad influence on Renoir's own later style, on French poetic realism more broadly, and even beyond national practices.[18] Unlike *On purge bébé*, for *La Chienne* Renoir had complete artistic control. However, after filming, the producers, expecting a light comedy, were unhappy with the material, and temporarily barred him from the editing room. They ultimately returned control to him after they found they could not successfully edit the film themselves.[19] *La Chienne* has since become one of Renoir's most highly regarded films of the early 1930s, and is one of the films that connects Renoir most closely to poetic realism. The film is about an unhappily married bourgeois man, Michel Legrand (Michel Simon), who is introverted and socially awkward. He falls in love with a prostitute, Lulu (Janie Marèse), who, together with her pimp boyfriend Dédé (Georges Flamant), takes advantage of Legrand's naiveté to obtain money from him. When Legrand realizes he is being used, he murders Lulu in her apartment. Dédé is accused of the murder and is sentenced to death, and Legrand ends up as a hobo on the street. The film's cinematography and use of direct sound are key markers of Renoir's naturalistic style, which highlight the class differences between Legrand and Lulu through a realistic portrayal of the seedy Parisian streets and bars where Dédé and Lulu spend their time. In *La Chienne*, diegetic music serves a number of important functions. But, rather than provide atmosphere to the lower-class settings like the examples discussed earlier, the music instead mostly serves to critique the confines of the bourgeois society that Legrand comes from.

Diegetic Music and Cinematic Artifice

One important difference from other early poetic realist films was Renoir's use of music to highlight the artifice of cinema as a storytelling medium. The film opens with a Guignol puppet show (a French style of puppet theater similar to Punch and Judy, featuring a character named Guignol). Guignol puppet shows are typically participatory, with audiences responding to questions voiced by the puppets. But here, the puppet show serves more as a point of entry into the cinematic spectacle, through a specifically French style of street performance. The show serves as a narrative framing device, introducing the characters of the drama and declaring that the story is neither a comedy nor a tragedy. An upbeat melody in 3/4 time, with strings, accordion, and brass, begins to play even before the opening credits start. As the music and credits end, we see a curtain. The music begins again, this time as part of a puppet show. The puppets describe each of the main characters in the film, as an image of each character's face is superimposed on the puppet show curtain, and a brief musical accordion scalar flourish punctuates each line.

This opening is highly theatrical, and the music serves to underline its artifice. It is in stark contrast with the realist aesthetic of the rest of the film; it nods to the *théâtre filmé* aesthetic, but departs from it immediately afterward. The film ends with a closing curtain, a fleeting reference to the film's opening diegetic performance. By opening with a puppet show, and ending the drama with a closing curtain, Renoir implies that the film's story, though in some respects highly realistic, is nevertheless heightened drama for spectators' pleasure. Although there are no other moments as explicitly theatrical elsewhere in the film, the other scenes with diegetic music help articulate the tension between complete realism on the one hand, and manipulated drama on the other.

Music and the Confinement of Bourgeois Culture

In several scenes, diegetic music highlights the constraints of Legrand's bourgeois world, a world in which he neither seems happy nor particularly comfortable. Though brief, these musical moments are important for establishing Legrand's social standing, which are contrasted with Lulu's. In the opening scene, Legrand is at a meeting for the company where he works. As the meeting ends, someone puts on a phonograph, which is seen in close-up. We hear the light operatic voice of a man singing Enrico Toselli's "Serenata" (1900). As the song plays softly in the background, Legrand converses with the men from his firm. They clearly find him odd, and try to joke with him, but he is serious and refuses to go out with them. The musical style is restrained, and in the opening scene Legrand has a similarly reserved demeanor. Its light operatic style lends the song an air of respectability, contrasting Legrand's world with the very different side of Paris depicted soon after. Legrand speaks poetically about the pleasures of life, while his comrades discuss how they just want to have fun. The song's lyrics are nostalgic, evoking "dreams and memories," and anticipating the sense of loss that will come for Legrand later in the film.[20] Because the music was direct recorded at the same time as the dialogue, with no possibility of mixing in postproduction, the music's volume is higher than would typically be expected for a dialogue scene, which serves to emphasize Legrand's shy, soft-spoken, awkward personality.

In a later scene, after Legrand has become involved with Lulu, we see him shaving in his house, a task that is part of his daily routine. In the background, a young girl in the apartment across the street practices piano, and we hear her play Clementi's Sonatina in C, movement 3, the sound wafting through Legrand's open window. The piece is again one of complete restraint: its typical classical style features perfectly balanced phrase structures. The girl's belabored attempt at the piece parallels Legrand's efforts at keeping up appearances: he has been struggling to financially provide the lifestyle Lulu wants. As the music continues, he surreptitiously steals money from his wife's savings to give to Lulu. The seemingly unremarkable situation of a young girl practicing mundane music, playing along in the background as Legrand completes mundane tasks, is in sharp contrast with the dramatic narrative moment of his stealing the money. But his action is rendered completely normal at this particular moment because of the way Legrand progresses so smoothly from the act of shaving to stealing. The bourgeois piano music first complements, then provides counterpoint to, Legrand's actions.

Music also foreshadows Legrand's decline from his social standing, through a musical occurrence that aggressively intrudes on the narrative space. Alexis, Legrand's wife's first husband, was a war hero presumed dead. Alexis has sought out and found Legrand, and the two sit in a café drinking beer. Alexis says he would like to get back together with his wife but needs money, as he has been living a less than honest life since he faked his own death during the war. Legrand, eager to free himself from his marriage so he can devote himself to Lulu, hatches a plan. He will encourage Alexis to steal money from Legrand's house, so he will be discovered and, with the first husband back in the picture, Legrand will be freed from his marital ties. As the two converse, a tinny player piano begins playing loudly in the background. We do not see its source at first, but the music plays loudly alongside their conversation. Its mechanical, upbeat dance melody is unemotive, unchanging in tempo or volume, throughout their discussion. The effect is particularly striking as Alexis tries to extort money from Legrand. The music starts up again, this time much louder, as Alexis leaves the bar, and we finally see the source of the music—the player piano on the other side of the bar's empty dance floor. One anonymous couple dances to the music, their faces devoid of emotion. Then the camera cuts to a close-up of the player piano itself, visually highlighting the mechanism by which it plays (Figures 5.2a–b). The music and the image dissolve to the next scene, as we see and hear the cuckoo clock in Legrand's apartment and soon see him drunkenly stumbling home. The player piano, a seemingly gratuitous musical intrusion into the narrative, is unsettling because it holds no immediate apparent meaning. (The reason for its intrusion is less clear than the player piano in *Le Quatorze Juillet*, for example.) It highlights the working-class setting of the bar where Legrand and Alexis meet, providing musical realism to the scene. But its intrusion into the soundscape of the scene is too aggressive for it to be explained purely as atmosphere. It also points to the machinations at work in Legrand's downfall. This scene also foreshadows the friendship Legrand and Alexis will strike up at the end of the film, when Legrand has lost everything and is a tramp living on the street. The two of

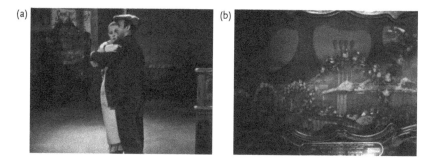

Figures 5.2a–b: Dancing Couple and Player Piano, *La Chienne* (1931)

them, whether voluntarily or not, will abandon their social standing and as a result become much freer, regardless of how much they lose in the process. Perhaps the player piano, in its mechanical rigidity, points to the shackles of their lives they will have to throw off in order to experience true liberation.

Though Renoir depicts bourgeois life critically, Lulu is eager to attain this social stature that would deliver her a life without want. Renoir illustrates this point with piano music, in a scene where Lulu and Dédé meet with art dealers. Lulu and Dédé have been selling Legrand's amateur paintings to an art dealer, pretending they are by Lulu. At the party, they are clearly out of their element, their situation made all the more awkward when the art dealer tells Lulu that a wealthy man would like to commission her to paint his portrait. She angrily refuses (mostly out of fear), and walks over to a man sitting at the piano. She absentmindedly hits a few notes, then asks the man to play something nice on the piano. He begins playing a simple waltz, and Lulu looks on and listens. Dédé stands up to talk to Lulu, and begins dancing with her. They talk as they dance, and he pressures her to take the commission, asking for a healthy advance in order to get close to the wealthy patron. Their dance is, according to Kelley Conway, "stiff and intense," which drives home how manipulative Dédé has been toward Lulu and how quickly Lulu is willing to submit.[21] The intensity of their dancing is at odds with the simplicity of the piano music. Not only does the music accompany the dance that highlights the power dynamic in Dédé and Lulu's relationship, but it also indicates how uneasily they fit into their surroundings at that moment, and how they will never comfortably achieve the lifestyle they had both, in different ways, been hoping for. The waltz resumes just as Lulu sits with the prospective client, right before she tries to seduce him, making the music complicit in the couple's exploitation of their innocent victims. In all of these scenes, music serves to highlight, even exacerbate, the differences in class and in social expectations, which brings the tragedy of Legrand's downfall, Lulu's death, and Dédé's demise into further relief.

La Chienne's Realist Singer

The film's most famous musical moment is the scene where Legrand murders Lulu. This scene incorporates street musicians, including a street singer, into the narrative and the soundtrack. This song has very different social meaning than the bourgeois music heard in other scenes. Although related to the realist singer type found in other early poetic realist films, Renoir's treatment of the realist singer contains a few important differences. For one, the singer is male, which means the gendered cultural connotations found in the female realist singer type are absent. Additionally, the action does not stop for the street singer's performance and the singer is never seen in close up, instead acting as a distanced, abstracted entity. Lastly, the singer's presence prompts a complex web of simultaneous, and at times contradictory, interpretations of the scene that unfolds as the singer performs.

Legrand has just arrived at Lulu's apartment to tell her he forgives her for sleeping with Dédé, which he assumes she has only done for money. He says he is now in a position to offer her a better life. But she demands that he finish his painting, and Legrand realizes that she has been manipulating him. At this moment, the camera cuts to the street below, and we see a couple of street performers—a woman with a violin and a man with a guitar—begin playing. A crowd begins to gather around them (Figures 5.3a–b). The scene cuts back to the apartment. Then a man begins singing the "Sérénade du Pavé," a song popularized by Eugénie Buffet (and, later, Édith Piaf). The song's lyrics are from the point of view of a singer, who sings below the window of a *chère inconnue* (dear unknown). The song has the trappings of a love song, but the singer acknowledges that the relationship between a singer and a listener is

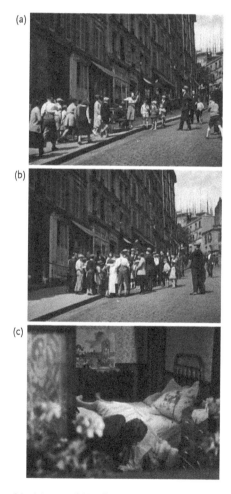

Figures 5.3a–c: Street Musicians and Murder Scene, *La Chienne* (1931)

not one of love; it only matters that the listener throw the singer a coin or two for the song:

Sois bonne, ô ma chère inconnue	Be good, my dear unknown
Pour qui j'ai si souvent chanté.	For whom I have so often sung.
Ton offrande est la bienvenue.	Your gift is welcome.
Fais-moi la charité.	Give me charity.
Sois bonne, ô ma chère inconnue	Be good, my dear unknown
Pour qui j'ai si souvent chanté.	For whom I have so often sung.
Devant moi, devant moi, soi bienvenue.	Before me, before me, be welcome.

The lyrics, to a certain extent, parallel Lulu's feelings toward Legrand. We never see the singer clearly, so his voice remains acousmatic, becoming, much like René Clair's opera singers in *Le Million*, a voice of commentary on the actions taking place.

Lulu shows no remorse about manipulating Legrand, and begins laughing in his face. He yells at her to stop, and we see a close-up of a knife. Their conversation increases in volume and intensity. At that moment, the image cuts back to the street performers and the crowd surrounding them. The camera slowly pans up to the bedroom window, then fades to black. It then travels into the bedroom, where Lulu, bloodied and dead, is sprawled across the bed, Legrand kneeling over her (Figure 5.3c). He leaves the apartment undetected because the crowd is distracted by the street musicians. Moments later, Dédé drives to Lulu's apartment and parks his car right in the middle of the crowd, interrupting the spectators' sight of the musicians and drawing attention to himself. Due to his conspicuous arrival, he will soon be accused of the murder. The musicians continue, unaware of what has just taken place, until the landlady goes upstairs to deliver Lulu's mail. She shrieks upon discovering Lulu's dead body, which interrupts the music, and shouts out the window to the crowds below.

The presence of the street musicians in this scene is so prominent they almost overshadow the murder that takes place off screen. Their music covers up any sounds that might be heard, and their image becomes the visual stand-in for the event that is taking place. The inclusion of the street singer during this scene has been interpreted in many ways. In a literal sense, we can interpret the music as anempathetic to the events on screen, as a means of commenting on broader social issues. Christopher Faulkner, for instance, calls the scene an example of Brecht's *Verfremdungseffekt*, a musical contrast to Legrand's violently repressed sexual frustration that takes the spectator out of the heat of the moment by showing the street musicians "and their courtly love song at the very moment of the murder."[22] As a result, the music pulls the spectator out of the dramatic moment. It is true that during this scene it is difficult to empathize with any of the characters. However, the song is not just about courtly love: it is a comment on how songs about courtly love are performed for money, which makes their abstract message of love ring false and brings the music close to the level of prostitution. Alexander Sesonske offers a different perspective, suggesting that the use of music here helps to "universalize the dramatic situation."[23] The audience for the street performers becomes the stand-in for the audience of the film, placing them extremely close to the action to encourage them to identify with Legrand's suffering. The street musicians also contribute to the film's realism. According to Kelley Conway, the choice of a street singer, rather than a different ensemble or style, lends the scene "an element of authenticity rooted in the realm of culture. . . . To viewers of the 1930s, the realist singer was a contradictory but authentic emissary of the margins, worthy of our sympathy and our respect."[24] All of these interpretations reveal the rich multivalence that the music brings to this scene, enacting meaning in simultaneous and contradictory ways.

Interestingly, this scene was apparently the only one in the film where the music was recorded after the fact and mixed with the dialogue.[25] If Renoir were aiming purely for realism, the scene would have unfolded in silence, or with realistic direct-recorded sounds. If he had incorporated nondiegetic underscoring, it is difficult to imagine how the music could have achieved these various simultaneous functions. The fact that it cannot comment emotionally on the action brings home the point that, although the characters think they are acting of their own free will, their actions are beyond their control, much like the puppets in the opening scene, determined by the external social forces around them.

MUSICAL HUMOR, EROTICISM, AND *BOUDU SAUVÉ DES EAUX* (1932)

In *Boudu sauvé des eaux*, Renoir also critiqued bourgeois culture, but this time in the form of satire. As a result, Renoir's approach to diegetic music in the film is quite different from *La Chienne*. Just as in *La Chienne*, music provides commentary on the actions and characters, as well as class critique; but in *Boudu sauvé des eaux*, music is also used as a source of humor and irony, and as a symbol of eroticism and sexual frustration. The film, which was freely adapted from a play by René Fauchois, recounts the story of Édouard Lestingois, a bourgeois bookseller, who rescues a free-spirited tramp named Boudu from a suicidal plunge into the Seine after he loses his beloved dog. Lestingois brings Boudu to live in his house, and he, his wife, and his servant and mistress Anne-Marie try to mold him into a proper bourgeois man. He disrupts the foundations of the household and all of the relationships inside it, refusing to accept what he sees as arbitrary social customs. He seduces both the maid and Madame Lestingois. After Boudu wins the lottery, the Lestingois couple urges him to marry Anne-Marie, which would smooth over the tensions in the household caused by the various infidelities committed. However, in the final scene, Boudu leaves the wedding by capsizing their rowboat and swimming away, back to his old carefree life.

Music as a Bourgeois Symbol: Blurred Boundaries, Humor, and Sexual Tension

Just as in *La Chienne*, Renoir opens *Boudu* with a theatrical device, an explicit reference to live stage performance. In this case, the theatrical opening serves to satirize the main characters. Renoir explicitly plays on the diegetic ambiguity of a musical source in order to point to the bourgeois pretentions of the film's characters, but also to highlight the artifice of cinematic storytelling.

As the opening credits finish, we hear a solo flute, which the title credits announce is played by flutist J. Boulze. The modal melody is rhythmically free, sounding something like an etude (Example 5.2). A title card reads "Boudu." Then we see a stage with a backdrop, a pair of columns that are very clearly part of a set, and a portly-looking satyr dancing around with a nymph (Figure 5.4a). The audiovisual pairing could very well have been an intentional reference to Debussy's *Prélude de l'après-midi d'un faun*. If so, it is a humorous one, since the satyr is neither graceful nor good-looking.

The satyr carries a set of panpipes, but he places it down and continues dancing, all while the flute solo plays. The satyr embraces the nymph, and the image dissolves to a couple embracing in a bookshop. It is Monsieur Lestingois and his maid, Anne-Marie. He declares his feelings for her in an over-the-top profession of love, complete with references to Greek mythology, and throughout his dialogue, the flute plays softly underneath (Figure 5.4b). Then, the camera cuts to a man playing the flute as he looks out his window, which finally grounds the solo flute in a diegetic source (Figure 5.4c). When the man stops playing, the background noise of the busy city street enters, and Lestingois closes his window. The flutist neighbor has been practicing this whole time.

Alex Clayton suggests that this flute solo is "heard variously—and sometimes at once—as diegetic and non-diegetic, physical and ethereal, imagined and real."[26] Perhaps the practicing neighbor's melodies prompted Lestingois's flight of fancy as he clandestinely met with his mistress, inspiring his flowery,

Example 5.2: Flute Melody, *Boudu sauvé des eaux* (1932)

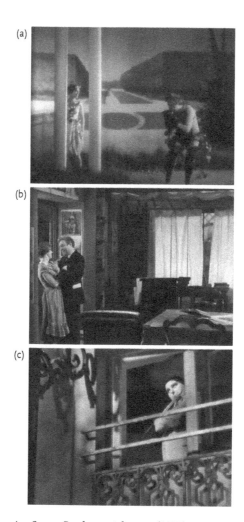

Figures 5.4a–c: Opening Scene, *Boudu sauvé des eaux* (1932)

poetic language. Perhaps the melody begins as an expression of Lestingois's interiority, only to be suddenly made exterior through the visual presentation of the practicing neighbor. This opening scene creates an effective multi-layered audiovisual joke—the visual equivalence (seen as ridiculous) between Lestingois and a satyr, the distorted reference to a well-known symbolist ballet, and the suggestion that this poetic-musical representation of his literary fantasy in fact emanated from a very real source. The melody takes on additional meaning—and irony—as the film continues.

The flute music (and flutist character) reappears several times in the film, and comes to represent the erotic energy that Boudu infuses into the Lestingois household, appearing when characters experience sexual tension or anticipation. On Boudu's first night in the house, we see the flutist practicing at his window, then get a glimpse of each member of the household having trouble sleeping. Boudu is not accustomed to sleeping on a soft sofa, and ultimately moves to the harder, cooler floor. Madame Lestingois is restless, alone in her bed with pent-up sexual frustration. Anne-Marie is awake, expecting a nighttime visit from Monsieur Lestingois. And Monsieur Lestingois waits for an appropriate amount of time to pass to get up and pay Anne-Marie a visit, only to be thwarted by Boudu's presence on the floor. The flute plays again the next morning, as we see first a shot of Notre Dame, then the flutist, then the Lestingois family eating breakfast. Once more we hear the flute when Boudu paces outside the bookstore, after he has seduced Madame Lestingois. In all these instances, if taken literally, the flutist character must be a somewhat lecherous voyeur, playing flute as he looks out his window and seemingly observes a great deal of the action taking place, just as Monsieur Lestingois spies on ladies on the street with a telescope. More symbolically, the flutist comes to represent a nonverbal narrator of sorts—his music wafts through the neighborhood, which somehow reaches and influences the different members of the Lestingois household. The flute serves as a phallic musical stand-in for the act of seduction. It underscores the Lestingois household's fantasy that they can somehow tame Boudu and the chaos he embodies, even as they simultaneously seem unable to resist it. It is also a constant critique of the pretenses of the bourgeois culture the Lestingois household represents. Moreover, by associating the flute with a critique of bourgeois pretense, Renoir's explicit musical joke also points to the artifice of the cinematic mode of storytelling.

Throughout the film, music represents the contrast between bourgeois society and the more carefree world of Boudu. For instance, early in the film, Anne-Marie sings in the study as she cleans, with Monsieur Lestingois present. He tells her to clean the piano, and she asks why they have a piano if no one plays it. Lestingois replies, "We have a piano because we are respectable people." She plunks out a melody on the piano as Lestingois looks through a telescope, where he ultimately spots Boudu about to jump off the bridge. The piano is visible in multiple scenes, although no one plays more than a few notes. Music is symbolically significant for the Lestingois family, even if no one actually makes any music. On the other hand, music sonically represents the more carefree, vivacious life that Boudu represents and the Lestingois subconsciously yearn for. This contrast is also highlighted in the brief melodies that different characters sing: Anne-Marie sings "Les fleurs du jardin," which Alexander Sesonske suggests represents domestication, and Boudu sings "Sur les bords de la Riviera," which is an expression of liberation.[27]

Narratively Intrusive Music as a Representation of Sexual Frustration and Fulfillment

The scenes featuring Madame Lestingois are perhaps the most pointed in their use of music for a humorous and symbolic representation of sexual frustration and satisfaction. In one scene, Madame Lestingois lies sprawled out on the bed, exhausted after dealing with Boudu's destruction of her kitchen. Suddenly, we hear the upbeat music of a barrel organ emanating from the street. We see a shot of the organ grinder playing on the street below. The scene then crosscuts between Madame Lestingois and Boudu, who is walking to a barber to have a shave and haircut. The implication, if not apparent immediately, soon becomes clear: Madame Lestingois will give in to her lust and embrace a more vivacious side to life, aided by Boudu.[28] Unlike the organ grinder in *Cœur de Lilas*, here the barrel organ does not seem necessary for creating mood or atmosphere. It is also not necessarily anempathetic. Instead, it seems to be present to cue the spectator into the joke, and to suggest that we should not take Madame Lestingois as seriously as she takes herself.

When Boudu returns from the barber and seduces Madame Lestingois, music becomes a more literal stand-in for the act of seduction. She yells at him for the destruction he caused, and he approaches her aggressively. She protests at first, but the two of them fall out of the frame. As they fall below the frame, the camera focuses on a painting of a trumpet player on the wall in the apartment, and the scene cuts abruptly to a brass band playing outside the window. We then see Monsieur Lestingois, who seems perturbed that a loud band is disrupting his reading. When the camera cuts back to the room upstairs, Boudu and Madame Lestingois reappear in the frame, the lady of the house looking happy and full of energy for the first time in the film (Figures 5.5a–c). The cut-away to the diegetic marching band serves as a stand-in for the act of seduction taking place in the apartment. The music is triumphant and jubilant, which humorously exaggerates her feelings at the end of the scene. We later learn that the band is there to honor Monsieur Lestingois's selfless act of saving Boudu, made all the more ironic by the fact that the audience knows the music is covering up the sounds of his wife's infidelities. The painting becomes a conspicuous visual stand-in for the music, and it does not take much for the spectator to imagine the real action taking place below the frame. Unlike the rape scene in *Paris-Béguin*, in which the music seemed heartlessly unresponding to the actions unfolding, here the music tells us how the characters feel before we see them, making the triumph of Boudu's sexual act absolutely clear, and shown as something worth celebrating (as problematic as that may seem to a modern-day spectator).

Music as a Symbol of Liberation

In the final scene, music once more serves to reinforce the contrast between Boudu and the other characters, highlighting Boudu's choice to return to his more liberated, prebourgeois life. The main characters are in a rowboat, rowing down the river to the wedding of Boudu and Anne-Marie. On the shore, we

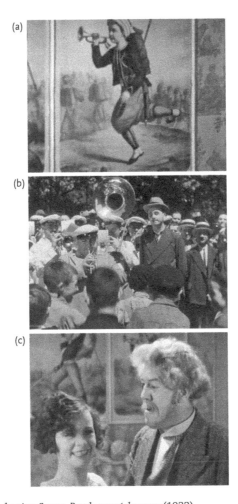

Figures 5.5a–c: Seduction Scene, *Boudu sauvé des eaux* (1932)

see a wedding ensemble, which begins playing the *Blue Danube* waltz. The camera zooms out to show a greater expanse of the river. The music fades out as Boudu capsizes the boat (it is unclear whether this action is intentional or not). Chaos ensues as the members of the wedding party make their way to the riverbanks, as Boudu literally goes with the flow, floating downstream with no attempt to turn around or rejoin his bride-to-be. He ends up on the shore, some distance away from the wedding, and he slowly transforms back to his tramp persona, as music accompanies his actions. For the first time in the film, there is no obvious diegetic source for the music. Perhaps it is still the wedding band's music, but it could not realistically be heard from so far away. Boudu exchanges his clothing for the tattered clothes of a scarecrow. We briefly see the wedding party, and the music—"Sur les bords de la Riviera" (a tune that Boudu had previously sung to himself throughout the film)—seems to be grounded in a source yet again, although we do not see the wedding band this time. The music becomes louder, and we see a number of men who appear to be hobos walking in the city. They sing together, and they walk out of the frame, the camera's low angle focusing on the expansive sky. Ending the film with singing men is somewhat out of place with the purported realism of the rest of the film, but the implication here is that Boudu, and by extension these men, live in a world that merits nondiegetic music, a fantastical, antirealist world, one that the Lestingois family will never inhabit. The music in this final scene is incisive, serving as a reminder that throughout the film, diegetic music that provides humor can simultaneously critique.

Although Renoir's approach to music differs subtly from film to film, important commonalities reveal his emerging aesthetic priorities that continued through the 1930s. Though his use of music was sparse, it was significant in its ability to critique, particularly social class. It often served a literal purpose and a more symbolic one, while pushing the limits of the aesthetic of cinematic realism epitomized in direct sound. Renoir's approach had much in common with other early examples of poetic realism—particularly his use of music for atmosphere and the ways in which diegetic music could intrude on the narrative—but his approach often reflexively called attention to cinema's artificiality, even within an otherwise naturalist film.

CONCLUSION

At the same time that *théâtre filmé* was dominating a great deal of French filmmaking in the first years of synchronized sound, Renoir, along with Grémillon, Duvivier, Feyder, and others, experimented with music's role in realist cinema. Music was an important tool for achieving one of poetic realism's primary features: the representation of the harsh, unsympathetic social conditions and settings of interwar France. Source music played a nuanced role. It could highlight mood or atmosphere. It could reveal the desires and wishes of the characters, or it could universalize the characters' situations. It could add a layer of irony or contrast, often for tragic or poignant effect. And it could help the spectator understand the interior state of the characters. This multivalent use of diegetic music, paired with the aesthetic affinity for direct sound in France more broadly, profoundly shaped the poetic realist aesthetic that increased in prominence with the rise of the Popular Front in the mid-1930s, leading up to World War II.

Although Renoir has been considered the paradigm of such an approach, as my analysis reveals, his treatment of music in film was part of this broader set of aesthetic and narrative concerns and experiments in the early sound era.

But as the 1930s progressed, directors took these early musical approaches in multiple directions. Renoir was one of the only filmmakers to maintain such a dogged commitment to diegetic music.[29] Music as part of the narrative world of the film remained an important element in poetic realist cinema, although more sparingly: *Pépé le Moko*, Julien Duvivier's 1937 film set in an Algerian casbah, for instance, uses source music for setting and atmosphere, and also features one of the most memorable instances of the realist singer in 1930s French cinema. However, nondiegetic musical scores played an increasingly significant role in poetic realism as the transition era waned. In films such as Marcel Carné's *Le Quai des brumes* (1938) and *Le Jour se lève* (1939), the atmospheric scores by composer Maurice Jaubert (the subject of chapter 6) play a significant role in communicating the psychological state of the protagonist. And some directors opted for little to no music—in films like Jacques Feyder's *Pension Mimosas* (1935), for instance—instead relying on the other elements of the soundtrack to convey audiovisual realism. Renoir, on the other hand, continued to use diegetic music to point to the artifice of cinematic storytelling and to further his acerbic attack on the bourgeoisie, which would reach its apotheosis in his 1939 film *La Règle du jeu*. In this film, his interest in diegetic music manifested in a fascination with mechanical musical instruments, a preoccupation that began in his earlier sound films, and, as I argue in the next chapter, was a broader fixation of directors in early sound cinema in France.

As my analysis of a number of films from the early 1930s makes clear, for early poetic realist directors, realism was rarely conceived of as a pure aesthetic, and diegetic music helped contribute in substantial ways to a more stylized, poetic element to the soundtrack, through an ostensibly realist source. The debates about realism and fantasy discussed in this and the previous chapter continued into the mid-1930s. In chapter 6 we shall encounter one particularly well-known example of a film, released in 1934, whose blend of realism and stylization through its music (both diegetic and nondiegetic) prompted controversy. The role of music in synchronized sound film was far from fixed: debates about music's function in French cinema continued to rage on even in the mid-1930s.

CHAPTER 6

"The Music Has Something to Say"

The Musical Revisions of L'Atalante (1934)

Once nearly forgotten, *L'Atalante* is a legendary part of the cinematic mythos. The second collaboration between French director Jean Vigo and composer Maurice Jaubert, and Vigo's only feature-length film, it has become a staple in the cinephile canon, cementing Vigo's posthumous reputation as a prominent figure in 1930s French cinema. The film follows Jean, the captain of a barge called *L'Atalante*, and Juliette, a country girl who marries Jean and comes to live with him on the barge but is tempted by the excitement of the big city. Vigo's telling of this simple love story infuses the lives of these working-class characters with moments of lighthearted humor, blending gritty realism and dreamlike whimsy, and making *L'Atalante* an oft-cited early example of French poetic realism. Both Vigo's film and Jaubert's lyrical score went on to inspire a generation of postwar French filmmakers.

Yet few audiences in 1934 saw the director's original version. Before *L'Atalante* was released, its producers attempted to make it more accessible, replacing parts of Jaubert's score with the hit song "Le Chaland qui passe" (The Passing Barge) and renaming the film after the song. Their tactic failed, for the film did not gain commercial traction. Three weeks after *L'Atalante*'s premiere, Vigo died of tuberculosis, aged twenty-nine, believing his film to have been an utter failure.[1]

Following its initial rapid disappearance, from 1940 onward, a number of restoration projects began to rescue *L'Atalante* from obscurity, leading to its ultimate mythologizing by filmmakers and critics alike. By the 1950s and 1960s, Vigo was being hailed by the French New Wave as one of France's most innovative early directors.[2] Biographer Michael Temple has called him a "patron saint and martyr of French film culture,"[3] and since 1951 a yearly Prix

Jean Vigo has been given in his honor to a promising young French director. *L'Atalante* continues to be a favorite of filmmakers and critics, despite—or perhaps because of—the film's simplicity, rough edges, and unpretentious plot and characters, the story behind its disastrous beginnings making its later success all the more poignant. *L'Atalante* has also proven a fertile subject for scholarly interpretation, playing a prominent role in film studies discourse since the 1940s (though it is rarely mentioned in film music studies).[4] Yet scholars have overlooked an important narrative and musical subtext in the film—a reflexive fixation on the recent arrival of synchronized sound film in France, given voice through a sustained focus on musical playback technologies and their magical qualities.

In this chapter I argue that both versions of the film—Vigo's and the producers'—attempted in different ways to define the role of music in synchronized sound film. At a time when the economic, technological, and aesthetic disruptions in Hollywood caused by the transition to synchronized sound had mainly subsided, *L'Atalante* reflects the broader concerns about sound that persisted in the French film industry even in 1934.[5] Although Jaubert's music for Vigo's original version of *L'Atalante*—a combination of lyrical instrumental underscoring and folk-like diegetic song—is seemingly simple in its structure and harmonic language, it contributes substantially to narrative, mood, and character development, while helping to shape the film's blend of realism and fantasy. *L'Atalante* also reflects on musical machines and their ability to captivate, using recorded music to distinguish between different cinematic "modes": a realist mode with a social message and a dreamlike one with fantastical possibilities. Throughout the soundtrack Vigo and Jaubert comment reflexively on sound film as a new medium with unique capabilities, experimenting with the range of ways in which mediated music could prompt seemingly magical events. Their approach to film music in *L'Atalante* folds sound cinema into a broader historical lineage that encompasses the many rapid changes in music's technological mediation and circulation in the early twentieth century (including radio and phonography), many of which initially appeared equally magical.

The producers' version, which today survives in a single copy at the Cinémathèque Royale de Belgique in Brussels, tells a very different story about sound, one that has significant aesthetic and interpretive ramifications. It reveals how a seemingly straightforward musical decision—the addition of a popular song to the soundtrack—could transform the film's meaning and tone. While Vigo was fascinated with mediated music and its ability to create a magical cinematic world, the distributors pursued a different goal, namely to fit the film's music into a commercially successful paradigm. Yet these differing approaches to the soundtrack are more complex than a simple "art vs. commerce" binary. (Jaubert and Vigo, as we shall see, did not eschew popular music in their soundtrack and story.) Rather, the different versions of *L'Atalante* reflect broader concerns about how recorded sound would affect French cinema during sound film's early years.

VIGO, JAUBERT, AND SYNCHRONIZED SOUND

Jean Vigo began his brief career in the throes of the debate about synchronized sound in France, a debate that, as I have argued throughout this book, was driven by a deep ambivalence felt by many French filmmakers and critics. He was the son of a well-known anarchist, Miguel Almereyda, who when Vigo was twelve was arrested for treason and later found strangled in his prison cell.[6] Although Vigo's politics were never as radical as his father's, it is perhaps not surprising that each of his four films contains, to varying degrees, political undercurrents, articulating protests against unjust aspects of society. According to Siegfried Kracauer, Vigo "was a rebel, on two counts: against the screen formulas and, even more intensely, against the established order of things. He used the camera as a weapon, not as an anesthetic."[7] In his 1930 talk "Toward a Social Cinema," Vigo expressed his cinematic ideals by advocating social documentary, urging filmmakers to deal with "society and its relationships with individuals and things."[8]

Alongside his desire to make political films, Vigo experimented with narrative cinema's stylistic possibilities, believing that a poetic cinema could most effectively reveal social truths. He advocated a cinematic style that favored "reality"—that is, an emphasis on the concreteness of space and things, the specificity of realistic characters, and real-world exteriors, as a means of bringing his political statements into focus—combined with poetic, distinctly cinematic techniques.[9] This is apparent from his very first film, the twenty-minute nonnarrative silent film *À propos de Nice* (1930). A montage of footage shot in Nice in the style of the city symphonies of the 1920s, *À propos de Nice* has a social and political message—a critique of the idle rich and their pastimes set against the toiling of the working classes. It also contains surrealist visual jokes and moments of lighthearted humor, revealing the influence of avant-garde filmmakers such as Luis Buñuel on Vigo's aesthetic.[10] Vigo was not interested in pure documentary realism, even if he valued nonfiction film. He believed that a playful, poetic cinematic style was a means of pointing to social problems. This insistence on poetry shaped his approach to the soundtrack in his subsequent films.

Maurice Jaubert shared Vigo's commitment both to socially significant cinema and to film's poetic potential.[11] Jaubert, who would become one of France's preeminent film composers of the 1930s, was born in Nice in 1900 and began studying piano at the age of five.[12] He moved to Paris in 1916 to study law at the Sorbonne, but within a few years decided to leave his law career behind and fully devote himself to composing music. He was soon connected with French musical modernist circles, becoming friends with Honegger and Ravel (who was best man at his wedding) and writing favorably about Les Six in music reviews for *Le Petit Niçois* under the pseudonym Maurice Gineste.[13] As a reviewer he praised Auric and Poulenc in 1924 for "having opened a clear path toward a new kind of music."[14] Around this time, he began composing concert music and music for the theater, and in 1925 was hired by the Pleyel piano company to oversee the recording of piano rolls for the Pleyela, their player piano. He wrote a concert piece, *Le Magicien prodigieux* (1925), for Pleyela, voice, and drums, which was praised in a review by Honegger.[15] While Jaubert produced a number of concert works, he is mainly remembered today for his film scores. From 1931 to 1935 he was the music director of the production company Pathé-Cinéma, composing many scores and conducting countless others.[16] He would go on to write some of the most memorable poetic realist film scores—among them those for Marcel Carné's *Hôtel du Nord* (1938), *Le Quai des brumes* (1938), and *Le Jour se lève* (1939)—and continued composing for film until he was recalled for military duty in 1939. He was killed in combat in 1940.

Significantly, while Jaubert's harmonic and melodic musical language mostly remained traditional, he was unquestionably modernist when it came to his approach to technology.[17] Jaubert was interested in the increasing importance of music technology for the composition of both concert and film music. In addition to his embrace of mechanical musical instruments, as indicated by his position at Pleyel, he was intrigued by the compositional possibilities of the phonograph. He was one of the first to use the term *phonogénie*, describing the "happy and fortuitous meeting between the possibilities of the phonograph and the qualities of an orchestra and a voice," and suggesting that in the future "the phonograph will no longer be just a reproducer, but a creator."[18] He recognized the new musical potential of the sound film medium, and he took care to write film music that would not only sound good live but also record well.

Jaubert's fascination with recording technologies and film scoring went beyond mere attention to details of timbre. He experimented radically with the soundtrack in his first collaboration with Vigo, *Zéro de conduite* (1933). Depicting the rebellion of a group of schoolboys against repressive boarding school authorities, *Zéro de conduite* elicited polarized responses, provoking both applause and boos and hisses, and was promptly banned from distribution by the French Board of Censors on account of its political content.[19] Jaubert's most famous musical experiment occurs in the scene where the boys begin their revolt in the dormitory. Vigo shot the scene in slow motion, and to match the surrealist quality of the images Jaubert composed a theme, recorded the melody, reversed it, transcribed it so that the musicians could play it backward, recorded it again, and reversed it once again in postproduction. The resulting melody plays from beginning to end, but with an eerie fade-in of each note instead of a precise attack. This almost unprecedented manipulation of the soundtrack has been referred to as an early precursor to *musique concrète*.[20] The soundtrack draws attention to itself, and Jaubert made no attempt to hide the technological manipulation that went into the scene's music. Although in 1933 spectators might not have known exactly how the eerie and dreamlike musical effect was achieved, they would have been well aware that it could not have been recreated live. Jaubert's score for *Zéro de conduite* reveals a composer who was not only interested in the concept of *phonogénie* but also intrigued by the possibilities of recorded sound as a narrative and aesthetic "creator."[21]

Even so, Jaubert, like Vigo, claimed to favor cinematic realism, not wanting music's role in the soundtrack to detract from a film's narrative plausibility. In a lecture delivered in 1936 titled "Music on the Screen," he described what he saw as the ideal relationship between music and image in cinema, providing a valuable window into his own approach to film scoring.[22] Though the essay represents his thoughts as a more seasoned film composer (it was delivered two years after his work on *L'Atalante* and after the chaos of the transition period had mostly subsided), his comments are largely consistent with his own compositional approach in his earlier film scores. First, he rejected Hollywood film-scoring paradigms of the period (particularly those established by Max Steiner), suggesting that music "brings an *unreal* element which is bound to break the rules of objective realism."[23] Claiming that music should serve the images rather than govern them, he went on to suggest that music used indiscriminately could destroy the realism of cinema. He argued that the task of nondiegetic music is not to be expressive, but to be "decorative," adding a mood instead of calling attention to itself or making itself redundant to the information in the image.[24]

Still, he allowed for an important exception, a particular case where music's function is heightened. Music has the power, he suggests, to trigger a different cinematic mode:

> [J]ust as the novelist sometimes interrupts the telling of a story with an expression of his feelings, argumentative or lyrical, or with the subjective reactions of his characters, so does the director sometimes move away from the strict representation of reality in order to add to his work those touches of comment or of poetry which give a film its individual quality, descriptions, movements from one point to another in space or time, recalling of earlier scenes, dreams, imaging of the thoughts of some character, etc. *Here the music has something to say*: its presence will warn the spectator that the style of the film is changing temporarily for dramatic reasons. All its power of suggestion will serve to intensify and prolong that impression of strangeness, of departure from photographic truth, which the director is seeking [my italics].[25]

In other words, he embraced music's power to generate a dramatic shift—a different kind of cinematic mode that departs from realism. Precisely as in *Zéro de conduite*, where his foregrounded music prompted an alternative cinematic mode, music can, claimed Jaubert, announce the surrealist possibilities of cinema to the spectator, providing an "impression of strangeness," and helping to depart from the "photographic truth" of realism.

L'ATALANTE'S MUSICAL DEVICES

The music of *L'Atalante* does precisely this, prompting the film's frequent "touches . . . of poetry."[26] It is not just any music that brings about the shift away from realism, however. Musical *media*—radios, phonographs, player pianos, loudspeakers—signal change and act as borders between different cinematic worlds, reflexively pointing to the power of music technology to access new cinematic possibilities. These musical devices are closely linked to cinema: not only do they present a lineage of recorded music that sound film had recently become a part of, but many of the devices had also played a role in accompanying or providing synchronized sound for films in the not-so-distant past.[27] Vigo and Jaubert weave a rich variety of technologies of sound into the film's story, giving recorded music, and by extension the medium of synchronized sound film, a great deal of agency in shaping narrative possibilities.

L'Atalante follows the trials and tribulations of the newlyweds Jean (Jean Dasté) and his bride Juliette (Dita Parlo) as they adjust to life together on the barge, with the first mate Père Jules (Michel Simon) and the cabin boy (Louis Lefebvre). The story's focus on the real hardships of a working-class couple lent the film a political edge. But within a mostly realist portrayal of the couple's world the musical machines add whimsy and fantasy to the depiction of their story. In various ways throughout the film musical media differentiate Juliette, who craves the modernity of city life, from Jean, who is content with his premodern lifestyle on the barge and initially unsympathetic to his wife's yearnings. After a period of crisis and separation they reunite, now able to communicate and love as a mature couple. Musical machines play an important role in aiding their evolution as individuals and their subsequent joyous reunion. In this way, Vigo and Jaubert explored audiovisual expressions of wonder and amazement, by integrating a series of reflexive experiments with the soundtrack directly into the narrative.

Although *L'Atalante* was based on a preexisting scenario, the focus on music reproduction technology was not in the original synopsis by Jean Guinée, but was added by Vigo and his creative team.[28] Vigo adapted the script, keeping the basic premise but substantially changing the tone and many details. In Guinée's scenario, Juliette is tempted to run away to Paris when she meets a young sailor. Vigo changed this character to a traveling salesman (Gilles Margaritis), who sells the idea of Paris through a song while trying to sell his many wares. Guinée's Juliette runs away to Paris, but after spending her money on "innocent pleasures" leads a lonely life. The first mate, Jules, finds her in a small chapel, praying, and brings her back to the barge. Vigo substantially altered the character of Jules, turning him into Père Jules, a sailor with a colorful past and a fascination with musical machines, as portrayed by renowned Swiss film actor Michel Simon.[29] Père Jules ultimately finds Juliette not in a church but in a Pathé Song Palace, a store where customers pay to listen to popular songs through headphones. Vigo's changes preserved the simplicity of Guinée's original scenario but gave a depth to Juliette's coming-of-age story and a playful quality to the ordinary lives of ordinary people. They also added a previously absent element of the fantastical, which allowed for poetic magical sequences triggered by musical devices.

An abundance of musical playback media is not unique to L'Atalante. As we have seen, in the late 1920s and early 1930s filmmakers were constantly exploring the possibilities of sound film technology, thematizing it in highly self-conscious ways. For fear that audiences would not accept music that seemed to come from out of nowhere, a shot of someone turning on a phonograph gave filmmakers the excuse to play music during a scene, establishing explicitly diegetic musical sources through visual cues. This strategy of explicitly diegetizing a musical source was common in early Hollywood sound films, but became a particularly prominent feature of French sound film, especially in early poetic realist films, as we saw in the previous chapter.[30] Indeed, Charles O'Brien writes, "It is difficult to think of a French film of the [1930s] with a contemporary setting that doesn't include a moment when a character places a needle on a spinning phonograph."[31] Machines could also deceive or malfunction, and some filmmakers, perhaps most notably René Clair, called attention to this possibility.[32] For others, the very idea of synchronism was marvelous. Michel Chion calls this phenomenon the "New Rapture of Synchronization," writing, "Synchronism of sound and image in the brand new sound film was still something magical, an enchanted encounter between two entities."[33] Some films explored how mechanically reproduced sound could be employed with exuberance and even a brash experimentalism, sometimes folding these techniques into the plot in significant ways. Vigo and Jaubert's experiments thus reflect this approach. The analysis that follows examines Jaubert's score, then turns to each of the musical devices in L'Atalante—a radio, music boxes, spontaneous song, a player piano, a phonograph, and a song palace—to demonstrate the range of musical and sonic experiments in the film and their narrative multivalence.

Examples 6.1a–b: Themes of A and B sections of "Le Chant des mariniers," *L'Atalante* (1934)

Jaubert's music is never purely incidental.[34] While the music is harmonically simple, its impact, as Russell Lack points out, "lies in its structural daring."[35] The score has four themes that recur and one distinct melody that appears only once. The economy of musical themes gives each one a specific set of connotations, linking characters, actions, and events; but the different manners in which these themes appear add to the story's interpretive flexibility.

The most ubiquitous theme is the "Chant des mariniers," first heard during the opening credits.[36] The song's lyrics, written by Charles Goldblatt (who also wrote lyrics for *Zéro de conduite*), are peppered with popular language to describe the hard work that characterizes life on the barge, as well as the young women whom the bargemen convince to leave dry land and join them. The song has two main sections: an upbeat A section with a "tempo di marcia," featuring a staccato melody in the style of a workers' march, and a B section, with a more lyrical, sweeping, legato melody in a slow, lilting 6/8 (Examples 6.1a–b).

A section

Nous n'somm' pas sur les pénich' pour y flâner	We're not on the barges to laze around,
Faut travailler	We have to work,
Nous n'somm' pas sur les canaux pour s'balader	We're not on the canals to stroll,
Faut naviguer	We have to navigate,
Les fesses sur la barre	Our butts on the helm,
C'est nous les malabars	We're the muscle men.
Quand le sourire d'une belle	When the smile of a beautiful woman
Nous retient et nous appelle	Catches and calls to us,
Et si le temps nous dur'	And if time drags on for us,
Il faut bien qu'on endur'	We must still endure
Quand on a le cœur gai	When we have a happy heart
Le métier de marinier	The job of a bargeman.

B section

Les jeun' fill' se sont embarquées	The young girls came aboard
Sur les pénich' pour bien longtemps	On the barges for quite a spell.
Leurs joues commenc' à se hâter	Their cheeks begin to age
Et leurs yeux sont couleur du temps	And their eyes are the color of time.
Les mariniers les ont volées	The bargemen stole them
Sans aucun remords à la terre	From the land with no remorse.
Par les fleuv' les ont emportées	They took them on the rivers,
Leurs amours voguant vers les mers[37]	Their loves sailing toward the seas.

The "Chant des mariniers" is first heard during the opening credits and recurs throughout the film, appearing diegetically in various contexts. Two accordionists play it during Jean and Juliette's wedding procession; the inhabitants of the barge sing it to pass the time (sometimes accompanied and sometimes not); Père Jules plays it on the accordion when Juliette explores his room; it is heard as background music in the bar called the Quatre Nations; and in the film's climactic reunion scene it plays in the song palace where Jules finds Juliette. The B section theme and other related melodic fragments are also woven into the instrumental underscoring at various moments in the film. This theme, with its barcarolle rhythms and melodic repetition, is closely linked to water and the river, an important element in this story about the progress of a barge (and a relationship) along the Seine. Much of the music is heard through the musical devices that appear in the film, which serve in different ways to establish tension and heighten the contrast between Jean's and Juliette's desires, particularly in relation to the powerful effect that modern technology has on Juliette.

After listening to a radio program announcing news from Paris, Juliette becomes fascinated by modern technology and the big city, developing an obsession with Paris. Jean turns on the radio and an announcer's voice calls out, "*Allô, ici Paris!*" Jean is disillusioned with urban life, just as he is no longer impressed by the radio's ability to transmit faraway voices. Juliette, on the other hand, is captivated, both with the content of the announcer's message (ladies' fashion, shopping on the Boulevard Haussmann) and with the presence of the Parisian voice within their own small barge bedroom (Figure 6.1). The scene establishes the primary conflict between Jean and Juliette: Jean, beholden to tradition and the timelessness of work on the barge, finds modern technology unremarkable, and even seems to resent it, whereas Juliette, who yearns for the modernity of the city, has a childlike fascination with the radio's ability to render distant people and places closer. Through the radio, Paris and the modernity it proffers become both graspable and unattainable: so near and yet so far.

Music boxes and a *bon homme* musical conductor marionette serve as sources of wonder and bring together Juliette and Père Jules, the older, worldlier first mate. Jules, who is connected to many of the musical media in

Figure 6.1: *"Allô, ici Paris!," L'Atalante* (1934)

the film, himself acts as a kind of mediator between Jean and Juliette, helping them to reunite at the end of the film. He also serves as Juliette's link to the city through his stories and strange possessions, many of them musical. When Juliette explores Père Jules's room, her discovery of his musical machines adds to his mysterious allure and marks the beginning of their friendship.

Jules's cabin is filled to the brim with objects that he has collected in the course of his travels, revealing his colorful past. Together the pair wind up and play his many music boxes (Figure 6.2a). Jules shows her his *bon homme*, uncovering an almost life-sized, slightly grotesque torso of an orchestra conductor automaton.[38] He winds it up and operates it to Juliette's amazement (Figure 6.2b). Juliette's exploration of other mysterious objects in Jules's room prompts stories about where and how he acquired them. A few moments later Jean bursts into the room, angry with both his wife and his first mate, and breaks the spell that Jules's magical den had cast. Yelling at them, he begins to throw Jules's objects on the floor, each with a loud crash, expressing his anger verbally, physically, and sonically. This scene precipitates the married couple's conflict and adds an ambiguity to the relationship between Juliette and the older Père Jules. It also sets Jules apart, contrasting him with Jean's smaller, sober worldview. Jules gives Juliette a glimpse into a different life—less monotonous, more enchanting, and indeed more musical than the life of barges and docks. Music boxes initiate the interaction between the two characters, allowing them to build a connection that becomes important for the film's later resolution.

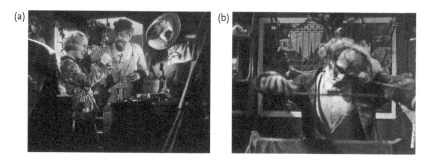

Figures 6.2a–b: Music Boxes and the *bon homme, L'Atalante* (1934)

L'Atalante also features a spontaneous "performed" song. While spontaneous song is not a musical machine like a radio or phonograph, it is nevertheless a musical "device" that engages with recorded music in a different
sense—a new narrative means of presenting music on film that became possible only with the arrival of synchronized sound. The peddler's performance
stands out from the grittier portrayal of barge life, setting the peddler apart
from the rest of the characters through his charm, whimsy, and what he
represents—life in the bustling, exciting, modern city.

According to accounts by Vigo's creative team, the inclusion of a song was
at least partly dictated by the distributors at the Gaumont film studios. A large
percentage of French films featured popular songs well into the 1930s—
Charles O'Brien suggests it may have been as many as half of France's national cinematic output[39]—and the producers presumably believed that the
insertion of a song would make the film more marketable. Singers were also
common characters in 1930s films, on account of the popularity of musical
comedy and operetta; and as Colin Crisp has pointed out, many French films
of the 1930s focused on a protagonist whose singing talent set him apart from
the other characters as the "natural object of romantic love."[40] The presence
of a singer character could also give narrative justification for the inclusion of
one or more diegetic songs.

Vigo's response to this request was the "Chanson du camelot" (The Peddler's
Song). Sung to Juliette and Jean at the Quatre Nations dance hall, the song
mocked the kind of performance that the producers had in mind. First of all,
it was sung by a minor character instead of a protagonist, and it had deliberately silly lyrics chock full of puns (written by Charles Goldblatt).[41] It would,
as Marina Warner points out, "have been so much more expected to have him
sing a love song,"[42] but instead he sings about his knick-knacks. As a song
about useless things the "Chanson du camelot" takes the mockery of cinematic singing even farther, perhaps poking fun at the very idea itself: the practice of song plugging, or selling a song, within a film.

At the same time, with the arrival of the song *L'Atalante* takes an almost
surrealist turn. The peddler begins to sing without any narrative justification,

conveying Juliette's wonder at and enchantment with the man and his stories of Paris. The peddler's fast-paced sweet talk is intended to help sell his wares, but it accomplishes more than that: it plants the seeds of Juliette's desire to explore outside the barge. The song, which flows out of his conversation with Jean and Juliette, is delivered directly to them, until the image cuts to a long shot in which the peddler and his objects occupy the entire dance floor.

Actor Gilles Margaritis was not a singer, and he in fact protested when he was told he would sing in the film.[43] His untrained voice results in a delivery that is situated somewhere between speech and song, turning the song into an extension of his fast-talking dialogue. The speech leading up to the song seems to carry a musical quality, while Jaubert's music heightens the speechlike effect of the vocal part, in which the peddler lists off the various items he has for sale in rapid, repetitive, rhythmic text. While this kind of spontaneous transition from speech into song later became a fixture of film musicals, it stands in sharp contrast to the rest of the singing in L'Atalante. Vigo subverts the narrative expectations established up to that point by creating a filmic world in which a peddler entices Juliette with descriptions of the wonders of the big city presented in a song. In the next scene he appears as a one-man band, equipped with bass drum on his back and trombone in hand, further demonstrating the ease with which his character expresses himself through music. Unlike the diegetic musical performances that the other characters participate in, the peddler's mode of musical delivery—a rendering of his thoughts into spontaneous song—links his character with the fantastical. Thanks to the new medium of sound film technology, a character can convey his enchanting stories musically, through song.[44]

In the same scene at the Quatre Nations dance hall a *piano mécanique* is prominently featured. It is humorously portrayed as quaint and antiquated, contrasting with the more modern music reproduction technologies in the film. While Jean and Juliette are walking to the dance hall, the "Chant des mariniers" plays at a brisk pace. A number of couples dance to the music, and the source of the music, a Limonaire mechanical café piano, can be seen in the background. Limonaire organs and pianos were commonly found in dance halls, providing what came to be known as a "characteristically 'Parisian' sound."[45] The Limonaire transforms the "Chant des mariniers"—which until this point had remained closely linked to barge life—into Parisian dance hall music. The free-floating presence of this mediated music serves to draw Jean and Juliette toward the Quatre Nations, and likewise Juliette toward Paris.

After the peddler has finished his song, a *java*—an instrumental dance in an upbeat 3/4 time—begins to play on the Limonaire. The peddler pulls Juliette onto the dance floor, and as they dance he begins to talk to her about Paris. In the middle of the piece the music abruptly stops. Someone urgently calls out that a coin must be fed into the piano's slot for the music to continue. The music begins where it left off, and the couples return to dancing.

The moment is brief and could easily pass unnoticed. Yet the urgency of the request for money suggests that if the music stops the peddler's spell over Juliette will be broken: it is the music itself that grants the peddler's words their import. It also emphasizes yet again the commercial contract that gives rise to song and music in film, through the literal exchange of money for music.[46] In fact, the java comes to represent Juliette's later disillusionment with alienating city life, as it next appears when she is walking around Paris, penniless, looking unsuccessfully for work.

The *piano mécanique* is a more antiquated form of musical reproduction technology than the phonograph and the radio. The Limonaire brothers stopped making pianos and organs in 1930, and player pianos, once a symbol of modernity in classical music (in works such as Antheil's *Ballet mécanique* and Stravinsky's *Étude pour pianola*), were by 1934 in decline. Jaubert himself was very familiar with pneumatic keyboards, having overseen the recording of piano rolls at Pleyel; but his interest in pianolas had by this time been supplanted by sound cinema. In a broad sense, amplified music reproduction, the technology that made sound film possible, precipitated the player piano's demise. The presence of the Limonaire, then, has multifold meanings. It comments on the poignantly outdated form of music played in the provincial bar, far from the modernity of Paris; it is an obsolete symbol of modernity that dupes Juliette into becoming enchanted with the city; it is a brand of mechanical music that is less sophisticated than the phonograph or sound film technology; but it also participates in the magic of the film's musical media, by connecting the protagonists to distant places and transforming a provincial musical idea into a more modern one.[47]

To an even greater extent than either the radio or mechanical musical instruments, a phonograph figures prominently in the plot's unfolding. Père Jules constantly references his broken phonograph; he follows his friend Rasputin to the shore to buy a new record; and he steals a phonograph horn from a bar in Paris when he is drunk. Jules is almost obsessed with the machine as an object, buying a record with no concern for its musical content. When Rasputin comes to sell him a record, announcing that he has a new disc for Jules, Jules's first question is *"Il est long?"* But the record he buys is not played until near the end, when the phonograph takes on magical powers.

Père Jules tries to distract Jean, who has become catatonic with grief over leaving Juliette behind in Paris, and says to the cabin boy that if only his phonograph worked it might help to cheer Jean up. He grabs the record he bought earlier from Rasputin and absentmindedly runs his finger across it. Miraculously, music seems to emanate from it: an accordion playing the B theme of the "Chant des mariniers." He lifts his finger and the music stops (Figure 6.3a). He tries it again, running his finger across the disc, and the music starts up again. He lifts his finger and it stops. In amazement, he tries it one more time, but this time when he lifts his finger the music continues. The

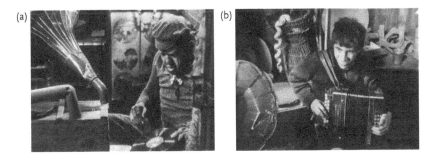

Figures 6.3a–b: Père Jules's Amazement and the Boy's Prank, *L'Atalante* (1934)

image then cuts to the boy, who is playing the accordion. He stops, laughing at his own joke made at the skipper's expense (Figure 6.3b). Père Jules responds defensively: "Go ahead and laugh, but I've seen more amazing things than playing a record with a finger" ("Tu peux te marrer, mais on avait vu des choses plus fortiches que faire marcher un disque avec un doigt").[48]

As Jules plays the record with his finger the inanimate music played by a musical machine and the organic music played live by a human being become one, and are made interchangeable. This reflexive moment lays bare the audiovisual artifice of sound cinema and its material heterogeneity. But more than just an audiovisual gag, Père Jules's finger becomes the needle, a visual manifestation of his own desire for his phonograph to work again and cheer Jean up. This kind of cinematic event became possible only with synchronized sound, but phonographs themselves were relatively recent phenomena, and sources of fascination and anxiety in their own right. As Carolyn Abbate has argued, French modernist works such as Ravel's *L'Enfant et les sortilèges* were, among other things, "meditations on mechanical reproduction," which posed the larger question of "how musical mechanism might shift our sense of voice, subjectivity, and their representations" in the early twentieth century.[49] Whereas Ravel's music contained traces of mechanical music, Jaubert's music literally becomes mechanical music, and it does so as a means of reflecting on sound cinema's possibilities.

Later in the scene, Jules finally fixes his broken phonograph. He oils it and repairs a misplaced spring, and suddenly it works. He winds it up and a waltz by Jaubert emanates from the machine. The music continues as a surrealist underwater sequence begins. Earlier Juliette had told Jean that if you open your eyes under water you will see the person you love, so Jean dives off the side of the boat (Figure 6.4a). In this sequence, as Jean swims around, an apparition—Juliette dressed in a flowing white dress—suddenly appears (Figure 6.4b).

The music that issues from the phonograph becomes the accompaniment to Jean's dreamlike underwater sequence. Jean climbs out of the water, and we then see the phonograph again, where a handful of cats, fascinated, have

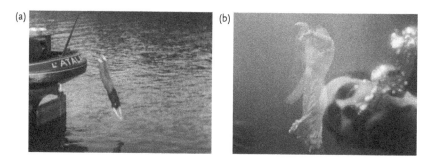

(a)   (b)

Figures 6.4a–b: Jean Dives Overboard and Surrealist Underwater Sequence, *L'Atalante* (1934)

gathered around to listen. One even sits in the phonograph horn (Figure 6.5).[50] Next, Père Jules and the boy carry the phonograph, while it continues to play, across the roof of the barge, with the horn pointing to the shore, a literal depiction of the phonograph's ability to disseminate music across great distances. They sit down with Jean, and, as if to prove to him that it works, lift the needle and begin to play the record again.

The transition between reality and fantasy is thus precipitated by recorded music. The miracle of the phonograph rouses Jean from his catatonia and inspires him to want to find Juliette again. Jean and Juliette's love overcomes the distance between them and their inability to find one another—much as the phonograph, as a playback medium, overcomes the spatial and temporal displacement of the acts of performance and listening. The phonograph scene is followed by a cross-cutting between Jean and Juliette, each restless in bed, separated spatially but connected in their thoughts, as they think sensuously of one another. The music in this scene, a swelling of the lyrical theme that has underscored an earlier scene combined with the B theme of the "Chant des mariniers," does not directly emanate from the phonograph; yet, extending from the previous scene into this one, the phonograph nevertheless continues to act as an uncanny communicator. Jean and Juliette, though spatially distant, are connected through their thoughts and through the music. Jaubert's interest in *phonogénie* resurfaces as a narrative trope, and the phonograph becomes not just a reproducer but a creator.

But perhaps the most profound moment of musical media magic in *L'Atalante* comes at the end of the film. Père Jules decides to search for Juliette. He almost tracks her down at the Hôtel l'Ancre, where she is living, but she is not at home. Juliette, now nearly penniless, wanders into a Pathé Song Palace, a shop where people pay to listen to records through headphones—an early version of a jukebox. The setting evokes a sense of both modernity and isolation.[51] Customers must listen individually through headphones, and the soundscape of the scene is remarkably quiet, with only a few barely audible conversations. Juliette cautiously approaches one of the booths advertising the "Chant des mariniers" in large letters. She turns the dial to the song, puts

Figure 6.5: The Cats and the Phonograph, *L'Atalante* (1934)

a coin in the machine, and holds the headphones up to her ears. Here, the song appears in an unexpected context, allowing Jules to find Juliette and reunite the married couple. Suddenly, there is what Kelley Conway has called a "magical intervention" on the part of Père Jules and a popular record.[52] Juliette hears the song that has come to represent her life with Jean on the barge—the "Chant des mariniers," sung unaccompanied by herself and her husband. The scene cuts to the outside of the song palace, where a loudspeaker projects the music Juliette hears. Père Jules, still searching for her, happens to walk by and hear the music, and enters the store. When she sees Jules, Juliette drops the headphones, but the song continues on the soundtrack as Jules throws her over his shoulder and carries her out of the store, to the protests of the other customers (Figures 6.6a–d).

This scene plays out several impossibilities. First of all, the folksong originating in the local world of the provincial barge is somehow suddenly available for listening to at a Parisian song palace. Second, the song that Juliette hears through headphones, intended for her personal consumption, is broadcast through the loudspeakers for Jules to hear as well. Third, Juliette's experience transforms from an isolated modality of listening to a communal one. The loudspeaker acquires its own agency and subjectivity, is literally given a voice, as it seems to be directing the sound specifically toward Jules. Finally, the version of the song that comes through Juliette's headphones is

Figures 6.6a–d: The Pathé Song Palace, *L'Atalante* (1934)

an unaccompanied performance, sung by herself and her husband, musically recalling an earlier intimate moment when the two had sung together on the barge.[53] In the unrealistic sonic environment of the scene, the personal rendition of the song turns the commercial expectations of the song palace setting on its head. The Pathé Song Palace, a business devoted entirely to listening to recorded popular music, takes on the most fantastical powers of any mode of musical production in the film, allowing for the impossible discovery of Juliette that ultimately reunites the married couple (with Jules again acting as the mediator). Jaubert, who was music director for Pathé-Cinéma, might have had a hand in the choice of location for this final climactic scene;[54] but the scene even so proposes a cinematic narrative world where mechanically mediated music can acquire the agency to respond to a character's yearnings. Juliette's desire to reunite with her husband is so strong that it changes the laws of space and time, as manifested in a sound design whose reach goes well beyond cinematic realism.

Jean and Juliette's conflicts, their process of self-discovery, and their happy reunion are made possible only through these various musical media—the radio, music boxes, player piano, phonograph, and song palace loudspeaker. While each musical device is employed in the film's narrative to different effect, taken as a whole they suggest a particular approach to music's role in sound cinema. Music need not be diegetically justified. It can connect distant people and places, even if unrealistically, or at times deceptively. It can distinguish characters and elucidate their desires. It can even trigger impossible events, by emphasizing, in Jaubert's words, an "impression of strangeness, of departure from photographic truth." In the hands of Vigo and Jaubert, *phonogénie* is integral to the sounds of the film, to its narrative, and to its very form and content.

LE CHALAND QUI PASSE

Before the film was released its soundtrack underwent changes. *L'Atalante*'s brutal shooting schedule on location during the cold winter months precipitated Vigo's illness, and he became bedridden almost immediately after the crew finished shooting. Cinematographer Boris Kaufman and editor Louis Chavance finished editing the film, in frequent consultation with Vigo.[55] But according to Vigo biographer P. E. Salles Gomes, at a company preview for representatives from Gaumont, Parisian cinema owners, and provincial distributors on April 25, 1934, at the Palais Rochechouart, the reaction was cold: the industry representatives found it too long, narratively incoherent, and unmarketable in its existing form.[56] A few critics wrote positively about *L'Atalante* after the company showing, but their praise did not generate enough attention to satisfy the producers at Gaumont, and the company demanded significant changes in order to increase the film's commercial appeal.[57] Vigo was too weak to protest.

Taking the project out of Vigo's hands, the Gaumont producers added a popular song that seemed thematically related to the film, "Le Chaland qui passe," composed in 1932 by Cesare Andrea Bixio under the title "Parlami d'amore, Mariù" and used in an Italian film in that same year.[58] The song was published in France with French lyrics by André de Badet also in 1932, and was popularized by the well-known chanteuse Lys Gauty in a recording of 1933.[59] Hoping the song's success would rub off on the film, Gaumont inserted it in several places, replacing Jaubert's score, and renamed the film after the song. Preexisting popular songs were commonly featured in French films in the early 1930s, often, according to Charles O'Brien, "grafted on to a film's soundtrack in the late stage of post-production" and "reflecting strictly commercial rather than artistic motives."[60] But the changes to *L'Atalante* were unusually extreme. Press releases for the September opening of the film in its refurbished version highlighted the presence of Bixio's song. A *Notice d'exploitation*, sent to distributors by Gaumont, suggested that local presses publicize the film with a sample blurb: "Thanks to the famous song by C. A. Bixio, so admirably sung by Lys Gauty, *Le Chaland qui passe* . . . will surely not pass unnoticed! Its picturesque motifs can already be heard in the streets. We will not be surprised if as a film *Le Chaland qui passe* attains the same considerable success."[61]

The producers' attempts to save the film were not successful, critically or financially; and unlike its eponymous song, *Le Chaland qui passe* passed relatively unnoticed.[62] In addition to Gaumont's changes, the film fell victim to substantial cuts by distributors after its release. Despite a few favorable reviews it was a commercial failure, and after a run at the Colisée in Paris lasting only a couple of weeks it disappeared into obscurity.[63] On October 5, three weeks after the film's premiere, Vigo died. According to one account, in a morbidly ironic twist of fate a street musician was playing "Le Chaland qui passe" outside Vigo's apartment as he lay dying.[64]

Scholars frequently refer to *Le Chaland qui passe* as a "mutilated" or "maimed" version of *L'Atalante*. While it is impossible to know exactly which version the public saw in 1934, since cuts were notoriously widespread and varied from one distributor to another, the eighty-five-minute *Le Chaland qui passe*, located today at the Cinémathèque Royale de Belgique, preserves Gaumont's musical changes. Gaumont left most of the visuals and continuity intact. And although the producers' musical changes are haphazard in many places, they also show clear attempts to avoid disrupting Jaubert's compositional aesthetic, even while adding the new song. Ultimately, however, these seemingly superficial alterations, swapping one melody for another, transformed the film, resulting in a soundtrack that functions quite differently.

Le Chaland qui passe differs musically from Vigo's *L'Atalante* in several respects (see Table 6.1). The producers' version replaced the "Chant des mariniers" with "Le Chaland qui passe" five times, and the song replaced other themes by Jaubert twice. "Le Chaland" was also added in two previously silent moments, and one diegetic occurrence of the "Chant des mariniers" was also removed and replaced with direct sound. Finally, Gaumont replaced the "Chanson du camelot" with a take of a different stanza of the song, which Vigo had filmed but later discarded.

The new title song, in its French-language version, is a waltz about the love of two people on a barge who leave their cares on the shore, as revealed in the lyrics of the first stanza and refrain:

Stanza 1

La nuit s'est faite, la berge	Night has come, the bank
S'estompe et se perd,	Fades and loses itself,
Un bal-musette, une auberge,	A *bal-musette*, an inn,
Ouvre leurs yeux pers;	Open their blue-green eyes;
Le chaland glisse sans trêve	The barge glides without rest
Sur l'eau de satin.	On satin water.
Où s'en va-t-il? Vers quel rêve?	Where is it going? Toward which dream?
Vers quel incertain	Toward which uncertain
Du destin? . . .	Destiny? . . .

Refrain

Ne pensons à rien, le courant	Let's not think of anything, the current
Fait de nous toujours des errants;	Makes us forever wanderers;
Sur mon chaland, sautant d'un quai,	On my barge, jumping from a quay,
L'amour peut-être s'est embarqué,	Love has perhaps embarked,
Aimons-nous ce soir sans songer	Let's love each other tonight without thinking
À ce que demain peut changer:	About what could change tomorrow:
Au fil de l'eau point de serments:	No vows as we sail:
Ce n'est que sur terre qu'on ment![65]	Lies are only uttered on land!

The song's stanza is in a fairly fast, minor 3/4, which transitions into a more relaxed refrain in the parallel major key (Example 6.2). The carefree nature of the barge described by the music and lyrics, considered "schmaltzy" by Vigo scholars,[66] contrasts with the "Chant des mariniers," whose harmonic simplicity, marchlike tempo, and lack of rubato convey lyrical meaning without dramatic excess, recounting the hard work entailed in life on the barge. By replacing the "Chant des mariniers" with "Le Chaland," the social comment on the characters' working-class status is weakened. More subtly, whether intentionally or not, the altered soundtrack affects the music's aesthetic relationship to the images and the music's diegetic sources.

Some of the producers' changes to the audiovisual aesthetic of the film were relatively small and superficial. For instance, throughout *L'Atalante*,

Example 6.2: Refrain of "Le Chaland qui passe," by Cesare Andrea Bixio and André de Badet (Paris: Bourcier, 1932)

Table 6.1 MUSICAL DIFFERENCES BETWEEN *L'ATALANTE* AND *LE CHALAND QUI PASSE*

Scene Description	Timing of musical segments (based on Criterion DVD)	Music in *L'Atalante*	Music in *Le Chaland qui passe*
Opening credits	0:56–2:16	"Chant des mariniers" (orch. and chorus)	"Le Chaland qui passe" (orch.)
Wedding procession	3:04–4:29	"Chant des mariniers" (diegetic; accordions)	No change
Wedding procession (cont.)	4:29–5:28	Lyrical theme (orch.)	No change
Père Jules and boy wait at barge	6:09–6:20	"Chant des mariniers" (diegetic; accordion)	No change
The barge leaves	9:07–11:07	Lyrical theme, later in counterpoint with "Chant des mariniers" B theme (orch.)	"Le Chaland qui passe" (orch.)
The next morning on the barge	11:18–12:39	"Chant des mariniers" (diegetic; accordion and voice; sung by Jean, the boy, and Jules, then by Jean and Juliette)	No change
Jules and boy leave with Rasputin	16:03–16:12	"Chant des mariniers" (diegetic; a cappella)	Music removed, direct sound (ambient) added
Radio scene	20:56–21:00	Brief instrumental music	No change
Arrival in Paris	30:25–31:43	Paris Waltz (orch.)	No change
Père Jules's room	31:57–33:27	Music box music (diegetic)	Music box music (diegetic)
	36:39–36:49	"Chant des mariniers" B theme (diegetic; accordion)	"Le Chaland qui passe" (diegetic; accordion)
Père Jules drinking in Paris; his drunken return	43:38–43:48	Brief diegetic music in bar	No change
	44:05–46:41	"Paris" (by R. Mercier and Millandez) (diegetic; a cappella, sung by Père Jules)	
Quatre Nations dance hall	48:15–49:21	"Chant des Mariniers" (diegetic; player piano)	"Chant des Mariniers" (diegetic; player piano)
	51:04–52:21	"Chanson du camelot" (orch. and voice, intimate verse sung to Jean and Juliette)	"Chanson du camelot" (guitar, orch., and voice; "performed" verse)
	52:22–55:36	"Java" (diegetic; player piano)	"Java" (diegetic; player piano)

Peddler's apology	56:26–56:57	"Chanson du camelot," brief percussion and trombone (diegetic; played by peddler)	No change
Peddler leaves; Jean paces	[58:03–58:33]	No music	"Le Chaland qui passe" interlude (orch.)
Jean discovers Juliette missing	[1:00:16–1:00:33]	No music	"Le Chaland qui passe" interlude (orch.)
Juliette in Paris	1:01:46–1:04:08	"Chanson du camelot" (jazzy variation) (orch.)	No change
Juliette looking for work	1:05:31–1:06:50	"Java" (variation) (accordion)	"Le Chaland qui passe" (accordion)
Jean depressed; Père Jules fixes phonograph	1:09:22–1:09:47	"Chant des mariniers" (B theme) (diegetic; accordion)	"Le Chaland qui passe" (diegetic; accordion)
	1:10:45–1:14:32	Waltz ("Chant des mariniers B theme variation incorporated) (diegetic [phonograph]; orch.)	Waltz ("Chant des mariniers" B theme variation incorporated) (diegetic [phonograph]; orch.)
Juliette and Jean think of each other	1:14:32–1:16:05	Lyrical theme (variation) combined with "Chant des mariniers" B theme (orch.)	No change
Père Jules searches for Juliette	1:21:55–1:23:34	Lyrical theme (variation) (orch.)	No change
Pathé Song Palace	1:24:32–1:25:12	"Chant des mariniers" (diegetic [loudspeaker]; a cappella)	"Le Chaland qui passe" (diegetic [loudspeaker]; accordion)
Embrace; aerial shot of the river; end credits	1:26:53–1:27:40	"Chant des mariniers" B theme (orch. and wordless female voice)	"Le Chaland qui passe" (orch. and voice, sung by Line Marlys)

Jaubert's instrumental music mainly served to comment on the action or characters through melodies that had earlier been introduced diegetically. But in *Le Chaland*, in places where nondiegetic music was added, the music serves as an interlude or transition between scenes. This subtle change was perhaps a result of the need to retroactively fit the music into a predetermined image track, but it introduced a musical practice into the film that Jaubert himself deplored: he was dismissive of musical interludes, claiming that using music to fill the "gaps" in the sound in a scene was an "elementary conception" of the soundtrack.[67] Additionally, minor differences between the two versions hint at a different approach to sound editing. One example is the audiovisual joke of Père Jules's playing the record with his finger. In *L'Atalante*, when the music stops and restarts the sonic effect is as if someone had hit and then released a pause button: the melody stops every time Père Jules lifts his finger, beginning where it left off the moment he places his finger back down. In *Le Chaland qui passe*, it rather sounds as if someone is lowering and raising the volume: after a silence, the melody begins again where it would have done had the music continued. It is not clear why this change was made—perhaps as a more expedient method of dubbing the soundtrack—but it creates a stop-and-start timing that sounds impossible for an amateur musician to produce live.[68] The joke is still present, and the obvious splicing brings the materiality of sound film to the forefront, but Jules's moment of confusion between man and machine becomes less plausible, erasing the magical effect of the exchange. These somewhat minor musical changes reveal traces of differing approaches to the soundtrack.

Others of Gaumont's changes, however, had a much more profound narrative effect. For one thing, *Le Chaland qui passe* essentially has two theme songs—the eponymous song, and the "Chant des mariniers," which was still present in *Le Chaland*'s soundtrack in several places. The existence of two theme songs most drastically affects the final scene at the Pathé Song Palace. In Vigo's version the couple are miraculously brought together again through the emanation of their own voices from the song palace's speakers, reunited by a song that is quite possibly in Juliette's imagination. In *Le Chaland qui passe* the music coming through the loudspeaker is instead an instrumental accordion arrangement of the new title song. Although "Le Chaland qui passe" is omnipresent throughout this version of the film, Jean and Juliette never sing or play it for each other, and it therefore carries no personal meaning for them, nor does it lead to their reunion through a psychic musical connection. Juliette's character—her naive, childlike fascination with musical machines and her strong linking of music with place—is altered by the musical changes. In some ways this version of the scene aligns much more closely with audio-visual conventions and expectations. The manner in which the music appears in this version is perhaps more literally believable. Why would Juliette not pay to listen to a popular song in a song palace? And why would that song not be emanating from the loudspeakers, perhaps as a means of attracting new customers? But by removing the ambiguity of diegetic sources, this version never fully explains why Juliette would be so strongly taken by the song, or why it would suddenly have the kind of emotive power over her and Jules that the "Chant des mariniers" has in Vigo's version.

But that is likely not what the producers were trying to do. Their version proposes a different kind of role for music in sound film. It creates a fluidity between what the spectator hears throughout the film and what the characters hear, at this point folding what had mostly been background underscoring directly into the diegesis. There is a self-conscious acknowledgment of cross-marketing, the intermediality between songs and films that was common during the transition to sound, highlighting the manner in which the film and music industries were intertwined.[69] The song palace is in many ways a perfect setting to make this point. But it does not trigger a surrealist musical cinematic moment as Vigo's version does.

Anxiety over the diegetic source of music may also have been the reason for one of the other major musical changes in *Le Chaland qui passe*, the substituting of a different stanza of the "Chanson du camelot." Vigo had opted to use the second stanza, addressed intimately to Jean and Juliette, unrealistic in its delivery but representative of Juliette's overactive imagination, which is ignited by the peddler's description of Paris. In *Le Chaland qui passe*, for reasons unknown, the producers replaced it with the first stanza, which Vigo had filmed but rejected. This discarded and reinstated stanza begins with a shot from above, showing the peddler preparing for his performance. He sings facing the camera (although not directly to it), and strums a guitar before beginning his song. The lyrics begin in a presentational manner, with "C'est moi, le cam'lot de Paris." Performing to a crowd of spectators in the dance hall, he begins the song by playing his guitar, but then it flies out of his hands and the nondiegetic orchestra takes over (Figures 6.7a–b).

This version self-consciously establishes a diegetic source for the accompaniment through the presence of the guitar, even if it is quickly removed. The song is clearly performed to the crowd, making the act of singing more deliberate, despite its cheeky irreverence. In this version the song functions in a manner more typical of the way songs were often introduced in films of the early 1930s, existing in the filmic world in a manner that is perhaps easier to explain. If justified by narrative framing, even tenuously, in a space that is at least reminiscent of a stage, a song was thought to be more believable within a "naturalistic" filmic world.[70] Both versions of the scene attempt to present an unrealistic song within a "realist" context, but with very different aesthetic solutions, Vigo opting for an intimate exchange that almost mimics conversation, while the producers chose a more overt performance.

While the alterations made by Gaumont were in part additive, intended to make the film more marketable, they also in a sense *removed* certain elements.

(a)   (b)

Figures 6.7a–b: "La Chanson du camelot" (first stanza), stills from *Le Chaland qui passe*, from the documentary *Les Voyages de l'Atalante* (dir. Bernard Eisenschitz), *The Complete Jean Vigo* (Criterion Collection), DVD

They affected the freedom with which the music created and enhanced meaning, and they redefined the fluidity of the boundaries between "realistic" and "unrealistic" music. More broadly, they changed the surrealist sound film aesthetic proposed by the original version. The insertion of the title song was intended to bring narrative unity into the film where producers felt it was not strong enough to begin with. But its power was perhaps greater than they realized, in that it not only added to the film but also altered the existing narrative.

CONCLUSION

In some ways, it is no surprise that *Le Chaland qui passe* was a commercial failure. Audience members who were expecting the popular song would have been disappointed, as the star used to market the film, Lys Gauty, did not appear on screen or even on the soundtrack. Yet one might still wonder why the producers' tactic did not work better than it did, considering that the practice of adding a popular song generally met with great success in movies at the time. While it is impossible to know what prompted Gaumont to make the changes, it might very well be that Vigo and Jaubert's approach to the soundtrack—its multivalence, interpretive flexibility, and the magical powers of music in the film's cinematic world—was precisely what led Gaumont's producers to believe that the film could survive the musical alterations.

The story of the film's revisions is also difficult to extricate from the story of Vigo's untimely death. Within a few years of *L'Atalante*'s initial failure both Vigo and his final film had become mythologized, and the mistreatment of *L'Atalante* came to signal a creative genius who had been fundamentally misunderstood during his lifetime. Soon after Vigo's death, attempts were made to rescue *L'Atalante* from obscurity through a number of restoration projects, its first major rerelease in France taking place in 1940.[71] Thanks in part to the advocacy of Cinémathèque Française founder Henri Langlois and Vigo biographer Salles Gomes, a generation of postwar French filmmakers "rediscovered" Vigo and his films. The newfound appreciation of *L'Atalante* went hand in hand with the rise of the New Wave. Agnès Varda's *La Pointe courte*, sometimes referred to as the film that jump-started the New Wave, was premiered in Paris in 1956 alongside Vigo's *À propos de Nice*.[72] Vigo was later lionized by the New Wave, in particular by Jean-Luc Godard and François Truffaut, both of whom acknowledged his influence on their work. Truffaut called *L'Atalante* a "masterpiece," suggesting that in filming "prosaic words and acts" Vigo had "effortlessly achieved poetry" by reconciling realism and aestheticism.[73] Truffaut even suggested that the true descendant of *L'Atalante* was Godard's trailblazing New Wave film *À bout de souffle* (1960).[74] Both Godard and Truffaut, at different points in their careers, also incorporated Jaubert's music into their films, as a musical homage to the director they revered.[75]

But the Vigo myth may actually serve to obscure our understanding of the film. It has been easy to approach the producers' changes with a sense of outrage, believing that they destroyed the artistic essence of Vigo's film. And it is not difficult to understand why. At the same time, as my analysis of the two versions reveals, it is valuable to consider the *different* aesthetics attempted by the two versions, the manner in which these differences embodied broader debates about sound film in France in the early 1930s, and the resonances of these differing approaches in later cinematic practices. The connections between Vigo and Jaubert's formal experimentation with the soundtrack and that of the French New Wave directors are clear. Additionally, Vigo's version of *L'Atalante* suggested a magical role for the soundtrack—a role where the cinema allows music to connect and bring together otherwise distant people, places, and ideas in a manner that may not be fully explicated in the narrative. In many respects this kind of approach later became a mainstay of the film musical genre, though with very different aesthetic ramifications. But it did not sit easily with the expectations of the producers at Gaumont. They made musical realism a greater priority, and this ultimately came to dominate the approach to the soundtrack of much classical cinema in both France and Hollywood.

Additionally, the two versions of the film seem to anticipate two major models of film music in the later twentieth century—the pop compilation soundtrack and the director-composer collaboration. Though their method of execution might not have been ideal, the producers presented an aesthetic that allowed a preexisting popular song to shape a film's meaning and narrative through the song's external connotations.[76] Vigo and Jaubert prefigure the approach of many close director–composer collaborations that we have come to associate with the auteur model of filmmaking, such as Alfred Hitchcock and Bernard Herrmann, Truffaut and Georges Delerue, Steven Spielberg and John Williams, and Christopher Nolan and Hans Zimmer. Both the pop soundtrack model and the director–composer collaboration model allow for music to shape meaning in a film substantially, but they do so in different ways and at different stages in the production process.

Consideration of the different aesthetics of the two versions of *L'Atalante* from this perspective reveals much about the core debates in French cinema during the transition to synchronized sound in the 1930s, and the manner in which these debates have continued to resonate throughout much of film music's history. Additionally, *L'Atalante* provides a window into the central role of music in film practitioners' attempts to grapple with technological changes. The upheaval caused by crucial technological junctures such as the transition to sound offers an opportunity for artists to renegotiate the possibilities of artistic forms: the anxiety surrounding the uncertainty of sound resulted in many fascinating and experimental approaches to the soundtrack. And this film's troubled history serves as a reminder that throughout these debates the music did, indeed, have something to say.

Conclusion

Alternative Paths for Sound Film

The films covered in this book reveal the range of diverse responses to the arrival of synchronized sound film in France. Among these varied examples, music offered many possibilities for filmmakers in the negotiation of audiovisual aesthetics. It could be a narrative tool, establishing setting and providing important information or context. It could take over the soundtrack, replacing dialogue or natural sounds, or it could coexist on the soundtrack alongside dialogue and sound effects. Music could inject lighthearted humor, magic, or fantasy into film, or become important as an abstract, "poetic" presence contrasting with the realism of spoken dialogue. It could also be used to confront the boundaries between liveness and mediation, as a tool for commentary on the technology of recorded sound itself. The filmmakers discussed in each chapter represent a range of perspectives on, and approaches to, music in sound cinema, as filmmakers overtly explored various possibilities for music in synchronized sound film. From the filmmakers, composers, and critics conceptualizing sound film before its arrival in France, to Cocteau and Buñuel's incorporation of music in surrealist sound cinema, to the internationally produced French-language *opérettes filmées*, to the theater-cinema debate between Clair and Pagnol, the multivalent use of diegetic music in the early poetic realist films of Renoir and others, and the conflicting approaches to the soundtrack in the two versions of *L'Atalante*, music played a significant role in the negotiation of sound film's ontology and aesthetics.

Examining the multifaceted interaction between music and cinema during this important technological juncture not only nuances our understanding of 1930s French musical and artistic culture more broadly but also provides a new perspective on the development of later audiovisual practices in France. Music was a crucial tool in establishing a French national cinematic style in the era of sound, in ways that would continue to resonate for decades. As the last two chapters described, the soundtrack of French poetic realist cinema, the style of filmmaking that emerged with the rise of the Popular Front in the mid-1930s, had its roots in transition-era audiovisual experiments. Additionally, an examination of music in transition-era French cinema allows us to reconsider postwar French cinematic innovations, particularly those of the New Wave, as outgrowths and developments out of these earlier audio-visual experiments. The radical approaches undertaken by New Wave directors like Jean-Luc Godard and François Truffaut occurred much in the same spirit as those of the early sound era. Just like the directors experimenting with sound in the early 1930s, New Wave filmmakers wrote prolifically, acting as theorists, critics, and directors. They challenged dominant practices in the French film industry and proposed new ways of constructing an audiovisual cinematic experience, often with brazen reflexivity. Direct sound took on a heightened importance, and music was used in this context for a range of effects. Instead of being a radical break, we can see a real affinity between the experiments emerging from the 1950s and 1960s New Wave directors and those of the early 1930s.

Examining film music in France during the transition era also uncovers the sounds of French music during a liminal period of French musical history. Just as the film industry was in transition, so too was French composition: the political, social, and stylistic priorities of French music shifted significantly between the heyday of the musical avant-garde in the 1910s and 1920s and the dominant Popular Front aesthetics of the mid-1930s. Many of the changes came about because of global political and economic factors, including the Depression and the buildup to World War II. Our periodization of French musical history tends to leave out the early 1930s, precisely because it was a moment in French music history that was pulled in both of these directions. *French Musical Culture and the Coming of Sound Cinema* has helped bridge this gap, showing how cinema became a site for the negotiation and contestation of varying musical styles. An examination of the film scores of the transition era can thus provide a window into changing musical practices and debates in French music of the late 1920s and early 1930s more broadly.

These films contain an impressive range of musical genres and styles: classical works from the canon, French modernist composition, *chansons*, music-hall, French popular dance styles, operetta, and opera. Each style carried a different set of cultural and aesthetic connotations, informing the sound-track, its relationship to the image, and its relationship to other art forms, in different ways. For some filmmakers it mattered a great deal what the music sounded like. The changes made to turn *L'Atalante* into *Le Chaland qui passe* were intensified by the differences in musical style between the two theme songs. In other cases, the director was more interested in what music could do, how it interacted with the image and the narrative, than what exactly it sounded like. Clair's films are perhaps the clearest example of this, but so are Renoir's to some extent. Directors and producers collaborated with composers who had varying degrees of commitment to sound film as an outlet for new composition, and directors themselves played important roles in shaping the sounds of their films. The coexistence of such a variety of musical styles within early sound cinema reveals music's integral role for filmmakers who each, in different ways, attempted to define sound film's possibilities and potential.

Although composers with diverse backgrounds and styles were involved in cinema during the transition period, by the mid-1930s perceptions of French film composition had shifted. Although a number of modernist composers had become involved in composing for films in the silent era and first years of sound (including Honegger and Milhaud), by the end of the transition era, demands of the industry led a handful of composers to "transition" to film composition more fully. Composers like Georges Auric, Georges Van Parys, and Maurice Jaubert, though involved in varying degrees with film music during the transition era and before, became known almost exclusively (at least for some time) as film composers. Reception history has not looked kindly on this shift, which has been perceived as a move from "art" to "commercial" music. I hope my analysis has complicated the dichotomy between art/commercial music, revealing the blurriness of the boundary between the two, and the manners in which mainstream films, their scores, and their composers could be experimental, while films that were more formally adventurous in their audiovisual construction often engaged with very popular, "commercial" musical styles.

French Musical Culture and the Coming of Sound Cinema has proposed a nonteleological history of sound cinema. The range of possibilities within these examples reinforces the uncertainty of the aesthetic outcome of synchronized sound. Of course, there have been many other important technological developments and periods of aesthetic uncertainty in cinema before and after the early sound era—filters and zoom, color, widescreen, surround sound, and 3D, to name several—but none of these developments so fundamentally altered filmmaking aesthetics and practices as did the addition of the recorded soundtrack. The experimentation in the first few years following the technology's widespread introduction presented myriad possibilities for the new form. Because of the medium's uncertainty, the films of this period present a multiplicity of paths for sound film. Each film became its own aesthetic statement, its own articulation or definition of what sound film could (or should) be. By examining the first years of synchronized sound in this light, we can see multiple simultaneous paths for sound film that began to develop, even if ultimately only a few of these paths continued beyond the transition years.

But many of the creative and inventive ideas that these innovators proposed for the interaction of music and image did not become common practice. As such, despite the acclaim that many of these films received and continue to receive by scholars and film buffs alike, they always remain, to a certain extent, marginal in the history of film sound. They are considered "transitional" films, worthy of appreciation but ultimately anomalous. Calling these films transitional reinforces a historical trajectory that narrows our thinking about how music is "supposed" to function within film. But the evidence of the period tells a different story. Filmmaking practices and the resulting sound-image relationships *might* have evolved in a number of different directions, and the openness of the late 1920s and early 1930s underlines this fact. The early sound era should remind us that the relationship between sound and image is, and always was, fluid and unfixed.

A transformation reminiscent of the transition to sound film has been repeating itself, in a sense, in the digital age. Today, in a time of rapidly changing film technologies, including digital projection, 3D cinema, and the plethora of digital media platforms like YouTube that radically redefine what a "film" can be, cinema is undergoing a similar identity crisis. Today's new media open up tremendous possibilities, but leave both old and new forms in an uncertain state. Just as the subjects of my chapters did over eighty years ago, contemporary artists are negotiating the challenging terrain of balancing old and new, adapting to new technology while trying to determine what should be maintained from older forms, as they define new media in the twenty-first century. Perhaps that is why the narrative of the early sound period continues to be so captivating. Artists today are working through ontological questions about cinema in very much the same way proponents and opponents of sound film did in the 1920s and 1930s, rearticulating debates and questions that resonated then.[1] As was the case with the figures examined in this book, the debates are sometimes explicit, through writings or interviews, and sometimes they are to be deciphered within the works themselves. Such moments of change are both chaotic and thrilling. As we live through the present sea change and negotiate other future media transitions, we might keep in mind the lessons learned by reexamining the experiments of the 1920s and 1930s and recapturing that moment of possibility. Reconsidering and nuancing its history is thus all the more important.

NOTES

INTRODUCTION

1. All translations are my own unless otherwise noted. The song was written by the film's composer, Wolfgang Zeller, with lyrics by Jean Boyer and René Sylviano. Brooks's voice was dubbed throughout the film, her singing voice provided by Hélène Regelly.
2. Crafton, *The Talkies*; Altman, *Silent Film Sound*; Altman, with Jones and Tatroe, "Inventing the Cinema Soundtrack: Hollywood's Multiplane Sound System"; Lastra, *Sound Technology and the American Cinema*; Gomery, *The Coming of Sound: A History*; Bordwell, Staiger, and Thompson, *The Classical Hollywood Cinema*.
3. Spring, *Saying It with Songs*; Slowik, *After the Silents*; Fleeger, *Sounding American*.
4. Several scholars have made important inroads into our understanding of French film music of the 1920s and 1930s. Claudia Gorbman and Martin Marks have undertaken isolated case studies of film scores and overviews of filmmaking practices during the transition era; film historians Richard Abel, Dudley Andrew, Colin Crisp, Ginette Vincendeau, and Allan Williams have documented a range of aspects of the transition era in France, from theoretical debates to industry practices, economics to France's star system; additionally, several film and music scholars in recent years have focused on particular aspects of the soundtrack in 1930s French film, including Charles O'Brien, Kelley Conway, and Colin Roust. See Gorbman, *Unheard Melodies*; Marks, *Music and the Silent Film*; Abel, ed., *French Film Theory and Criticism*, vol. II; Andrew, *Mists of Regret*; Andrew, "Sound in France"; Crisp, *The Classic French Cinema*; Crisp, *Genre, Myth, and Convention in the French Cinema*; Vincendeau, *Stars and Stardom in French Cinema*; Williams, *Republic of Images*; O'Brien, *Cinema's Conversion to Sound*; Conway, *Chanteuse in the City*; Roust, "'Say it with Georges Auric'"; Roust, "Sounding French." My work bridges and builds upon these scholarly contributions, providing a focused and detailed narrative of changing musical practices and debates in French film music during the transition era.
5. Bordwell, "The Musical Analogy."
6. Émile Vuillermoz, "Before the Screen" ("Devant l'écran" *Le Temps*, November 29, 1916, 3), translated and reprinted in Abel, ed., *French Film Theory and Criticism*, vol. I, 131.
7. Saint-Saëns's and Satie's film scores are analyzed in Marks, *Music and the Silent Film*. Daniel Albright also analyzes Satie's score in relation to other art movements in *Untwisting the Serpent*, 216–25.
8. Paulin, "On the Chaplinesque in Music," esp. ch. 4.
9. See Perloff, *Art and the Everyday*; Kelly, *Music and Ultra-Modernism in France*; Davis, *Classic Chic*. For more on the history of film music in France, see Lacombe and Porcile, *Les Musiques du cinéma français*.
10. Abel, *French Cinema: The First Wave*, 252.

11. Ibid., 257–60.

12. For a discussion of the international disputes on sound film technology and the effect it had on the French film industry, see Andrew, "Sound in France"; Abel, ed., *French Film Theory and Criticism*, vol. II, 5–142; Crafton, *The Talkies*, 418–41; Crisp, *Classic French Cinema*, esp. 1–42; Icart, *La Révolution du parlant*; O'Brien, *Cinema's Conversion to Sound*; and Gomery, "Economic Struggle and Hollywood Imperialism," 113–23. Kristen Thompson has written about the exportation and distribution of American films in the world during this period, and Emily Thompson has explored the complicated politics left in the wake of American sound engineers who wired movie theaters for sound technology around the world. Thompson, *Exporting Entertainment*; Thompson, "Wiring the World."

13. Alexandre Arnoux, "J'ai vu, enfin, à Londres un film parlant," *Pour Vous*, no. 1 (previously *L'Intransigeant*), November 22, 1928, Collection Rondel, RK 657, BNF–AS, also found in Icart, *La Révolution du parlant*, 190.

14. Barrios, *A Song in the Dark*, 4.

15. Abel Gance, *Ciné-Miroir*, no. 217, May 31, 1929, in Icart, *La Révolution du parlant*, 141.

16. See Delluc, *Photogénie* (1920), and Epstein, "On Certain Characteristics of *Photogénie*" (1924, originally published as "De quelques conditions de la photogénie"), reprinted in Philip Simpson, Andrew Utterson, and K. J. Shepherdson, eds., *Film Theory: Critical Concepts in Media and Cultural Studies*, 4 vols. (London: Routledge, 2004), 1:49–51, 52–56.

17. Conway, *Chanteuse in the City*.

18. On artistic collaboration, see Howard S. Becker, *Art Worlds* (Berkeley: University of California Press, 1982).

19. The narrative of the period as a moment of total crisis or breaking point has existed since the transition era itself, and has been perpetuated in popular retellings of the period, perhaps most famously in the Hollywood film *Singin' in the Rain* (1952). In recent decades, many scholars have demonstrated the various points of technological, aesthetic, and economic continuity between silent and sound film. See, for instance, Bordwell, Staiger, and Thompson, *The Classical Hollywood Cinema*; Gomery, *The Coming of Sound*; Lastra, *Sound Technology and the American Cinema*; O'Brien, *Cinema's Conversion to Sound*; and Wurtzler, *Electric Sounds*.

20. Marvin, *When Old Technologies Were New*, 8.

21. This is particularly the case for theories of the voice in cinema. See Chion, *The Voice in Cinema*; Mary Ann Doane, "The Voice in the Cinema"; Neumeyer, *Meaning and Interpretation of Music in Cinema*.

22. Classic cinema in the American context has been characterized by Bordwell, Staiger, and Thompson, *The Classical Hollywood Cinema*, and in the French context by Colin Crisp, *The Classic French Cinema*. Crisp does include the transition era in his definition of "Classic French cinema," but acknowledges throughout that it was a time of flux.

CHAPTER 1

1. Alexandre Arnoux, "J'ai vu, enfin, à Londres un film parlant," *Pour Vous*, no. 1 (previously *L'Intransigeant*), November 22, 1928, Collection Rondel, RK 657, BNF–AS, also found in Icart, *La Révolution du parlant*, 190.

> J'aime le cinéma profondément. Ses jeux de noir et de blanc, son silence, ses rythmes enchaînés d'images, la relégation, par lui, de la parole, ce vieil

esclavage humain, à l'arrière-plan, me paraissaient les promesses d'un art merveilleux. Voici qu'une sauvage invention vient tout détruire. Qu'on me pardonne quelque amertume, quelque injustice. Après avoir tant travaillé, tant espéré, pour revenir, en fin de compte à une formule aussi éculée que le théâtre, se resoumettre à la tyrannie du verbe et du bruit, aggravée encore par un intermédiaire mécanique!

2. According to James Buhler and David Neumeyer, the transition from silent to sound film in Hollywood took from 1926 until about 1930, but it was not until 1933 or even later that many technical and aesthetic issues were resolved. Hollywood studios completely changed over production to sound by the fall of 1929, and production of silent films had mostly ended by the end of 1929, but films were still often released in two prints (one sound and one silent) as late as 1930. Only 60 percent of theaters were wired for sound by the spring of 1931. Buhler and Neumeyer, *Hearing the Movies*, 154–55.
3. Arnoux, "J'ai vu, enfin, à Londres un film parlant."

> Nous ne pouvons rester indifférents. Nous assistons à une mort ou à une naissance, nul ne pourrait encore le discerner. . . . *Seconde naissance ou mort*? Voilà la question qui se pose pour le cinéma.

4. The bibliophile Auguste Rondel, who was passionate about theater and the arts, compiled his own books of clippings by subject. These include multiple book-length volumes on "Le film sonore et le film parlant," organized by year. See, for instance, Rk 656, Rk 657, Rk 659, Rk 660, Rk 666, Rk 667, Rk 670, Rk 671, Rk 675, Rk 676, Rk 680, and Rk 681, Fonds Auguste Rondel, BNF–AS. Many articles from the period have also been compiled and excerpted in Icart, *La Révolution du parlant*.
5. Bordwell, "The Musical Analogy."
6. Much of the discourse describing these disputes used war terminology, and the corporate struggle surrounding sound film was often referred to in the press as a "battle"; see Andrew, "Sound in France"; Gomery, "Economic Struggle and Hollywood Imperialism."
7. On the international disputes surrounding sound film technology and its effect on the French film industry, see Abel, ed., *French Film Theory and Criticism*, vol. II, 5–37; Andrew, "Sound in France"; Crafton, *The Talkies*; Crisp, *The Classic French Cinema*; Gomery, "Economic Struggle and Hollywood Imperialism"; Icart, *La Révolution du parlant*; and O'Brien, *Cinema's Conversion to Sound*.
8. While American and German imports were commercially successful, the reaction of the press suggests that French audiences were also ambivalent about what sound meant for the future of French cinema.
9. Andrew, "Sound in France," 98.
10. Abel, *French Cinema: The First Wave*, 61.
11. Ibid. In January 1929, L'Herbier's film *L'Argent* was released with a phonograph recording of crowd noises and airplane roars, much like the soundtrack to *Wings*.
12. According to Richard Abel, "Demand reached the point where French film producers were forced to initiate sound film projects as a regular feature of their production schedule" (ibid.). The first French sound films were either silent films sonorized in France or produced and filmed in England or Germany.
13. According to Abel, "Within a year, the changeover was nearly complete: of the ninety-four French films produced in 1930, seventy-six were talkies" (ibid., 62).

Most of the others were rereleased silent films with synchronized soundtracks, films that were mostly ignored in the press.

14. Eugen Weber notes that movie theaters were still wiring for sound in the mid-1930s. By May 1934, 1,738 movie houses were wired for sound, and by December 1934, the number had increased to 2,077; in 1935, nearly one-sixth of movie theaters in France still showed silent films (Weber, *The Hollow Years*, 67). Urban centers were much quicker to transition: Richard Abel claims that by 1932, sound projection equipment was installed in 95 percent of Paris cinemas, but less than half of French cinemas nationwide (Abel, *French Cinema*, 64).

15. O'Brien, *Cinema's Conversion to Sound*, 68–70.

16. Jacques Feyder, "Je crois au film parlant," *Pour Vous* (June 20, 1929), translated and published in Bandy, ed., *Rediscovering French Film*, 55.

17. Sacha Guitry, *Ciné-Miroir*, no. 213, May 3, 1929, in Icart, *La Révolution du parlant*, 165–66.

> Jusqu'ici, je n'ai été intéressé que par très peu de films. Mais je crois que l'avènement du cinéma parlant est une chose extrêmement importante. Importante pour tout le monde: pour les acteurs de cinéma d'abord, qui, s'ils se trouvent incapables de bien interpréter les dialogues des films, peuvent être du jour au lendemain remplacés par des acteurs de théâtre. Pour le public, auquel le cinéma parlant apportera à la fois la voix et le jeu d'acteurs qu'il n'aurait peut-être jamais pu aller entendre au théâtre. Enfin, les directeurs de théâtre qui donnent des pièces médiocres vont avoir à se défendre contre une concurrence très grave.

18. Marcel Pagnol, "The Talkie Offers the Writer New Resources," *Le Journal*, May 17, 1930, translated and reprinted in Abel, ed., *French Film Theory and Criticism*, vol. II, 56.

19. The kinds of theatrical productions produced for the screen were limited, however. For instance, most were either part of the "legitimate" theater or sourced from popular venues. Though France had a long-standing tradition of experimental theater, beginning perhaps with Alfred Jarry's *Ubu Roi* (1896), and continuing with Dada and surrealist stage works and the experimental multimedia productions put on by the Ballets Russes and Ballets Suédois, these types of works rarely found their way onto the screen. On theatrical traditions in France, see Edward Forman, *Historical Dictionary of French Theater* (Lanham: Scarecrow Press, 2010).

20. François Mazeline, "Le Cinéma parlant," *Rumeur*, April 30, 1928, Collection Rondel, RK 656, BNF–AS.

> Cet effroyable monstre est né. Aux Etats-Unis déjà, et bientôt en France, seront installés des appareils de projection, synchronisés avec des appareils d'émission phonographique. Le Cinéma est, par définition, Art muet. Il est une sorte d'écriture idéographique; le contraire du verbe. Créer le cinéma parlant, c'est créer un mauvais concurrent du théâtre pour quartiers pauvres. . . . L'avenir du cinéma parlant est donc limité. Le monstre est inoffensif et impuissant.

The choice of the word "monster" here is revealing. Scholars have argued that monsters often appear in popular culture as symbolic expressions of cultural anxiety; Jeffrey Cohen, for instance, claims that interest in monsters "is born of the twin desire to name that which is difficult to apprehend and to domesticate (and therefore disempower) that which threatens." "Preface," in Cohen, ed., *Monster Theory: Reading Culture* (Minneapolis: University of Minnesota Press, 1996), ix.

21. L. P., *Ami du peuple*, August 24, 1928, Collection Rondel, RK 656, BNF–AS.

> Le Cinéma est l'art du geste.
> Le théâtre est l'art du verbe.
> Je m'explique: au théâtre, l'élément verbal importe seul. Tout le reste, mise en scène, jeu de l'acteur, etc., ne sert qu'à mettre en valeur l'élément verbal.
> Or, le verbe est l'ennemi du geste.

22. Robert Desnos, "Les Rayons et les ombres: Films parlants," *Soir*, June 26, 1928, Collection Rondel, RK 656, BNF–AS.

> Le film parlant est trouvé et l'on nous annonce la transformation totale du cinéma.
> Le cinéma! Il devait être tout entier au service du rêve. Voici qu'il tombe aux mains de la sale littérature et du réalisme.

23. Marcel L'Herbier, *Mon ciné*, no. 361, January 17, 1929, in Icart, *La Révolution du parlant*, 139–40.

> J'avoue que le film parlant, tel qu'il existe actuellement, m'intéresse peu. La reproduction fidèle des paroles d'un acteur ou de l'entrée en gare d'une locomotive n'a pas de réelle valeur artistique. . . . Le cinéma est devenu—avec quelles peines—un art original, indépendant. . . . Il serait désastreux qu'il profitât d'un progrès technique pour revenir en arrière, artistiquement parlant.

24. Henri Chomette, *Ciné-Miroir*, no. 224, July 19, 1929, in Icart, *La Révolution du parlant*, 154.

> Il est certain que, grâce au film parlant, on voudra enregistrer des pièces de théâtre, des opérettes, des revues de music-hall et procéder ainsi à une sorte de vulgarisation et de diffusion artistique de certaines œuvres. Cela peut être d'un intérêt commercial considérable, mais, à mon sens, l'avenir du film parlant n'est pas là. Du fait que nous pouvons maintenant joindre la parole et le son à l'image, ne commettons pas l'erreur de reléguer brusquement l'image au rôle du parent pauvre. Une pièce de théâtre filmée et sonorisée, ce ne serait qu'un "dialogue accompagné d'images," où tout serait sacrifié au dialogue.

25. Benjamin Fondane, "From Silent to Talkie: The Rise and Fall of the Cinema," *Bifur*, April 1930, translated and reprinted in Abel, ed., *French Film Theory and Criticism*, vol. II, 53, 48.

26. Lucien Wahl, *Cinémagazine*, no. 25, June 15, 1928, in Icart, *La Révolution du parlant*, 186. "Le cinéma est toujours pur quand il se tait!"

27. Bordwell, "The Musical Analogy," 142.

28. Abel Gance, *Ciné-Miroir*, no. 217, May 31, 1929, in Icart, *La Révolution du parlant*, 141.

> Le film dialogué ne sera pas la mort de l'art. J'ose prédire ceci: pendant un temps assez long, le cinéma mondial essaiera péniblement, avec ses acquisitions actuelles, de rejoindre la musique universelle et le drame parlé. Mais de cette révolution naîtra, comme presque toujours, un

ensemble de choses meilleures. . . . J'exclue délibérément du cinéma
futur le film dialogué, mais j'appelle passionnément la grande symphonie
visuelle et sonore qui, grâce au synchronisme aura capté le mouvement et
le bruit universels, pour les offrir à nos oreilles et à nos yeux émerveillés
comme un don magnifique et divin.

29. Abel Gance, "Images of Yesterday, Voices of Tomorrow," *Cinéopse* 125, January
1930, translated and reprinted in Abel, ed., *French Film Theory and Criticism*, vol.
II, 41–42.

30. Jean Epstein, *Cinéa-Ciné pour tous*, December 15, 1929, in Icart, *La Révolution du
parlant*, 144.

Le cinématographe visuel en noir et blanc a gagné sa vraie place, compris
son rôle: d'opposer, de réunir de très simples images selon des rythmes,
des recoupements qui signifient. Le rôle du film sonore me paraît
être également dans l'écriture de telles évolutions des sons, de leurs
groupements significatifs, de leurs compositions et parentés, de leur
scissions et filiations.

31. Marcel L'Herbier, in interview with Georges Altman, "'Vers une musique
supérieure,' espère Marcel L'Herbier," *Monde*, December 21, 1929, Collection
Rondel, 8-RK-667, BNF–AS.

La musique et le cinéma marcheront de pair, seront liés par un contrat qui
les unit par la même pellicule. La musique qui deviendra partie intégrante
du film, sera faite pour lui.
Aussi arriverons-nous à une "musique supérieure," à une véritable
ORCHESTRATION DE LA VIE.

32. Germaine Dulac, *Ciné-Journal*, no. 983, June 29, 1928, in Icart, *La Révolution du
parlant*, 150.

L'Art du cinéma n'est-il pas l'art de la beauté visuelle dans la combinaison
du mouvement et de la lumière? Leur adjoindre le verbe, c'est le détruire
dans son sens le plus profond. C'est une régression, non un progrès.
L'idiotisme en usage dans chaque pays est une frontière morale. . . .
Quand nos images seront dépendantes du verbe, ce que je ne peux imag-
iner, les spectacles cinématographiques seront incompréhensibles pour
beaucoup . . .
Mais le grand progrès sera, sinon le film parlé, du moins le film musical. Harmonie de sons. Deux modes d'expression profondément
humains et internationaux dépassant les frontières du langage. Autant je
réprouve le film parlé, autant je saluerai avec enthousiasme l'avènement
du film musical.

33. Henri Diamant-Berger, qtd. in René Lebreton, "Faut-il condamner le 'film parlé,'"
Comœdia, July 27, 1928, Collection Rondel 8-RK-657, BNF–AS.

La parole n'est pas indispensable au cinéma. Je lui préfère la musique. Le
film est une symphonie visuelle dont la parole ne suivra pas le rythme à
la cadence utile. Le film se marie beaucoup mieux à un développement
orchestral qu'à des mots.

34. See Kraft, *Stage to Studio*; Slowik, *After the Silents*, 80–86.

35. Antoine, "Menace pour les musiciens," *Journal*, December 4, 1928, Collection Rondel, RK 656, BNF–AS.

> [S]i plus d'un spectateur encore ne conçoit guère le film sans musique, les premières expériences ne sont pas sans inquiéter la corporation des musiciens. On signale déjà quelques licenciements d'orchestre et, si l'on réfléchit que les travailleurs de ce genre ne sont pas moins de dix mille rien que pour Paris, la gravité de la crise possible apparaît.

36. G.D., "Ombres . . . Noires. Les musiciens en péril: Ce que pense leur Syndicat des films sonores," *Soir*, December 3, 1928, Collection Rondel, RK 656, BNF–AS.

> La musique mécanique, c'est plus qu'un danger pour nous. Si elle se développe, elle constituera pour notre corporation une véritable catastrophe. . . . Le cinéma qui nous avait ouvert tant de débouchés va-t-il maintenant nous rejeter, nous mettre au rebut? Il ne nous restera que les théâtres et les music-halls.

37. *Ciné-Journal*, no. 1006, December 7, 1928, in Icart, *La Révolution du parlant*, 175–76.

> Un grand danger (le plus grand peut-être depuis qu'il existe des musiciens professionnels) menace la corporation.
> La musique mécanique tend à se substituer à l'exécution directe et humaine. Tous sont menacés, déjà des orchestres de cinéma sont supprimés et remplacés par des appareils à bande sonore. D'autres suivront.
> Aucun musicien, aucun chef d'orchestre ne doit rester indifférent devant une pareille menace. . . .
> Les bandes sonores dureront peut-être davantage; un répertoire se créera qui, un jour, supplantera presque complètement l'exécution par orchestre.

38. *Ciné-Journal*, no. 1062, January 3, 1930, in Icart, *La Révolution du parlant*, 176–77.

> Considérant que les films sonores et parlants de provenance étrangère sont présentés au public français en langue étrangère et avec un accompagnement musical presque exclusivement composé de musique étrangère;
> Considérant qu'une exclusion aussi marquée de la langue et de la musique françaises, sur le sol français, constituerait, si elle se généralisait, une grave offensive contre la culture française et l'art français:
> Emet les résolutions suivantes:
> 1° Les films parlants représentés en France ne doivent utiliser que la langue français.
> 2° Une part importante de l'accompagnement musical des films synchronisés présentés en France doit être consacrée à la musique française.
> Et décident de poursuivre l'étude et l'adoption de toutes mesures utiles, en faisant appel, s'il le faut, aux pouvoirs publics et à l'opinion publique, afin d'éviter que le cinéma ne devienne en France, l'instrument de pénétration d'expressions étrangères à la culture nationale.

See also Louis Aubrun, "Après les exécutants, compositeurs et éditeurs de musique protestent," *Paris Soir*, December 27, 1929, Collection Rondel, RK 666, BNF–AS.

39. Léon Poirier, *Le Figaro*, cited by *Cinéa-Ciné pour tous*, May 15, 1929, in Icart, *La Révolution du parlant*, 142.

> Eh oui, à mon avis, le film sonore va rapidement fondre avec la musique. Il y introduira d'une façon rythmique et précise l'antique "bruit de coulisse," il l'enrichira de sonorités nouvelles, il complétera les ressources instrumentales et nous obtiendrons ainsi une amélioration sensible de l'atmosphère musicale du film. Ce sera là sans doute le véritable progrès, le progrès durable survivant à la période de bluff que nous subissons.

40. Marcel L'Herbier, *Mon ciné*, no. 361, January 17, 1929, in Icart, *La Révolution du parlant*, 139.

> Et enfin, l'enregistrement de l'orchestre serait d'un intérêt capital. . . . Les metteurs en scène seraient forts heureux si, grâce aux films sonores, leurs œuvres étaient automatiquement projetées dans toutes les salles avec une adaptation musicale, immuable, original.

41. Milhaud, "Experimenting with Sound Films," 11.
42. Milhaud, *La Revue du cinéma*, no. 5, November 15, 1929, in Icart, *La Révolution du parlant*, 177–78.

> Le film sonore n'est encore qu'à son début, mais déjà son application est d'une importance considérable. Qu'arrivait-il autrefois lorsqu'un compositeur écrivait une partition spéciale pour un film? Seuls quelques grands cinémas pouvaient avoir un orchestre assez important pour l'exécuter, puis, dans les petites villes, le film passait avec une adaptation quelconque et la partition disparaissait à tout jamais. Grâce au film sonore, elle sera enregistrée pour toujours et se déroulera partout en même temps que le film. Quelle énorme diffusion!

43. Georges Auric, "L'Avenir musicale du film sonore," *Pour Vous*, December 6, 1928, Collection Rondel, RK 657, BNF–AS.

> La musique et le cinéma ici s'accordent pour la première fois d'un façon absolue quant au synchronisme de l'écran et de l'adaptation. Premier point—et dont on comprendra l'importance. D'autre part, la suppression de la fosse d'orchestre permet une projection tout à fait directe et proche du spectateur, en même temps qu'elle apporte enfin au compositeur la certitude de ne plus perdre son temps et ses efforts s'il tente la difficile entreprise qu'a été jusqu'à maintenant la réalisation d'une partition ou même d'une adaptation. Enfin, voici, pour finir, un *style* nouveau—et c'est là le plus grand et le plus haut intérêt de ce que nous devinons dans cette première "bande sonore,"—un style où le compositeur dépassera la "musique pure" sans avoir besoin de se courber au devant des exigences de la comédie ou du drame lyrique.

44. Émile Vuillermoz, "Chronique cinématographique: Le film-parlant," *Temps*, October 20, 1928, Collection Rondel, RK 656, BNF–AS. "Nous pouvons envisager dès maintenant l'utilisation pratique du concert ou du récital donné par pellicule sonore."
45. Milhaud, *La Revue du cinéma*, no. 5, November 15, 1929, in Icart, *La Révolution du parlant*, 178.

1° un cinéaste compose un film comme on chorégraphe un ballet sur une œuvre musicale déjà écrite. Dans ce cas-là le musicien n'a pas à se préoccuper du film.

    2° un musicien écrit une partition pour un film déjà existant. Dans ce dernier cas, c'est toute une nouvelle technique de composition à étudier.

46. The Baden-Baden festival emphasized new technology's impact on music composition, and had focused on music and film in both 1927 and 1928. In 1928, Milhaud's score for *Actualités* premiered with a live chamber orchestra. In 1929, seven sound film accompaniments were premiered on the same program, including Milhaud's *La P'tite Lili*. For more on the Baden-Baden festival, see Alexandra Monchick, "Paul Hindemith and the Cinematic Imagination," *Musical Quarterly* 95, no. 4 (2012): 510–48.

47. Cavalcanti's film premiered in 1927 without musical accompaniment. The film was distributed worldwide with Milhaud's score. It also received an American performance in 1931, organized by Aaron Copland. See Carol Oja, *Making Music Modern: New York in the 1920s* (New York: Oxford University Press, 2000), 389.

48. Milhaud, "Experimenting with Sound Films," 13–14.

49. Jacques Ibert, *Pour Vous*, no. 170, February 18, 1932, in Icart, *La Révolution du parlant*, 180.

> La collaboration avec le musicien doit être étroite, la partition doit naître en même temps que les images: pourquoi le compositeur n'assisterait-il pas le metteur en scène, de même que le scénariste? Ses suggestions peuvent enrichir l'œuvre, amplifier les conceptions du réalisateur; de passive qu'elle est habituellement, sa collaboration doit devenir active.

50. Arthur Honegger, *Pour Vous*, no. 66, February 20, 1930, in Icart, *La Révolution du parlant*, 179. "[L]a partition écrite pour le film évolue parallèlement à lui, épouse son rythme image par image, appuie ses effets au moment opportun."

51. Ibid. "[N]ous ne serons pas arrêtés dans notre élan par l'impossibilité d'obtenir d'un orchestre des sonorités nouvelles."

52. Émile Vuillermoz, "Chronique cinématographique: Le Film-parlant," *Temps*, October 20, 1928, Collection Rondel, RK 656, BNF–AS.

> De même, il sera nécessaire de sélectionner avec plus de soin les timbres de l'orchestre qui ne se reproduisent pas tous avec la même perfection. La timbale, par exemple, détermine des résonances fâcheuses qu'il sera bon de corriger. Par contre, des instruments comme la flûte, la harpe, le violon ou le violoncelle sont traduits avec une parfaite pureté.

53. Milhaud, "Experimenting with Sound Films," 11.

54. R. L., "Les Débuts du 'film parlant' français," *Comœdia*, October 20, 1928, Collection Rondel, RK 656, BNF–AS.

> Le "film parlant" reproduit non seulement la voix humaine, mais encore la musique et, en résumé, toutes les sonorités.
>   Bien entendu, et c'est là l'intérêt de l'invention, les bruits divers sont rendus en synchronisme parfait avec les images du film. . . .
>   Moins heureux me paraît l'emploi du "film parlant" pour l'adaptation orchestrale. La musique ainsi rendue a des sonorités trop brutales.

55. Germaine Dulac, qtd. in Germaine Decaris, "'L'Art du mouvement et du silence ne peut mourir,' déclare Germaine Dulac," July 11, 1929, Collection Rondel, 8-RK-667, BNF–AS.

> J'estime que, par le film sonore, nous atteignons à une musique nouvelle. Il est fréquent que les partitions d'orchestre s'adaptent mal à la projection qu'elles accompagnent et fassent regretter le silence. Or, il y a du drame et de la poésie dans le bruit. Nous pourrons maintenant faire un double film qui sera le film musical, avec d'autres moyens que ce que l'on appelle ordinairement la musique.

56. Jean Lods, in interview with Georges Altman, "L'Écran se tait, l'écran parle: Une enquête sur le film parlant," *Monde*, December 21, 1929, Collection Rondel, 8-RK-667, BNF–AS.

> Rappelez-vous la saisissante démonstration de l'inventeur russe Theremine, à l'Opéra, l'homme maniant des ondes musicales, créant un véritable "bain" sonore avec des accents et des tonalités prodigieuses. Le film sonore permettra de faire baigner le film dans cette atmosphère musicale....
> Résultat encore: Joie pour le compositeur de *construire* sa musique, en découpant des morceaux de pellicule.

CHAPTER 2

1. Dudley Andrew suggests that Surrealism "so quickly attained cultural credit that even mainstream French cinema felt repercussions from its incipient program for the cinema" (*Mists of Regret*, 43).
2. Breton, qtd. in Albright, *Untwisting the Serpent*, 268.
3. Andre Breton officially defined surrealism in his 1924 surrealist manifesto, and again in 1929. See Breton, *Manifestoes of Surrealism.*
4. Short, *The Age of Gold*, 9. See also Kovacs, *From Enchantment to Rage*, 15.
5. Short, *The Age of Gold*, 10.
6. Susan Hayward, *Cinema Studies: The Key Concepts*, 3rd ed. (New York: Routledge, 2006), 404.
7. Breton, qtd. in Schiff, "Banging on the Windowpane," 163.
8. Steegmuller, *Cocteau*, 226.
9. Schiff, "Banging on the Windowpane," 158–61.
10. Chirico, qtd. in Schiff, "Banging on the Windowpane," 162.
11. Albright, *Untwisting the Serpent*, 289.
12. Jean-Paul Clébert, *Dictionnaire du surréalisme* (Chamalieres: Éditions du Seuil, 1996), 392. "Il n'y a pas de musique surréaliste."
13. On "art of the everyday," see Perloff, *Art and the Everyday*. See also Taruskin, "The Cult of the Commonplace"; and Garafola, *Diaghilev's Ballets Russes*.
14. Albright, *Untwisting the Serpent*, 275–310.
15. Taruskin, "Cult of the Commonplace," 1094, 1099.
16. See Chion, *Audio-Vision*, 8–9.
17. Taruskin, "Cult of the Commonplace," 1101–2.
18. Schiff, "Banging on the Windowpane," 154.
19. See Short, *The Age of Gold*, 25.
20. Kovacs, *From Enchantment to Rage*, 124–33. Kim Knowles, in *Cinematic Artist: The Films of Man Ray* (Oxford: Peter Lang, 2009), writes that Man Ray "saw the music as a fundamental element of the film's overall structure, contributing to the sense

of rhythm and visual dynamism, but also guiding the viewer's expectations and emotional responses" (88). Knowles suggests that this film is Dadaist in some elements and surrealist in others, thus suggesting a fluidity between the two movements (90).

21. Abel, *French Cinema: The First Wave*, 257–60.
22. Doane, "The Voice in the Cinema," 35; Altman, "The Material Heterogeneity of Recorded Sound."
23. Abel writes that by 1932, sound projection equipment was installed in 95 percent of Paris cinemas but less than 50 percent of French cinemas nationwide (*French Cinema*, 64).
24. The Vicomte and Vicomtesse were responsible for funding a number of modernist musical projects in the 1920s, including Poulenc's 1932 *Le Bal masqué*, one of the most frequently cited examples of musical surrealism. Both sound films that they funded bear marks of their patrons, through inside jokes or references (particularly Buñuel's reference to the Marquis de Sade, Marie-Laure's great-great-great-grandfather, at the end of *L'Age d'or*). See Laurence Benaïm, *Marie Laure de Noailles: La Vicomtesse du bizarre* (Paris: Bernard Grasset, 2001).
25. Buñuel described that his patrons' one condition for his making the film was that they had an agreement with Stravinsky to write the music to it. "'Sorry,' I replied, 'but can you imagine me collaborating with someone who's always falling to his knees and beating his breast?' (That's what people were saying about Stravinsky.) De Noailles's reaction was totally unexpected, and earned him my lasting admiration. 'You're quite right,' he said. 'You and Stravinsky would never get along. You choose your composer, and then go make your film. We'll find another project for Igor.'" Buñuel, *My Last Sigh*, 115.
26. Baxter, *Buñuel*, 47; Buñuel, *My Last Sigh*, 65.
27. Later, Buñuel suggested this decision was arbitrary: "The film was projected while I manned the gramophone. Arbitrarily, I put on an Argentine tango here, *Tristan and Isolde* there." Qtd. in Colina and Turrent, eds., *Objects of Desire*, 19.
28. Baxter, *Buñuel*, 104. Van Parys is not credited in the film. Linda Williams attributes "Gallito" directly to Van Parys in *Figures of Desire* (106). Paul Hammond also lists "occasional music" by Van Parys, but does not connect it to "Gallito," which he lists separately (*L'Age d'or*, 72).
29. Edwards, *A Companion to Luis Buñuel*, 35.
30. Buñuel, *My Last Sigh*, 118.
31. Hammond, *L'Age d'or*, 60.
32. Buache, *The Cinema of Luis Buñuel*, 23.
33. Jean-Paul Dreyfus, "*L'Age d'or*," *La Revue du cinéma*, 17 (December 1930): 55–56, translated and reprinted in Abel, ed., *French Film Theory and Criticism*, vol. II, 70.
34. Colina and Turrent, *Objects of Desire*, 23.
35. Buñuel, *Classic Film Scripts*, 28.
36. Ibid., 30.
37. Ibid., 44.
38. Buñuel wrote of this scene in his shooting script: "Insert of the young woman sitting on an immaculately white lavatory. (This location is only suggested and not made explicit, so that we have an uneasy suspicion that this is where she is, rather than a certainty. The young woman is dressed immaculately and everything about her conveys an impression of great purity.)" (ibid., 29).
39. Allen Weiss has discussed the scatological imagery and symbolism of the film in "Between the Sign of the Scorpion and the Sign of the Cross."

40. Buñuel, *Classic Film Scripts*, 7.
41. Buñuel, *My Last Sigh*, 20. Buñuel described that in Calanda,

> there are more drummers, around a thousand. They play for twenty-four hours straight without stopping. And by the end the skin on the hands breaks and blood flows through the sheer force of gravity; that's why you see the drums marked by large blood stains. The drummers walk around town, beginning at twelve o'clock on Good Friday and they do not stop until noon on Holy Saturday. In fact, the tradition is not that old. (qtd. in Colina and Turrent, *Objects of Desire*, 28)

42. Though the orchestra itself was not credited, Armand Bernard is credited as the "chef d'orchestre." Bernard was a silent film actor with musical training who became involved in arranging and recording sound film scores, arranging the music for René Clair's first sound films *Sous les toits de Paris* and *Le Million*. Therefore, it is highly likely that the orchestra was employed by Tobis-Klangfilm's Paris studio.
43. Though scholars have listed some of the works that appear in *L'Age d'or*'s soundtrack, they are incomplete (Williams, *Figures of Desire*, 106; Hammond, *L'Age d'or*, 72; and Kino International's DVD).
44. Buñuel, *Classic Film Scripts*, 65.
45. In this respect, *L'Age d'or* shares similarities with Stanley Kubrick's 1971 film *A Clockwork Orange*. Kubrick, too, juxtaposes disturbing, ultraviolent images with beloved classical works, particularly Beethoven's Ninth Symphony. On music in *A Clockwork Orange*, see, for instance, Christine Lee Gengaro, *Listening to Stanley Kubrick: The Music in His Films* (Lanham: Scarecrow Press, 2013), 103–46; Claudia Gorbman, "Ears Wide Open: Kubrick's Music," in Powrie and Stilwell, eds., *Changing Tunes*, 3–18; Kate McQuiston, "Value, Violence and Music Recognized: *A Clockwork Orange* as Musicology," in *Stanley Kubrick: Essays on His Films and Legacy*, ed. Gary D. Rhodes (Jefferson, North Carolina: McFarland, 2008), 105–22; and James Wierzbicki, "Banality Triumphant: Iconographic Use of Beethoven's Ninth Symphony in Recent Films," *Beethoven Forum* 10, no. 2 (Fall 2003): 113–38.
46. Barlow, "Surreal Symphonies," 31. See also Aranda, *Luis Buñuel*, 83.
47. Buñuel, *Classic Film Scripts*, 33.
48. City symphonies were experimental documentaries that portrayed a city's daily life. This avant-garde filmmaking style was influenced by musical symphonies in form and structure, and relied heavily on montage. The best-known city symphonies are Walter Ruttmann's *Berlin: Symphony of a Metropolis* (*Berlin: Die Sinfonie der Großstadt*, 1927) and Dziga Vertov's *Man with a Movie Camera* (1929). On city symphonies, see, for instance, Alexander Graf, "Paris—Berlin—Moscow: On the Montage Aesthetic in the City Symphony Films of the 1920s," in *Avant-Garde Film*, ed. Graf and Dietrich Schennemann (Amsterdam: Rodopi, 2007), 77–91.
49. Translation found in Arthur B. Wenk, *Claude Debussy and the Poets* (Berkeley: University of California Press, 1976), 304.
50. See James Buhler, "Wagnerian Motives: Narrative Integration and the Development of Silent Film Accompaniment, 1908–1913," in Joe and Gilman, eds., *Wagner and Cinema*, 27–45; and Scott D. Paulin, "Richard Wagner and the Fantasy of Cinematic Unity: The Idea of the *Gesamtkunstwerk* in the History and Theory of Film Music," in Buhler, Flinn, and Neumeyer, eds., *Music and Cinema*, 58–84. Perhaps the most well-known silent score to incorporate Wagner was Joseph Carl Breil's score to Griffith's 1915 film *Birth of a Nation*, which famously accompanied the Ku Klux Klan's ride to the rescue with the "Flight of the Valkyries." Wagner's music, too, had

appeared in Hollywood sound films. The 1929 First National film *The Squall*, which had a score consisting primarily of preexisting music, incorporated the *Tristan und Isolde* Prelude in its score. The Prelude, however, is not used in the context of a love scene; instead, it plays as Irma, one of the female characters, describes the chaos that has fallen upon the family since Numi, the gypsy woman, came to stay with them. It therefore does not seem to be drawing on any extramusical associations in its use of the theme.

51. Buñuel, *My Last Sigh*, 219.
52. Qtd. in Hammond, *L'Age d'or*, 46.
53. Kovacs has claimed that the "predominance of Wagner's music in these early films testifies to Buñuel's romantic faith in love" (*From Enchantment to Rage*, 231).
54. Cocteau, *Two Screenplays*, 3.
55. Many have interpreted Cocteau's work as surrealist. Daniel Albright, for instance, points out that most of the surrealist musical projects involved Cocteau (*Untwisting the Serpent*, 275).
56. He later published this journal: Cocteau, *Opium: Diary of His Cure*.
57. Ibid., 117.
58. Ramirez and Rolot, *Jean Cocteau*, 19. At the time, animated films were some of the most popular sound films in France. *Mickey Mouse* was one of the first sound film hits in France in 1929. See Weber, *The Hollow Years*, 212.
59. Ramirez and Rolot, *Jean Cocteau*, 19.
60. Ibid., 21.
61. Steegmuller, *Cocteau*, 407.
62. Cocteau, "Le Sang d'un poète," translated and reprinted in Abel, ed., *French Film Theory and Criticism*, vol. II, 91–92.
63. Steegmuller, *Cocteau*, 406.
64. Cocteau, *Two Screenplays*, 1968, 63.
65. Ibid., 36.
66. In a letter to Auric from Cocteau, he wrote that he "found a way to give even more of myself—I recorded my lungs, my bronchi, my heart" ("J'ai trouvé un truc pour donner encore de moi—j'enregistre ce soir mes poumons, mes bronches, mon Cœur"). Letter to Georges Auric from Jean Cocteau, Houghton Library, Harvard University.
67. Georges Auric, Préface, in Bourgeois, *René Clair*, 10.

> L' "ingénieur du son," personnage essentiel, nous semblait alors beaucoup plus redoutable qu'il ne l'était en réalité. Avant même d'entreprendre mon travail, j'étais convaincu que toutes sortes de contraintes devaient être observées: cet instrument s'enregistrait mal, cet autre, au contraire, devait être choisi sans hésiter; tel "aigu" ne "sortirait" jamais et telles "basses" allaient être sacrifiées, si l'on ne tenait rigoureusement compte des consignes de nos techniciens. C'est ainsi que je décidais de supprimer les "cordes" de mon orchestre et réunis une sorte d'orphéon: type idéal (j'en étais convaincu!) de ce que m'imposait le cinéma et ce fameux "micro."

68. Colin Roust discusses this fact in "Sounding French," 80.
69. Auric, qtd. in Preface, Caizergues, ed., *Correspondance Georges Auric—Jean Cocteau*, 6.
70. Ned Rorem, qtd. in Deaville and Wood, "Synchronization by the Grace of God?" 108.
71. See Roust, "Sounding French," and Deaville and Wood, "Synchronization by the Grace of God?" As Roust has pointed out, the effect of accidental synchronization is that certain sync points will inevitably seem to line up even if unintended.

72. Albright, *Untwisting the Serpent*, 190–91.

73. Deaville and Wood, "Synchronization by the Grace of God?" 110.

74. Cocteau wrote that the angel "is stretched out flat on his stomach on the cloak. This is accompanied by the sound of an airplane engine that gets louder and louder, splutters and roars, devastating the silence" (Cocteau, *Two Screenplays*, 50).

75. Roust, "Sounding French," 47.

76. In this respect, Cocteau's is a Bergsonian approach to time, an important component of Deleuze's concept of the time-image. See Henri Bergson, *Matter and Memory*, translated by Nancy Margaret Paul and W. Scott Palmer (Mineola, NY: Dover, 2004); Gilles Deleuze, *Cinema 2: The Time-Image*, translated by Hugh Tomlinson and Robert Galeta (Minneapolis: University of Minnesota Press, 1989 [1985]).

77. Deleuze, *The Time-Image*, 47, 56–57. On the subjectivity of time, see also Valtteri Arstila and Dan Lloyd, eds., *Subjective Time: The Philosophy, Psychology, and Neuroscience of Temporality* (Cambridge: MIT Press, 2014).

78. These principles were also part of broader international discussions about the role of sound and music in film and multimedia works, and other figures, like Bertolt Brecht in Germany and Sergei Eisenstein in the Soviet Union, experimented with similar concepts.

79. Chion, *The Voice in Cinema*, 125.

CHAPTER 3

1. Barrios, *A Song in the Dark*, 78.

2. On the MLV, see various essays in Higson and Maltby, eds., *"Film Europe" and "Film America"*; O'Brien, *Cinema's Conversion to Sound*; and Vincendeau, "Hollywood Babel."

3. Kelley Conway has argued that the musical film, of which the *opérette filmée* was a subgenre, was "crucial to the critical acceptance of sound cinema itself." Conway, "France," in Creekmur and Mokdad, eds., *The International Film Musical*, 30. On theories of transnational cinemas, see Durovicová and Newman, eds., *World Cinemas, Transnational Perspectives*.

4. Vincendeau, "Hollywood Babel," 142–43.

5. Martine Danan, "Hollywood's Hegemonic Strategies," 230.

6. This practice survived for a few years, and was used to export French films to the United States. For instance, Mordaunt Hall writes of *Il est charmant* that the two leads "appear in a prologue to give in English an idea of what the picture is about. . . . After the pictorial adventures are over the players appear again in a brief epilogue in which they concur in the belief that the audience has understood at least most of what has happened." Hall, "The Hotel Parade," *The New York Times*, April 17, 1932.

7. Vincendeau, "Hollywood Babel," 140.

8. Maurice Mairgance, "La Faiblesse du film parlant français," *Ami du peuple du soir*, August 2, 1930, Collection Rondel 8-RK-675, BNF–AS. "Après dix-huit mois d'efforts, il est vraiment regrettable que les deux meilleures productions qui passent en ce moment sur nos écrans soient des films américains en langue française."

9. Andrew Lamb, "Operetta," *Grove Music Online, Oxford Music Online*, Oxford University Press, accessed October 3, 2016, http://www.oxfordmusiconline.com.ezproxy.lib.utexas.edu/subscriber/article/grove/music/20386.

10. Duteurtre, *L'Opérette en France*, 101.

11. Ibid., 115.

12. Robert Ignatius Letellier, *Operetta: A Sourcebook*, Vol. 1 (Newcastle upon Tyne: Cambridge Scholars Publishing, 2015), 360.

13. Duteurtre, *L'Opérette en France*, 112.

14. There were a few noted early cases of playback—most famously in the Hollywood film *Broadway Melody* (1929)—but it was not common, and the practice had likely not yet arrived in France.

15. See Wolfe, "Vitaphone Shorts and *The Jazz Singer*."

16. On Hellmann see http://www.lib.utexas.edu/taro/uthrc/00739/hrc-00739.html#series1. The film was recorded using the American RCA Photophone sound system.

17. See http://filmographie.fondation-jeromeseydoux-pathe.com/18783-chacun-sa-chance.

18. Vincendeau, *Stars and Stardom in French Cinema*.

19. O'Brien, *Cinema's Conversion to Sound*, 57.

20. Ibid.

21. Jean Prudhomme, "Chacun sa chance," *Matin*, December 26, 1930, in "Documents about the film 'Chacun sa chance,' 1931," BNF–AS, 4-RK-2624. "Quelques chansons agrémentent ces scènes bien réalisées, alertes et gaies, que jouent le plus adroitement du monde André Urban, Renée Héribel, Gaby Basset et Jean Gabin."

22. L., "Chacun sa chance," *Ami du peuple*, January 2, 1931, in "Documents about the film 'Chacun sa chance,' 1931," BNF–AS, 4-RK-2624.

> C'est une opérette filmée (un sous-titre nous l'apprend) et il faut donc prendre ses précautions. Mais nous ne saurions en faire un grief à son réalisateur, Hans Steinhoff, et à l'adaptateur, M. René Pujol. Une fois admis le fait qu'il s'agit d'une opérette, nous nous plaindrons plutôt qu'on n'ai pas osé plus souvenu aborder le terrain de la fantaisie à outrance qui nous permet d'admettre plus facilement la simplicité de l'intrigue.

23. "Chacun sa chance," *Echo*, January 2, 1931, in "Documents about the film 'Chacun sa chance,' 1931," BNF–AS, 4-RK-2624.

> L'opérette filmée tient actuellement une place assez importante dans la production qui nous est offerte. . . . Nous avons employé à dessein l'expression "opérette filmée" parce que ce qualificatif semble rendre perceptible le souci qu'on (les réalisateurs) a de reléguer l'élément cinéma à un rang qui ne peut être le sien: le second. Est-ce que une tâche si délicate de faire s'accorder les lois essentielles sans lesquelles le cinéma n'est plus du cinéma et le sujet traité quel que soit ce dernier? Et est-il plus difficile de faire un film qui tout en conservant son caractère s'inspire de l'opérette, plutôt qu'une opérette cinématographique? Il est permis d'admettre cette hypothèse et *Chacun sa chance* n'est pas le seul film qui nous incite à penser ainsi. Dans *Chacun sa chance* qui d'ailleurs, il faut l'avouer, se voit sans ennui, le metteur en scène n'a pas plus cherché à demeurer dans le domaine cinématographique qu'à se débarrasser des effets purement scéniques.

24. The only major difference is the placement of the song "Le Chemin du paradis," sung by the leading couple. In the German version, the couple sings the song during the day. In the French version, they sing at night, in a slightly different placement in the story. This change likely had more to do with the logistics of filming than for any aesthetic reason: as with many MLVs, the same sets and leading actress were

in both versions, and filming would happen around the clock. In this instance, the French cast likely took the night shift. Otherwise, the two versions are remarkably similar.

25. *Le Chemin du paradis*, program, BNF–AS, 4-ICO CIN-15123.

> Premier Film-Opérette intégralement parlé et chanté en français; réalisé avec le concours d'une troupe d'artistes français. . . . UFA réalisera une série de grands films intégralement parlants français sous la direction de ses plus célèbres producteurs et metteurs en scène, assistés de metteurs en scène français, avec le concours d'écrivains, d'auteurs dramatiques français et de troupes d'artistes entièrement français.

26. For the German version, she acted alongside Willy Fritsch, and the pair became frequent costars in the early sound era. She spoke very little French, and there were plans to dub her dialogue, but while filming, people found her accent so charming that they decided to keep her voice.

27. Joseph Garncarz, "Made in Germany: Multiple-Language Versions and the Early German Sound Cinema," in Higson and Maltby, eds. *"Film Europe" and "Film America,"* 265.

28. Ibid. For biographical info, see also "Documents about Henri Garat," BNF–AS, 8-RK-18396; 4-RK-16902.

29. Antje Ascheid has suggested that some scholars see the film as a parody of the stage operetta genre, since it celebrates modernization and filmic innovation, and that the "dance numbers and comical performances . . . are staged for the camera and thus stress the film's modernist reflexivity." Antje Ascheid, "Germany," in Creekmur and Mokdad, eds., *The International Film Musical*, 52.

30. Jane Feuer has written of the Hollywood musical that, as the most complex genre of Hollywood film, it has paradoxically also been the one that attempts to offer the greatest illusion of spontaneity and effortlessness. Feuer, "The Self-Reflective Musical and the Myth of Entertainment," in *Genre: The Musical*, ed. Rick Altman (London: Routledge, 1981), 159–74.

31. Gaston Thierry, "Le Chemin du paradis," *Paris-Midi*, in "Documents about 'Le Chemin du paradis,'" BNF–AS, 8-RK 2821 (2) (III).

> Ce film parlant français—100 pour 100—réalisé en Allemagne, est d'une réussite complète. C'est une opérette, rien qu'une opérette, mais réalisée avec infiniment de goût, jouée à la perfection et accompagnée d'une partition plus qu'agréable. Si l'on ajoute que ce spectacle, qui est "un spectacle" dans toute l'acception du mot, demeure très souvent cinématographique, on comprendra notre indulgence pour un genre que nous avons maintes fois condamné, mais que des exceptions de cette valeur contribueraient à réhabiliter.

32. P. D., "Le Chemin du paradis," in "Documents about 'Le Chemin du paradis,'" BNF–AS, 8-RK 2821 (2) (III).

> Définitivement l'opérette semble trouver dans le film parlant une fraîcheur, et des possibilités nouvelles. . . . Enfin l'opérette trouve dans la juxtaposition de l'irréel, de l'arbitraire du théâtre "chanté" avec des décors naturels (un vrai ciel, de vrais arbres . . .) une atmosphère particulière que, pour notre part, nous trouvons fort agréable depuis la présentation du film *Le Chemin du paradis*.

33. J.-M. Aimot, "Film opérette," *Soir*, November 22, 1930, in "Documents about 'Le Chemin du paradis,'" BNF–AS, 8-RK 2821 (2) (III).

> "Le Chemin du paradis" . . . est également le chemin de la délivrance . . . Mais cette fois, si l'inspiration a été trouvé en dehors du cinéma, le cinéma a été utilisé sans se soumettre. . . . Un film opérette peut être un film.

34. Alexandre Arnoux, "Le Chemin du paradis," November 22, 1930, in "Documents about 'Le Chemin du paradis,'" BNF–AS, 8-RK 2821 (2) (III).

> Je ne voudrais pas que l'on crût que j'attache à *Chemin du paradis* plus d'importance qu'il ne convient. Œuvrette, je le répète et de peu de poids, mais gaie, vivante, et qui démontre que le cinéma, après un obscurcissement que l'on eût pu craindre définitif, reprend du poil de la bête, reconquiert les écrans d'où il menaçait d'être chassé, par usurpation.

35. Émile Vuillermoz, "Le Chemin du paradis," *Temps*, November 22, 1930, in "Documents about 'Le Chemin du paradis,'" BNF–AS, 8-RK 2821 (2) (III).

> Le livret et la partition ne sont pas d'une originalité extraordinaire, mais le mérite de cet ouvrage est de nous donner, pour la première fois, une véritable "opérette d'écran." Ici, le metteur en scène n'a renoncé à aucune des . . . richesses que nous voyons chaque jour sacrifiées au culte de microphone. Ici, le décor garde toute sa souplesse, toute sa mobilité, toute son ubiquité. Mais la trouvaille a consisté à assurer les mêmes privilèges à la musique. Jusqu'ici, à l'écran comme à la scène, la musique avait toujours été esclave de l'unité de lieu. Désormais la voici libérée de cette servitude. Un rythme peut s'envoler librement de son point de départ, atteindre au loin un autre objectif, sans ralentir ou presser son élan et imposer ainsi sa discipline à d'autres images et à d'autres actions. Un couplet d'opérette amorcé en plein air peut se poursuivre dans un salon, se continuer en auto et s'achever dans une usine. Un refrain peut galvaniser simultanément les êtres les plus divers; passer des uns aux autres avec une rapidité prodigieuse et mettre en branle un élément de gaîté dans les milieux les plus différents et ne conserver que la discipline de l'unité de temps. La musique devient ainsi une miraculeuse animatrice dont le fluide circule dans toutes les cellules du film. . . . Son rôle se trouve singulièrement magnifié et étendu. Cette conquête . . . nous ouvre des horizons imprévus sur l'avenir de l'écran lyrique.

36. J. F., "Le Chemin du paradis," *Comœdia*, November 27, 1930, in "Documents about 'Le Chemin du paradis,'" BNF–AS, 8-RK 2821 (2) (III).

> Ce qui motive mon enthousiasme, outre mon plaisir d'un soir, c'est que j'ai retrouvé-là, comme à la belle époque du muet, du *cinéma*, des quantités de raccourcis inexprimables au théâtre, des idées visuelles. C'est aussi du cinéma *parlant*, grâce au rythme qui rend le fantastique plausible, grâce à l'invention musicale qui est charmante.

37. Crisp, *The Classic French Cinema*, 23.

38. "Paramount et ses colonnes," *Minuit*, pp. 4–5, "Ceux qui ont animé le film 'Il est charmant,'" in "Documents about *Il est charmant*," BNF–AS, 4-RK 5253.

39. "Documents about Louis Mercanton," BNF–AS, 8-RK-480.

40. *Il est charmant*: Meg Lemonnier, BNF–AS, 8-RK-18738; 4-RK-17058; 8-RT-8957.

41. Rick Altman, *Silent Film Sound* (New York: Columbia University Press, 2004), 183.

42. L.-P. Coutisson, "Il est charmant," *Comœdia*, February 27, 1932, in "Documents about the film *Il est charmant*," BNF–AS, 8-RK 5253. "Car nous sommes dans la fantaisie pure de la première à la dernière image. C'est d'ailleurs ce qui fait le charme de ce film."

43. C. Tony, "A L'Odéon-Paramount: Il est charmant," in "Documents about the film *Il est charmant*," BNF–AS, 8-RK 5253.

> Voilà une opérette qui va mettre bien mal à l'aise des détracteurs du cinéma. . . . Car bon gré mal gré cette fois ils vont bien devoir avouer que voilà un film qui frôle de très près le chef d'œuvre d'humour, d'entrain et de gaîté. . . . Tout dans ce film d'ailleurs contribue à déchainer une gaîté "bien française" . . . *Il est charmant* est un modèle du genre et Paramount auteur responsable de cette délicieuse opérette cinématographique fait remporter là un très gros triomphe à la cinématographie française . . . puisque artistes, metteur en scène, *idées* tout est français dans *Il est charmant*. La musique est elle même française. Un peu plus que française . . . même puisqu'elle est signée par le compositeur marseillais Raoul Moretti, et l'on est doublement français quand on est de Marseille.

44. Paul Gordeaux, "Il est charmant," *Echo*, February 26, 1932, in "Documents about the film *Il est charmant*," BNF–AS, 8-RK 5253.

> En 1918, M. Albert Willemetz découvrait avec *Phi-Phi* la formule d'un nouveau genre d'opérette française, qui, pendant douze ans, allait donner à la scène lyrique tout un répertoire d'œuvrettes prestes, pimpantes, légères. En 1932, M. Albert Willemetz nous donne, avec *Il est charmant*, la formule de l'opérette française cinématographique. Cette formule est bonne.

45. Ibid.

> [J]e préfère une franche opérette, bien musicale et bien chantante de bout en bout, à ces comédies dont on nous a saturés depuis deux ans et où, brusquement, l'action, le rythme sont interrompus pour faire place à une chanson arbitrairement plaquée dans le film . . . tous "dans le mouvement" de cette opérette cinématographique qui constitue un des spectacles les plus agréables que l'écran nous ait offerts cette année.

46. Émile Vuillermoz, "Il est charmant," *Temps*, March 5, 1932, in "Documents about the film *Il est charmant*," BNF–AS, 8-RK 5253. "[C]ette formule représente une évolution très nette du goût dans l'histoire du divertissement cinématographique."

47. Ibid.

> De tout temps, nos auteurs, nos acteurs et nos musiciens ont excellé dans ces fantaisies aimables où la bonne humeur et l'ironie forment un mélange dont l'effervescence évoque irrésistiblement la mousse légère d'un de nos vins nationaux. Voilà bien longtemps que je déplore le peu d'empressement que montraient nos réalisateurs de films à accueillir dans leurs studios cet esprit parisien qui avait fait, jusqu'ici, la fortune d'une partie de notre théâtre et de notre chanson. . . . La nouvelle opérette de Paramount semble indiquer un revirement heureux de la part de nos éditeurs. . . . Le résultat est excellent. . . . [I]l y a là une réalisation qui commence à sentir

son terroir. Ce qu'il y a de particulièrement heureux dans cette technique, c'est un retour opportun à une certaine richesse de style cinégraphique complètement délaissée depuis quelque temps. Les professionnels du théâtre photographié, qui ignorent tout de la virtuosité technique de la pellicule silencieuse, avaient fini par discréditer la surimpression et les divers procédés de contrepoint visuel qu'on appelait, un peu à la légère, des "truquages." Louis Mercanton a eu l'intelligence et le courage de réhabiliter ces privilèges précieux de l'image mouvante. . . . J'aurais souhaité, pour ma part, voir cette collaboration complétée par un compositeur plus personnel que M. Moretti. . . . Mais s'ils manquent d'originalité, les refrains de M. Moretti sont au moins écrits d'une façon sérieuse et solide et ont un tour populaire très franc qui assurera leur succès immédiat.

48. Paul Granet, "Il est charmant," *Eve*, March 20, 1932, p. 12, in "Documents about the film *Il est charmant*," BNF–AS, 8-RK 5253. "Oui, *Il est charmant*, ce film léger, fantaisiste, très, très fou, mais toujours gai et toujours d'une bonne tenue. Charmante aussi la pimpante musique de Moretti. Bien des airs sont déjà fredonnés au phono."

CHAPTER 4

1. *The Broadway Melody* was advertised as the first "all talking, all singing, [and] all dancing" film. See Barrios, *A Song in the Dark*, 66.
2. Clair and his response to the arrival of synchronized sound film have been the subject of numerous scholarly studies. See, for instance, R. C. Dale, "A Clash of Intelligences: Sound vs. Image in René Clair's *À nous, la liberté*," *The French Review* 38, no. 5 (April, 1965): 637–44; Dale, *The Films of René Clair*, 2 Vols.; Fischer, "René Clair, *Le Million*, and the Coming of Sound"; Gorbman, "Clair's Sound Hierarchy and the Creation of Auditory Space"; Gorbman, *Unheard Melodies*; and O'Brien, "*Sous les toits de Paris* and Transnational Film Style: An Analysis of Film Editing Statistics," *Studies in French Cinema* 9, no. 2 (2009): 111–25.
3. Clair, "Three Letters from London," in *Reflections on the Cinema*, 94.
4. See Bowles, *Marcel Pagnol*.
5. Pagnol, qtd. and translated in Bowles, *Marcel Pagnol*, 14.
6. Marcel Pagnol, "The Talkie Offers the Writer New Resources," *Le Journal*, May 17, 1930, translated and reprinted in Abel, ed., *French Film Theory and Criticism*, vol. II, 56 (emphasis in original).
7. Marcel Pagnol, "Les Ennemis du cinéma parlé," *Comœdia*, June 6, 1930, BNF–AS Collection Rondel, 8-RK-671 (Le Cinéma sonore et parlant, 1er semestre 1930).

   Enfin, le film parlé a contre lui la plupart des producteurs des films parlés. Presque tous ceux qui travaillent pour le Nouvel Art font tout ce qu'ils peuvent pour nous en dégoûter. . . . Les gens du théâtre, de leur côté, comprendront bientôt que le "talkie," loin d'être un rival, n'est qu'un élargissement de leur art.

8. Marcel Pagnol, "The Talking Film," in Bandy, ed., *Rediscovering French Film*, 91.
9. Ibid.
10. Bowles, *Marcel Pagnol*, 61–64.
11. *Marius* was part of a trilogy including *Fanny* (1932) and *César* (1936). *César* was unique among the three because it was written as a screenplay, rather than being adapted from a stage version.

12. Bazin, "The Case of Marcel Pagnol," 204–5.

13. Waldman, *Paramount in Paris*, 78.

14. Roger Vignaud, *Vincent Scotto: L'homme aux 4000 chansons* (Gémenos: Éditions Autres Temps, 2006).

15. Ginette Vincendeau, "The Art of Spectacle: The Aesthetics of Classical French Cinema," in Temple and Witt, eds., *The French Cinema Book*, 138.

16. Andrew, *Mists of Regret*, 119.

17. Clair articulated his idea of "poetics of the screen" in Clair, *Reflections on the Cinema*, 60–66.

18. Clair was a prolific writer throughout his career, and he published collections of his writings, in which he reevaluated his earlier philosophies on cinema, a couple of different times in his life. See Clair, *Reflections on the Cinema*; and *Cinema Yesterday and Today*. Georges Charensol and Roger Régent also published interviews with Clair, in *Un Maître du cinema: René Clair* and *50 ans de cinéma avec René Clair*.

19. Clair, "Talkie versus Talkie" ("Le Parlant contre le parlant"), *Pour Vous*, 57, December 19, 1929, translated and reprinted in Abel, ed., *French Film Theory and Criticism*, vol. II, 39–40.

20. Clair, "Three Letters from London," in *Reflections on the Cinema*, 96–97.

21. René Clair, "Film Authors Don't Need You" ("Les Auteurs de films n'ont pas besoin de vous"), *Pour Vous*, 85, July 3, 1930, translated and reprinted in Abel, ed., *French Film Theory and Criticism,* vol. II, 57.

22. Ibid., 58.

23. Clair, "Three Letters from London," in *Reflections on the Cinema*, 94.

24. Ibid., 91–95 (emphasis in original).

25. While in the United States "vaudeville" refers to a music-hall variety show, in France, *vaudeville*, or *comédie en vaudeville*, was used to connote a French poem or song of satirical nature or a comedy enlivened through lyrics, and, later, to refer to the genre of musical comedy in which these "vaudeville" songs appeared. See Clifford Barnes, "Vaudeville," *Grove Music Online*, Oxford University Press, accessed May 21, 2013, http://www.oxfordmusiconline.com/subscriber/article/grove/music/29082.

26. Clair, quoted in Charensol and Régent, *Un Maître du Cinéma: René Clair*, 121–22.

> Pour conserver ce rythme à l'écran, il faudrait beaucoup trop de dialogue. Effrayé je demande à la Tobis d'arrêter les pourparlers avec les auteurs de la pièce. On me répond: "Trop tard. Depuis hier nous avons versé quatre-vingt mille francs." J'étais forcé de continuer. Devant cette nécessité, j'imagine qu'il doit être possible de retrouver l'irréalité du vaudeville en remplaçant les paroles par de la musique et des chansons. A partir de ce moment mon travail commence à m'intéresser. Je suis enchanté d'avoir découvert cette formule d'opérette où tout chantera sauf les personnages principaux. . . . Maintenant j'allais concevoir des éléments musicaux directement inspirés par l'action et cela posait un certain nombre de problèmes passionnants.

27. Parès, *33 tours en arrière et notes en vrac*, 101–2. Benoît Duteurtre describes Van Parys and Parès's stage works, such as *La Petite Dame du train bleu* (1927) and *L'Eau à la bouche* (1928), as "comédie[s] légère[s]" (*L'Opérette en France*, 167–71). Van Parys later became a prolific film composer. He went on to collaborate frequently with Clair, beginning a decade and a half later, when Clair returned to France after the war, with *Le Silence est d'or*, and continuing through 1961, with *Tout l'or du monde*.

Van Parys kept a journal throughout his career, which later was published under the title *Les Jours comme ils viennent* (1969). It appears to have been written contemporaneously with the events he describes, and traces the majority of the long span of his career as a film composer, particularly his relationship with Clair. Parès also published a memoire, *33 tours en arrière et notes en vrac* (1978), which recounted his experience collaborating with Van Parys and Clair from the distance of several decades. Parès never worked in film to the same extent as Van Parys; yet his experience with *Le Million* clearly left an impression on him. These two sources serve as valuable accounts of their working relationship both with Clair and with each other.

28. In some respects, this format has many ingredients of the "backstage musical." There is also a history, dating back to the nineteenth century, of "opera-house mysteries," from which stories like *The Phantom of the Opera* emerged. By setting the climax of a comedy backstage at an opera house, Clair may have been parodying this longer tradition. See, for instance, Margaret Miner, "Phantoms of Genius: Women and the Fantastic in the Opera-House Mystery," *19th-Century Music* 18, no. 2 (Autumn, 1994): 121–35. Another well-known parody appeared a few years later with the Marx Brothers' *A Night at the Opera* (1935). See Michal Grover-Friedlander, "'There Ain't No Sanity Claus!' The Marx Brothers at the Opera," in *Between Opera and Cinema*, ed. Jeongwon Joe and Rose Theresa (New York: Routledge, 2002), 19–37.

29. These two scenes were shot silent, and the music was added in postsynchronization.

30. Parès, *33 tours en arrière et notes en vrac*, 103.

> En prenant connaissance de ce découpage, je me souviens de notre étonnement. Depuis le début jusqu'à la fin, tout était prévu au point de vue musical, jusqu'au minutage exact de chaque intervention musicale et l'indication du moindre effet à faire. Les chœurs étaient écrits et nous ne devions pas en changer une virgule: c'était la première fois que je voyais ça au cinéma. Je ne l'ai du reste pas revu par la suite.

31. René Clair, "Le Million—Découpage technique." 1931. René Clair Collection, BNF–AS, 4-COL84-10 (1). Emanuelle Toulet provides a catalog of the René Clair collection in her article "René Clair dans les collections de la Bibliothèque Nationale de France," *1895*, no. 25 (September 1998): 169–91.

32. According to Charles O'Brien, Clair's shooting scripts were unique in their level of preparation and detail before shooting (*Cinema's Conversion to Sound*, 79–80).

33. Parès, *33 tours en arrière et notes en vrac*, 103.

34. Clair, *"Le Million," Cinémonde* 124 (March 5, 1931), translated and reprinted in Abel, ed., *French Film Theory and Criticism*, vol. II, 74.

35. Parès recounted in his memoire:

> During that time, (I am sure that young people in the cinema won't believe it), there was neither "playback" nor magnetic tape that we could cut or put back together at will, and we recorded all of the songs on stage with the orchestra, at the same time that we filmed the image. You must really believe that it wasn't easy and that we lost a considerable amount of time! (Parès, *33 tours en arrière et notes en vrac*, 106).
>
> *À cette époque-là, (je suis sûr que les jeunes du cinéma ne s'en doutent même pas), il n'y avait pas de "playback" ni de ruban magnétique que l'on puisse couper ou recoller à volonté, et on enregistrait toutes les chansons sur le plateau avec l'orchestre, en même temps qu'on tournait l'image. On doit bien penser que ce n'était pas facile et que l'on perdait un temps considérable!*

Certain songs in *Le Million* appear to have been recorded silent and postsynchronized (*film sonore*), but these scenes never show a close-up of the actors' mouths singing, so precise synchronization was not likely the goal.

36. Clair specified the scenes that would require a metronome in his shooting script: for the song "Millionaire," for instance, he indicated, "tourner au métronome d'après les temps musicaux." Clair, *Le Million*, découpage technique.

37. Van Parys, *Les jours comme ils viennent*, 133. "J'ai été aidé au maximum par le monteur René Le Hénaff, qui est un vrai musicien, et a assemblé tous les fragments des petits ensembles avec une précision étonnante."

38. Clair, "*Le Million*," 75.

39. Perhaps the songs were even intended to invite participation from the audience. While there is no account of audiences singing along during a screening of the film, it is conceivable that this could have occurred. Salabert published an entire piano-vocal score of the music from the film, which gave audience members access to the music, either in the theater or at home. Regardless, the simplicity of the music, alongside the fact that it was cross-marketed through sheet music and records, points to the music's exerptability, and its ability to act as a metaphor for the entire filmgoing experience, and an active, engaging experience at that. Georges Van Parys, Philippe Parès, and Armand Bernard, *Le Million, Partition d'Écran*. 1931, Éditions Salabert (Paris). BNF–M, Fol. VM7 24798-24800.

40. In this respect, Clair contributed to a long-standing discourse on the aesthetic affinities between opera and cinema, a connection that began in the silent era and has continued to interest scholars from both musicology and film studies. See Marcia J. Citron, *Opera on Screen* (New Haven: Yale University Press, 2000); Citron, *When Opera Meets Film* (Cambridge: Cambridge University Press, 2010); Grover-Friedlander, *Vocal Apparitions*; Joe and Gilman, eds. *Wagner and Cinema*; Joe and Theresa, eds., *Between Opera and Cinema*; David Schroeder, *Cinema's Illusions, Opera's Allure: The Operatic Impulse in Film* (New York: Continuum, 2002); and Jeremy Tambling, *Opera, Ideology and Film* (Manchester: Manchester University Press, 1987).

41. Carolyn Abbate and Roger Parker, in their book *A History of Opera* (New York: W. W. Norton & Company, 2012), suggest there is "in the entire corpus of cinema, no greater or more delicate expression of affection for opera, of delight in its absurdities and faith in its transformative powers," than in this scene (517).

42. Some of the most influential theoretical discussions of the voice in cinema, particularly the illusion of voice–body unity, are Chion, *The Voice in Cinema*; Doane, "The Voice in the Cinema"; and Silverman, *The Acoustic Mirror*.

43. Van Parys, *Les Jours comme ils viennent*, 128–29.

44. Ibid., 129.

> Pour Talazac, c'est une autre histoire. Elle n'a que la valse à chanter, en duo avec Stroesco, mais la malheureuse n'a plus qu'un brin de voix. . . . Le timbre de soprano, avec l'âge, est descendu jusqu'à une sorte de barytonnade enrouée. Comment s'en sortir, avec Stroesco qui, lui, est ténor? La valse est écrite dans une tessiture assez élevée, et je crains fort qu'elle ne parvienne pas à la chanter.

45. Ibid., 131–32. "[E]lle a perdu sa voix et ne peut absolument plus sortir la moindre note. . . . Pourtant, il me semblait que vous l'aviez engagée parce qu'elle était chanteuse?"

46. Ibid., 132.

Erreur, mon vieux. Erreur totale. Je l'ai engagée parce qu'elle a la silhouette idéale pour ce rôle. La grosse cantatrice à qui je vais flanquer des nattes et que l'on va pousser comme un wagon. La voix, vous pensez si je m'en fiche. . . . On va . . . trouver une vraie chanteuse qui la doublera. Le principal pour moi, c'est qu'on VOIE Talazac, ce n'est pas qu'on l'ENTENDE.

47. Pagnol, who in 1946 became the first filmmaker elected to the Académie Française, later nominated Clair in 1960 (Bowles, *Marcel Pagnol*, 128–29). Clair was the first figure elected exclusively for his work as a filmmaker.
48. See Dale, *The Films of René Clair*, vol. II, for representative reviews.
49. The only other "musical comedy" that Clair directed after the mid-1930s was *Les Belles du nuit* in 1952.

CHAPTER 5

1. Marcel Carné, "Cinema and the World" ("Le Cinéma et le monde"), *Cinémagazine*, November 12, 1932, 9–12, translated and reprinted in Abel, ed., *French Film Theory and Criticism*, vol. II, 102–103.
2. Andrew, *Mists of Regret*, 7.
3. On French poetic realism, see Andrew, *Mists of Regret*; Susan Hayward, "French Poetic Realism," in *Cinema Studies: The Key Concepts*, 3rd ed. (New York: Routledge, 2006), 170–72; Turk, *Child of Paradise*; and Williams, *Republic of Images*.
4. Andrew, *Mists of Regret*, 19.
5. Notable exceptions are McCann, "'(Under)Scoring Poetic Realism'"; and Conway, *Chanteuse in the City*.
6. O'Brien, *Cinema's Conversion to Sound*, 2. O'Brien also claims that direct sound is a characteristic of French cinema that has persisted throughout the decades.
7. Ibid., 118–19.
8. Renoir, *My Life and My Films*, 106.
9. Williams, *Republic of Images*, 232.
10. Andrew, *Mists of Regret*, 11.
11. O'Brien, *Cinema's Conversion to Sound*, 1–2.
12. Conway, *Chanteuse in the City*.
13. Langlois, *Les Cloches d'Atlantis*, 181–83.
14. Williams, *Republic of Images*, 164–65.
15. Renoir, *My Life and My Films*, 104.
16. O'Brien, "The Exception and the Norm: Relocating Renoir's Sound and Music," in Phillips and Vincendeau, eds., *A Companion to Jean Renoir*, 45.
17. Renoir, "On Filmmaking," in Bandy, ed., *Rediscovering French Film*, 112.
18. Andrew, *Mists of Regret*, 104.
19. Sesonske, *Jean Renoir: The French Films*, 77.
20. Kelley Conway suggests the lyric "foreshadows the loss that Legrand will experience." Conway, "Popular Songs in Renoir's Films of the 1930s," in *A Companion to Jean Renoir*, 201.
21. Ibid., 202.
22. Faulkner, *The Social Cinema of Jean Renoir*, 25. He suggests, "Renoir creates a fairly obvious synecdoche whereby the environment in which the murder takes place is larger than Lulu's room—by implication it is the whole of French society" (24).
23. Sesonske, *Jean Renoir*, 99.
24. Conway, "Popular Songs in Renoir's Films of the 1930s," 206.
25. Marie, "The Poacher's Aged Mother," 223.
26. Clayton, "From Within," 62.

27. Sesonske, *Jean Renoir*, 135–36.
28. Clayton suggests, "the lure of the street—with its bawdy banter and simple pleasures—is all but embodied in the mechanical energy of the barrel organ" ("From Within," 63).
29. According to Alan Williams, "Jean Renoir's early work with the new medium is more significant as the point of departure for his brilliant career in the French sound film's golden age than as an important example to his contemporaries of how to succeed in the talkies" (*Republic of Images*, 168).

CHAPTER 6

1. Jaubert died a few years later in combat during World War II. Although he had an illustrious career as a film composer throughout the 1930s, he too did not live long enough to see *L'Atalante* achieve acclaim.
2. The restored version of *L'Atalante* is available on the DVD collection *The Complete Jean Vigo* ([New York]: Criterion Collection, 2011).
3. Michael Temple, audio commentary on *À propos de Nice*, on *The Complete Jean Vigo* DVD.
4. Scholarship on *L'Atalante* includes Dudley Andrew, "The Fever of an Infectious Film: *L'Atalante* and the Aesthetics of Spontaneity," in *Film in the Aura of Art* (Princeton: Princeton University Press, 1984), 59–77; Andrew, *Mists of Regret*; David Baldwin, "*L'Atalante* and the Maturing of Jean Vigo," *Film Quarterly* 39, no. 1 (Autumn 1985): 21–27; Bourgeois, Benoliel, and de Loppinot, eds., *L'Atalante*; Conley, "Getting Lost on the Waterways of *L'Atalante*"; Lherminier, *Jean Vigo*; Salles Gomes, *Jean Vigo*, 149–94; Temple, *Jean Vigo*, 91–134; and Warner, *L'Atalante*. Russell Lack and Gregg Redner have briefly analyzed the film's music, and Claudia Gorbman has discussed the collaboration between Vigo and Jaubert with respect to their earlier film *Zéro de conduite*. See Lack, *Twenty Four Frames Under*, 98–104; Redner, *Deleuze and Film Music*, 25–46; and Gorbman, *Unheard Melodies*, 113–39.
5. Scholars typically consider Max Steiner's score for the 1933 film *King Kong* to be the first classical Hollywood film score, beginning an era of a relatively standardized approach to film composition. James Wierzbicki, for instance, writes that Steiner's score for *King Kong* provided Hollywood "with a model for scoring practice that would sustain itself at least for the next two decades" (Wierzbicki, *Film Music: A History*, 130). Similarly, Mervyn Cooke claims that Steiner's score "almost single-handedly marked the coming-of-age of nondiegetic film music [and] established a style and technique of scoring that was not only much imitated during the Golden Age, but continues to be reflected in mainstream narrative scoring practices to the present day" (Cooke, *A History of Film Music*, 88). Recently, Nathan Platte and Michael Slowik have problematized these claims. See Platte, "Before *Kong* Was King: Competing Methods in Hollywood Underscore," *Journal of the Society for American Music* 8, no. 3 (2014): 311–37; Slowik, "Diegetic Withdrawal and Other Worlds"; and Slowik, *After the Silents*.
6. Temple, *Jean Vigo*, 3–6. The mythology surrounding Vigo has been shaped by two important biographical details that profoundly influenced his career: the legacy of his father, and his chronic poor health. According to Vigo biographer Salles Gomes, the shadow of Vigo's father was cast over everything Vigo did throughout his short life. For more on Vigo's biography, see Salles Gomes, *Jean Vigo*, and Temple, *Jean Vigo*.
7. Siegfried Kracauer, "Jean Vigo," translated by William Melnitz, *Hollywood Quarterly* 2 (1947): 261.

8. Jean Vigo, "Toward a Social Cinema," translated and reprinted in Abel, ed., *French Film Theory and Criticism*, vol. II, 60–63. Vigo's talk, "Vers un cinéma social," was given at the Vieux-Colombier cinema on June 14, 1930.

9. Vigo singled out Luis Buñuel's 1929 *Un Chien andalou*, pointing out its "admirable confrontation between the subconscious and the rational" and calling it "an accurate and courageous film" (Vigo, "Toward a Social Cinema," 61).

10. In addition to Buñuel and other surrealist filmmakers, Vigo's style in this film was influenced by the Soviet montage theorists. He collaborated on *À propos de Nice* with Boris Kaufman, the brother of Soviet filmmaker Dziga Vertov, and Kaufman worked as cinematographer for Vigo's later films.

11. In many respects, Vigo and Jaubert made an incongruous pair. Vigo was an anarchist-leaning atheist, Jaubert a liberal, politically committed, pious Catholic. Yet their mutual commitment to cinema resulted in a fruitful collaboration and friendship (Salles Gomes, *Jean Vigo*, 90). They met through director Jean Painlevé at Amis du Cinéma, the film club in Nice that Vigo had helped to found, for a screening of Cavalcanti's *Le Petit Chaperon rouge* (1929), for which Jaubert had written the score. As it turned out, a print of the film had not arrived from Paris in time (Temple, *Jean Vigo*, 55).

12. In his biography of Jaubert, François Porcile has called the composer "a marginal musician" ("un musicien marginal"), suggesting that his success as a film composer has marginalized his position in French music history. Porcile, *Maurice Jaubert*, 92. See also Mark Brill, "Jaubert, Maurice," *Grove Music Online, Oxford Music Online*, Oxford University Press, accessed February 28, 2014, http://www.oxfordmusiconline.com/subscriber/article/grove/music/14203; McCann, "'(Under)Scoring Poetic Realism'"; and Surowiec, "Maurice Jaubert: Poet of Music."

13. Porcile, *Maurice Jaubert*, 23–37.

14. Quoted in Porcile, *Maurice Jaubert*, 32: "avoir ouvert une voie claire vers une musique neuve."

15. Ibid., 35–39.

16. Ibid., 45–56.

17. On defining musical modernism in terms of a composer's approach to technology rather than musical style, see Lewis, "'The Realm of Serious Art.'"

18. Quoted in Porcile, *Maurice Jaubert*, 43: "une heureuse et fortuite rencontre entre les possibilités du phonographe et les qualités de tel orchestre ou de telle voix"; "Ce jour-là le phonographe sera non plus reproducteur, mais créateur"; translated in Surowiec, "Maurice Jaubert," 88.

19. The premiere was on April 7, 1933, at the Cinéma Artistic. It was common for a film to be cut by censors, but a film's being banned outright in its entirety was a rare occurrence. We can only speculate as to the reason for the government's ban, but the possibilities are many. They might have objected to the film's scathing portrayal of authority figures and of France's educational system, to the scatological references and the brief shot of a penis, to the overall subversive content and style, or to the mere fact that Vigo was Almereyda's son. Whatever the motive, it was not shown again in France until 1945. It was screened without incident in Belgium soon after its premiere, however, and was well received there.

20. Russell Lack points out that the score for *Rapt* (1934), another notable precursor to *musique concrète* practices in which composer Arthur Hoérée cut and spliced a collage of musical storm sounds to make the orchestra almost unrecognizable, was perhaps inspired by *Zéro de conduite* (Lack, *Twenty Four Frames Under*, 106–7).

This process of musical and technological experimentation was intertwined with *Zéro de conduite*'s political message. Claudia Gorbman, in her compelling analysis of the music for the film, notes the manner in which this creative approach to the soundtrack contributed to the film's overall message: "To record a piece backwards makes chaotic non-sense of it: but to return it to its normal state via a second transformation restores it to a new order, creatively different from the original. It seems that *Zéro de conduite* accomplishes this in formal, thematic, and ethical terms" (Gorbman, *Unheard Melodies*, 139).

21. Jaubert also made certain orchestration decisions in an effort to compose a phonogenic score. Most notably, he used a reduced ensemble featuring woodwinds and brass rather than strings, and he stayed within limited pitch ranges. These kinds of concerns became increasingly unnecessary as the fidelity of recording, mixing, and reproduction technology improved.

22. Jaubert, "Music on the Screen." Jaubert's lecture, "La musique dans le film," which was given in London, was first printed in *Esprit* in April 1936, under the title "Le cinéma: . . . La musique" (April 1, 1936, 114–19).

23. Jaubert, "Music on the Screen," 109. Jaubert's main complaint concerned "mickey-mousing," a technique Steiner was known to employ frequently in his scores.

24. While Jaubert wrote in opposition to Hollywood practices, many of the prescriptive statements in his essay could indeed also describe classical film music in America.

25. Jaubert, "Music on the Screen," 109. For the original French passage, see Jaubert, "Le cinéma: . . . La musique," 116 (my italics):

> Mais, de même que le romancier interrompt parfois la narration du drame par l'exposé de ses vues personnelles, dialectiques ou lyriques, des réactions intérieures de ses personnages, de même le metteur en scène échappe parfois à la stricte reproduction de la réalité pour ajouter à son œuvre ces éléments documentaires ou poétiques qui donnent à un film son ton inimitable: descriptions, passage d'un point à un autre de l'espace ou du temps, rappels de scènes antérieures, rêves, figuration imaginaire des pensées de tel personnage, etc. . . . *Ici la musique a son mot à dire*: sa présence même va avertir le spectateur que le style du film change momentanément pour des raisons dramatiques. Toute sa puissance de suggestion va accentuer, prolonger l'impression de dépaysement, de rupture avec la vérité photographique que cherche le metteur en scène.

26. In his chapter "Jean Vigo: The Material and the Ideal," Michel Chion similarly writes, "the music serves as a springboard from which the film departs from realism and attains lyricism and poetry" (Chion, *Film, a Sound Art*, 62).

27. Orchestrion machines, player pianos, and phonographs were all employed as silent film accompaniment. Additionally, phonographs were an important part of early sound synchronization technologies, particularly Vitaphone. Jennifer Fleeger claims that Warner Bros. initially placed Vitaphone "within a particular narrative about the phonograph" in order to make the technology feel more familiar to the public (Fleeger, *Sounding American*, 31).

28. Vigo teamed up with an independent producer, Jacques-Louis Nounez, who had funded *Zéro de conduite* and believed strongly in Vigo's vision. Nounez provided financial backing and arranged for the use of Gaumont film studio's space and cameras, and he negotiated with Gaumont to provide hardware and studio time. But because of the financial loss he had suffered from the censoring of *Zéro de*

conduite, Nounez decided that for their next film Vigo should adapt a preexisting scenario rather than choose his own subject. Deliberately suggesting a script that he thought was banal and innocuous, Nounez believed he could prevent trouble with the censors. It was a brief synopsis registered at the Association des Auteurs de Films by the writer Jean Guinée. Vigo, initially unhappy with the script, became excited by the project when he realized that he could change the story extensively, using Guinée's synopsis only as a starting point. See Salles Gomes, *Jean Vigo*, 155.

29. Simon had recently played Boudu in *Boudu sauvé des eaux* (discussed in greater length in chapter 5), and the role of Père Jules was influenced by his portrayal of this lovable nonconformist.

30. The act of visually highlighting playback media was already established as a convention in the silent era, albeit with a different purpose than in sound film. A silent film might feature technologically mediated music and sound in its narrative, but it was primarily invoked visually or through intertitles.

31. O'Brien, *Cinema's Conversion to Sound*, 29.

32. Clair's 1931 film *À nous la liberté* is a notable example. The film focuses on a phonograph factory, and the assembly-line work is portrayed as dehumanizing. Furthermore, in one scene, Émile, one of the lead characters, hears a song and sees a beautiful woman, Jeanne, leaning outside a window. He assumes that Jeanne is the source of the song and immediately becomes infatuated. He continues to stare at the window, even after Jeanne has disappeared into the apartment, out of sight. The song continues while the image cuts to Jeanne, who, having just exited the apartment, walks down the street. Émile is unaware of her departure, and continues to stare at the window, the source of the sound. Suddenly, the song distorts as the music slows down. The image cuts to a shot of a phonograph, and an old lady, Jeanne's neighbor, comes over to turn the phonograph off. Émile has been duped by the musical machine. For more on the music of *À nous la liberté*, see Roust, "'Say It with Georges Auric.'"

33. Chion, *Film, a Sound Art*, 38. Early sound animation in particular took advantage of the magical possibilities of synchronization between sound and image.

34. Jaubert's autograph scores for the film's music are housed at the BNF–AS, FOL-COL-5/31 (1–3).

35. Lack, *Twenty Four Frames Under*, 100, 98.

36. Jaubert had composed the song by November 1933, before the film's shooting began, according to the dating of his autograph score.

37. French text transcribed from Jaubert's autograph score.

38. Vigo searched flea markets for bric-a-brac, and asked his cast and crew members to contribute, in order to fill Jules's room. Vigo added phonograph parts and the music boxes. Actor Gilles Margaritis found the conductor puppet at his uncle's house and brought it to add to the scene. See Salles Gomes, *Jean Vigo*, 163–64.

39. O'Brien, *Cinema's Conversion to Sound*, 29. This practice was ubiquitous in Hollywood, as Katherine Spring has examined in depth in *Saying It with Songs*.

40. Crisp, *Genre, Myth, and Convention in the French Cinema*, 170–71.

41. Michel Chion suggests the song was "arranged and rhymed in the style of the advertising jingles in which the surrealists took such pleasure" (*Film, a Sound Art*, 61).

42. Warner, *L'Atalante*, 49.

43. According to the accounts of those present on the set, they had to shoot the scene between twenty and thirty times because he kept forgetting the words.

44. Salles Gomes has suggested the purpose was "not to create poetry for its own sake but to make Juliette's enchantment seem credible," thereby "reject[ing] reality in order to communicate it" (*Jean Vigo*, 165).

45. Arthur W. J. G. Ord-Hume, "Limonaire," *Grove Music Online, Oxford Music Online*, Oxford University Press, accessed February 28, 2014. http://www. oxfordmusiconline.com/subscriber/article/grove/music/43924. The Limonaire brothers ceased to make fairground and dance hall organs in 1918 but continued the production of automatic café pianos until the business finally closed in 1930.

46. Jaubert reused the java theme in two subsequent films—Marcel Carné's *Le Quai des brumes* (1938) and *Hôtel du Nord* (1938)—in both cases as diegetic music (at a carnival in the former and at an outdoor Bastille Day celebration in the latter). This reuse of the java indicates that he might have viewed the piece as a generic piece of dance hall music, purely functional and therefore recyclable.

47. The comment on music boxes and mechanical instruments in *L'Atalante* is more nuanced than it is in a French film of the later 1930s that famously featured music boxes and musical automata, Jean Renoir's *La Règle du jeu* (1939). A satire of the upper classes banned by the French government on the eve of World War II, the film features a member of the landed gentry, Robert, who is obsessed with musical automata. The musical machines in this film help to deliver a broader critique of the upper class, and Robert's fascination with the machines is portrayed with cynicism: they represent an obsolete technology in the same way that his social class has become a thing of the past. Whether or not Vigo and Jaubert influenced Renoir's use of music boxes and automata, *L'Atalante* shows a different perspective on antique musical technologies. In 1934 they were outmoded and quaint; by 1939 they had become unambiguously obsolete.

48. This type of play with the ambiguity of music's source anticipates the famous gag in Woody Allen's 1971 film *Bananas*, in which a harpist in the hotel closet is discovered to be the origin of what had seemed to be nondiegetic underscoring.

49. Carolyn Abbate, "Outside Ravel's Tomb," *Journal of the American Musicological Society* 52 (1999): 473, 468.

50. This shot was a happy accident. As Salles Gomes writes, the cats, ubiquitous throughout the film, usually ran from the lights and were scared of the camera, but when the phonograph played they gradually moved closer and closer, sitting around it "as if listening attentively to the music. Vigo had no intention of missing a shot like that, and for once work went ahead without trouble from the cats. One of the kittens even nestled inside the loud-speaker, and at that point Vigo must have felt that all resistance to his creativity had ceased" (*Jean Vigo*, 171).

51. Marina Warner suggests that "its early juke-boxes, glass booths, brass dials, dangling earphones and polished irregular surfaces give [cinematographer] Kaufman his final opportunity to depict the graphic strength of the city of modern life—and these early pop music machines inspire powerful nostalgia today" (*L'Atalante*, 63).

52. Conway, *Chanteuse in the City*, 153.

53. The soundtrack for this scene differs in the recent rereleases of the film. In the 1990 restoration, music plays quietly in the background as Juliette walks into the Song Palace. The version of the "Chants des Mariniers" played through the loudspeakers is the opening credits music, sung by a male chorus to orchestral accompaniment. However, Bernard Eisenschitz, who led the 2001 restoration, changed the soundtrack to what I have described in my analysis, based on indications found in the screenplay. See note 71 of this chapter for more information on the history of the film's restoration.

54. Gregg Redner argues that the choice of location also speaks to Jaubert's position as an outsider in French modernist musical culture, "draw[ing] the world of the production team into the world of the film" (*Deleuze and Film Music*, 40). Marina Warner also posits, "The setting must have been chosen by Jaubert, who was Pathé Cinéma's director of music at the time" (*L'Atalante*, 63). It is curious that Gaumont would have permitted a scene at Pathé, one of their competitors. Gaumont did not, however, distribute records as Pathé did.

55. Temple, *Jean Vigo*, 102–3.

56. Salles Gomes, *Jean Vigo*, 185. Vigo's independent producer, Nounez, was happy with the film, but he was at the mercy of the distributors and could not afford another financial loss of the sort he had had with *Zéro de conduite*.

57. An example of positive criticism is Valéry Jahier's review, "L'Atalante," *Esprit* 26 (November 1934), translated and reprinted in Abel, ed., *French Film Theory and Criticism*, vol. II, 186.

58. The song's Italian lyrics were by Ennio Neri. Bixio was a popular Italian songwriter from the 1930s to the 1950s. His songs were performed by such famous singers as Beniamino Gigli and Luciano Pavarotti.

59. Gauty was a famous French chanteuse the height of whose popularity was in the 1930s and who even appeared in a talking film in 1930.

60. O'Brien, *Cinema's Conversion to Sound*, 75.

61. *L'Atalante*: Plaquette de présentation, 1934, BNF–AS, 4-ICO CIN-10040: "Déjà, grâce à la célèbre mélodie de C. A. Bixio, si admirablement chantée par Lys Gauty, 'Le Chaland qui passe . . .' est sûr de ne pas passer inaperçu! Déjà, ses pittoresques motifs courent les rues. Ne nous étonnons pas non plus que 'Le Chaland qui passe . . .' en tant que film, n'obtienne un succès considérable." Unsurprisingly, the publicity for the film suggested cross-marketing with record stores nearby, listing a number of different recordings of the popular song by Gramophone, Pathé, and Columbia recording companies, of artists including the Orchestre Marek Weber, Richard et Carry, Line Marlys, and Lys Gauty.

62. The small minority of filmgoers attracted by Vigo's name were, according to Salles Gomes, "puzzled by a film so mutilated as to be incoherent": Salles Gomes, *Jean Vigo*, 189.

63. Temple, *Jean Vigo*, 105.

64. Salles Gomes, *Jean Vigo*, 197.

65. French text transcribed from the performance by Lys Gauty on the CD *Ciné-stars: Le Temps des drames*, Orphée B003DEBHA2, 1993.

66. Marina Warner claimed the song was added "to give the film a proper feel of schmaltz" (*L'Atalante*, 75).

67. Jaubert, "Music on the Screen," 107.

68. The accordion arrangement of "Le Chaland" is more virtuosic than that of the "Chant des mariniers," with more flourishes, making it less "amateur" than the versions of the "Chant des mariniers" that Père Jules and the boy had played casually on the barge in Vigo's version. *L'Atalante* (Vigo's version) does not hide the amateur quality of their accordion playing. But added in postsynchronization, the diegetic accordion arrangement of "Le Chaland qui passe" sounds exactly the same every time, clearly coming from the exact same track and spliced in every time from the beginning of the track.

69. For a discussion of this practice in the American film industry, see Spring, *Saying It with Songs*.

70. See Conway, *Chanteuse in the City*, 1–25. As such, street singers would figure prominently in a story, giving diegetic space for musical performance in a more "naturalistic" setting. Colin Crisp suggests that the number of street singers in films increased over the course of the 1930s, "with a sort of musical apotheosis toward 1939" (*Genre, Myth, and Convention*, 91).

71. In 1940 Henri Beauvais, who had been administrator of Gaumont in 1934, became an independent producer with the society Franfilmdis and bought the rights. Perhaps in acknowledgment of guilt over his role in its alterations he rereleased the film, now under its original title, and reinserted Jaubert's music, but a number of scenes were still missing. This copy was the version the postwar generation of French cinephiles was most familiar with. In the 1950s, Cinémathèque founder Henri Langlois and Vigo biographer Salles Gomes released an enhanced version with additional scenes; and in 1990 Gaumont undertook a more thorough restoration of the film, after the discovery of a 1934 pre-changes copy in the British Film Institute. One more restoration was undertaken in 2001, revising some of the choices made in 1990, which Bernard Eisenschitz, who oversaw the 2001 restoration, considered errors of interpretation in guessing the intentions of the filmmaker. The film is now restored as closely as possible to Vigo's intentions, and is widely available on DVD. See Eisenschitz, "Los *Atalante*."

72. Richard Neupert, *A History of the French New Wave Cinema*, 2nd ed. (Madison, WI: University of Wisconsin Press, 2007 [2002]), 60.

73. François Truffaut, *The Films in My Life*, translated by Leonard Mayhew (New York: Simon and Schuster, 1978), 23–24.

74. Truffaut and Eric Rohmer, "Postface à *L'Atalante*," recorded for a 1968 French television broadcast of the film, available on *The Complete Jean Vigo* DVD. With a metacinematic approach typical of the New Wave, both directors made references to Vigo and his films in their own work—Truffaut's *Les Quatre Cent Coups* (400 Blows) is clearly indebted to *Zéro de conduite* and Godard's 1963 *Les Carabiniers* was dedicated to Vigo—cementing Vigo's importance for a new generation of avant-garde and formalistically experimental filmmakers.

75. Truffaut resurrected Jaubert's music in each of his films from 1975 to 1978, and used some of *L'Atalante*'s themes in *L'Histoire d'Adèle H* (1975). In 2001, Godard inserted part of *L'Atalante*'s soundtrack (both speaking and singing voices) into his film *Éloge d'amour*. On Truffaut's use of Jaubert's music, see Annette Insdorf, "Maurice Jaubert and François Truffaut: Musical Continuities from *L'Atalante* to *L'Histoire d'Adèle H*," *Yale French Studies*, no. 60 (1980): 204–18.

76. On the pop soundtrack since its emergence in the 1950s, see Smith, *The Sounds of Commerce*. On popular music and auteurism in contemporary cinema, see Arved Ashby, ed., *Popular Music and the New Auteur: Visionary Filmmakers after MTV* (New York: Oxford University Press, 2013).

CONCLUSION

1. Lev Manovich, in his text *The Language of New Media*, discusses the emergence of a new medium (the digital computer) through the lens of Dziga Vertov's 1929 silent film *Man with a Movie Camera*, explicitly drawing parallels between the digital revolution and the invention of cinema over 100 years ago. Manovich, *The Language of New Media* (Cambridge: MIT Press, 2001).

SELECT FILMOGRAPHY

Note: The year listed is the release year, except where noted otherwise. I have indicated DVD or VHS information, or other access information (if available at archives).

ABBREVIATIONS

BNF   Bibliothèque Nationale de France
CNC à la BNF   Centre National du Cinéma at the Bibliothèque Nationale de France
CNC Bois d'Arcy Centre National du Cinéma at Bois d'Arcy

1928
L'Eau du Nil (The Water of the Nile)
dir. Marcel Vandal
prod. Gaumont, Vandal et Delac
(CNC à la BNF)

1929
Le Collier de la reine (The Queen's Necklace)
dir. Gaston Ravel, Tony Lekain
mus. Febvre-Longeray, André Roubaud
prod. Gaumont, UFA

Le Requin (The Shark)
dir. Henri Chomette
mus. L. E. Szyfer
prod. Tobis
(CNC Bois d'Arcy)

La Route est belle (The Road Is Beautiful)
dir. Robert Florey
mus. André Gailhard, Joseph Szulc, Philippe Parès, Georges Van Parys
prod. Braunberger-Richebé

Les Trois Masques (The Three Masks)
dir. André Hugon
mus. Isidore de Lara
prod. Pathé
(CNC Bois d'Arcy)

1930

L'Age d'or (The Golden Age)
dir. Luis Buñuel
mus. Buñuel (compiler), Georges Van Parys
prod. Charles and Marie-Laure de Noailles
(DVD, Kino Video, 2004)

Chacun sa chance (Each His Own Luck)
dir. Hans Steinhoff and René Pujol
mus. Walter Kollo
prod. Pathé-Natan, Marcel Hellman
(VHS, René Château Vidéo, 1995)

Le Chemin du paradis (The Road to Paradise)
French language version of *Die Drei von der Tankstelle*
dir. Wilhelm Thiele
mus. Werner Heymann
prod. UFA
(DVD, René Château Vidéo, 2016)

Chiqué
dir. Pierre Colombier
mus. Jean Eblinger
prod. Pathé
(CNC à la BNF)

David Golder
dir. Julien Duvivier
mus. Walter Goehr
prod. Vandal et Delac
(available on *Julien Duvivier in the Thirties* DVD, Criterion Collection Eclipse Series, 2015)

L'Enfant de l'amour (Illegitimate Child)
dir. Marcel L'Herbier
mus. Raoul Moretti, Joseph Szulc
prod. Pathé-Natan
(CNC Bois d'Arcy)

Le Mystère de la villa rose (The Mystery of the Villa Rose)
dir. Louis Mercanton, René Hervil
prod. Les Établissements Jacques Haïk
(CNC Bois d'Arcy)

L'Opéra de quat'sous (The Threepenny Opera)
French-language version of *Die Dreigroschenoper*
dir. G. W. Pabst
mus. Kurt Weill
prod. Tobis-Klangfilm
(DVD, Criterion Collection, 2007)

La Petite Lise (Little Lise)
dir. Jean Grémillon
mus. Roland-Manuel
prod. Pathé-Natan
(VHS, René Château Vidéo, 1996)

Prix de beauté (Beauty Prize)
dir. Augusto Genina
mus. Wolfgang Zeller
prod. Sofar
(DVD, Kino Video, 2006)

Le Roi des resquilleurs (The King of the Gate Crashers)
dir. Pierre Colombier
mus. Ralph Erwin, Casimir Oberfeld
prod. Pathé-Natan
(CNC Bois d'Arcy)

Le Sang d'un poète (The Blood of a Poet)
(completed 1930, premiered 1932)
dir. Jean Cocteau
mus. Georges Auric
prod. Charles and Marie-Laure de Noailles
(DVD, Criterion Collection, 2000)

Sous les toits de Paris (Under the Roofs of Paris)
dir. René Clair
mus. Armand Bernard, Raoul Moretti, René Nazelles
prod. Tobis
(DVD, Criterion Collection, 2002)

1931
Allô Berlin, Ici Paris (Hello Berlin, This Is Paris)
dir. Julien Duvivier
mus. Karol Rathaus
prod. Tobis
(DVD, Gaumont, 2011)

La Chienne (The Bitch)
dir. Jean Renoir
prod. Braunberger-Richebé
(DVD, Criterion Collection, 2016)

Les Cinq Gentlemen maudits (The Five Cursed Gentlemen)
dir. Julien Duvivier
mus. Jacques Ibert
prod. Vandal et Delac
(DVD, LCJ Editions, 2007)

Cœur de Lilas (Lilac's Heart)
dir. Anatole Litvak
mus. Maurice Yvain
prod. FIFRA
(DVD, René Château Vidéo, 2008)

Le Congrès s'amuse (The Congress Dances)
French-language version of *Der Kongreß tanzt*
dir. Eric Charell, Jean Boyer
mus. Werner R. Heymann
prod. UFA
(VHS, René Château Vidéo, 1995)

Faubourg-Montmartre
dir. Raymond Bernard
mus. André Roubaud
prod. Pathé-Natan
(VHS, René Château Vidéo, 1995)

La Fin du monde (The End of the World)
dir. Abel Gance
mus. Arthur Honegger
prod. L'Ecran d'Art, V. Ivanoff
(CNC Bois d'Arcy)

Jean de la Lune (Jean with His Head in the Clouds)
dir. Jean Choux
mus. Lionel Cazaux, Claude Augé
prod. Georges Marret

Mam'zelle Nitouche (Miss Nitouche)
dir. Marc Allégret
mus. Hervé
prod. Vandor-Film, Ondra-Lamac Film
(VHS, Éditions Montparnasse, 1992)

Marius
dir. Alexander Korda
mus. Francis Gromon
prod. Les Films Paramount
(available on *The Fanny Trilogy* DVD, Kino Video, 2004)

Le Million (The Million)
dir. René Clair
mus. Armand Bernard, Philippe Parès, Georges Van Parys
prod. Tobis
(DVD, Criterion Collection, 2000)

À nous la liberté (Freedom for Us)
dir. René Clair

mus. Georges Auric
prod. Tobis
(DVD, Criterion Collection, 2002)

Nuits de Venise (Nights in Venice)
dir. Robert Wiene, Pierre Billon
mus. Max Niederberger
prod. Sofar, Tobis
(CNC à la BNF)

On purge bébé (Baby's Laxative)
dir. Jean Renoir
prod. Braunberger-Richebé
(available on *La Chienne* DVD, Criterion Collection, 2016)

Paris-Béguin (The Darling of Paris)
dir. Augusto Genina
mus. Maurice Yvain
prod. Osso
(VHS, René Château Vidéo, 1996)

Princesse, à vos ordres (Her Highness Commands)
French-language version of *Ihre Hoheit befiehlt*
dir. Hanns Schwarz, Max de Vaucorbeil
mus. Werner Heymann
prod. UFA
(CNC à la BNF)

Sola
dir. Henri Diamant-Berger
mus. Lionel Cazaux, Jean Lenoir
prod. Erka-Prodisco Films
(CNC à la BNF)

La Tragédie de la mine (The Tragedy in the Mine)
Released in Germany as *Kameradschaft*
dir. G. W. Pabst
prod. Gaumont-Franco-Film-Aubert, Nero Film
(DVD, UFA Klassiker Edition, 2006)

1932
L'Âne de Buridan (Buridan's Ass)
dir. Alexandre Ryder
mus. Jean Wiéner
prod. Pathé-Natan
(CNC à la BNF)

L'Atlantide (Atlantis)
dir. G. W. Pabst
prod. Nero-Film

mus. Wolfgang Zeller
(DVD, MK2, 2004)

Boudu sauvé des eaux (Boudu Saved from Drowning)
dir. Jean Renoir
mus. Raphaël, J. Boulze, Edouard Dumoulin
prod. Jacques Haïk
(DVD, Criterion Collection, 2005)

Chotard et Cie (Chotard and Co.)
dir. Jean Renoir
prod. Films R. F.
(DVD, René Château Vidéo, 2015)

Fanny
dir. Marc Allégret
mus. Vincent Scotto
prod. Braunberger-Richebé
(available on *The Fanny Trilogy* DVD, Kino Video, 2004)

Les Gaîtés de l'escadron (Fun in the Barracks)
dir. Maurice Tourneur
prod. Pathé-Natan
(VHS, René Château Vidéo, 1995)

Il est charmant (He Is Charming)
dir. Louis Mercanton
mus. Raoul Moretti
prod. Paramount
(DVD, Lobster Films, 2013)

La Nuit du carrefour (Night at the Crossroads)
dir. Jean Renoir
prod. Europa-Films
(DVD, René Château Vidéo, 2015)

La Petite Chocolatière (The Chocolate Girl)
dir. Marc Allégret
prod. Braunberger-Richebé
(CNC Bois d'Arcy)

Le Quatorze Juillet (Bastille Day)
dir. René Clair
mus. Maurice Jaubert
prod. Tobis
(DVD, Video Dimensions, 2011)

1933
L'Ami Fritz (In Old Alsace)
dir. Jacques de Baroncelli

mus. Roland-Manuel
prod. Les Films Artistiques Français
(CNC Bois d'Arcy)

Ciboulette
dir. Claude Autant-Lara
mus. Reynaldo Hahn
prod. Cipar-Films
(CNC Bois d'Arcy)

Le Coq du regiment (The Rooster of the Regiment)
dir. Maurice Cammage
mus. Fernand Heintz
prod. Fortuna-Films
(DVD, StudioCanal Vidéo, 2004)

Don Quichotte (Don Quixote)
dir. G. W. Pabst
mus. Jacques Ibert
prod. Vandor-Film
(DVD, Ripley's Home Video, 2007)

L'Homme à l'Hispano (The Man in the Hispano-Suiza)
dir. Jean Epstein
mus. Jean Wiéner
prod. Vandal et Delac
(VHS, René Château Vidéo, 1995)

Jofroi
dir. Marcel Pagnol
mus. Vincent Scotto
prod. Auteurs Associés
(VHS, Compagnie méditerranéenne de films, 1992)

Madame Bovary
dir. Jean Renoir
mus. Darius Milhaud
prod. Nouvelle Société de Films
(DVD, Gaumont, 2014)

Ces Messieurs de la santé (Men of Santé Prison)
dir. Pierre Colombier
mus. Jacques Dallin
prod. Pathé-Natan
(VHS, René Château Vidéo, 1995)

Un Soir de réveillon (One New Year's Eve)
dir. Karl Anton
mus. Raoul Moretti
prod. Paramount
(VHS, René Château Vidéo, 1996)

La Tête d'un homme (A Man's Head)
dir. Julien Duvivier
mus. Jacques Dallin
prod. Vandal et Delac
(available on *Julien Duvivier in the Thirties* DVD, Criterion Collection Eclipse Series, 2015)

Théodore et Cie (Theodore and Co.)
dir. Pierre Colombier
mus. Jane Bos
prod. Pathé-Natan
(VHS, René Château Vidéo, 1990)

Zéro de conduite (Zero for Conduct)
dir. Jean Vigo
mus. Maurice Jaubert
prod. Argui-Film/Gaumont
(available on *The Complete Jean Vigo*, DVD, Criterion Collection, 2007)

1934
Amok
dir. Fédor Ozep
mus. Karol Rathaus
prod. Pathé-Natan
(CNC à la BNF)

Angèle
dir. Marcel Pagnol
mus. Vincent Scotto
prod. Films Marcel Pagnol
(VHS, Compagnie méditerrannéenne de films, 1992)

L'Atalante
(Originally released as *Le Chaland qui passe* [The Passing Barge])
dir. Jean Vigo
mus. Maurice Jaubert
prod. Gaumont
(available on *The Complete Jean Vigo*, DVD, Criterion Collection, 2007)

Le Dernier Milliardaire (The Last Billionaire)
dir. René Clair
mus. Maurice Jaubert
prod. Pathé-Natan
(VHS, Pathé, 1989)

Le Grand Jeu (The Great Game)
dir. Jacques Feyder
mus. Hanns Eisler
prod. Films de France
(DVD, Eureka!, 2010)

Lac aux Dames (Ladies' Lake)
dir. Marc Allégret
mus. Georges Auric
prod. Société Parisienne de Production
(VHS, René Château Vidéo, 1995)

Prince de minuit (Midnight Prince)
dir. René Guissart
mus. Maurice Yvain, Pascal Bastia, Germaine Raynal
prod. Consortium du Film S. A.
(VHS, René Château Vidéo, 1995)

Rapt
dir. Dmitri Kirsanoff
mus. Arthur Hoérée, Arthur Honegger
prod. Cinédis
(on *Ramuz Cinéma*, DVD, Cin&Lettres, 2006)

Zouzou
dir. Marc Allégret
mus. Vincent Scotto, Georges Van Parys, Alain Romans
prod. Productions Arys
(DVD, Kino Video, 2005)

SELECT BIBLIOGRAPHY

ARCHIVES CONSULTED

Bibliothèque du Film, Cinémathèque Française, Paris, France (CF).

Bibliothèque Nationale de France, Paris, France (BNF).

Centre National du Cinéma, Bibliothèque Nationale de France, Paris, France (CNC à la BNF).

Centre National du Cinéma, Bois d'Arcy, France (CNC à Bois d'Arcy).

Cinémathèque Royale de Belgique, Brussels, Belgium (CRB).

Houghton Library, Harvard University.

SECONDARY WORKS

Abbate, Carolyn. "Sound Object Lessons." *Journal of the American Musicological Society* 69, no. 3 (Fall 2016): 793–829.

Abel, Richard. *French Cinema: The First Wave, 1915–1929.* Princeton: Princeton University Press, 1984.

———, ed. *French Film Theory and Criticism: A History/Anthology, 1907–1939. Volume I: 1907–1929.* Princeton: Princeton University Press, 1988.

———, ed. *French Film Theory and Criticism: A History/Anthology, 1907–1939. Volume II: 1929–1939.* Princeton: Princeton University Press, 1988.

Albright, Daniel. *Untwisting the Serpent: Modernism in Music, Literature, and Other Arts.* Chicago: University of Chicago Press, 2000.

Altman, Rick. "The Material Heterogeneity of Recorded Sound." In *Sound Theory/Sound Practice,* edited by Rick Altman, 15–31. New York: Routledge, 1992.

———. "Moving Lips: Cinema as Ventriloquism." *Yale French Studies,* no. 60 (1980): 67–79.

———. *Silent Film Sound.* New York: Columbia University Press, 2004.

Altman, Rick, with McGraw Jones and Sonia Tatroe. "Inventing the Cinema Soundtrack: Hollywood's Multiplane Sound System." In *Music and Cinema,* edited by James Buhler, Caryl Flinn, and David Neumeyer, 339–59. Hanover: Wesleyan University Press, 2000.

Andrew, Dudley. *Mists of Regret: Culture and Sensibility in Classic French Film.* Princeton: Princeton University Press, 1995.

———. "Sound in France: The Origins of a Native School." *Yale French Studies,* no. 60 (1980): 94–114.

Andrew, Dudley, and Steven Ungar. *Popular Front Paris and the Poetics of Culture.* Cambridge, MA: Harvard University Press, 2005.

Aranda, Francisco J. *Luis Buñuel: A Critical Biography.* Translated by David Robinson. New York: Da Capo Press, 1976.

Auric, Georges. *Quand j'étais là*. Paris: Bernard Grasset, 1979.

Bandy, Mary Lea, ed. *The Dawn of Sound*. New York: The Museum of Modern Art, 1989.

———, ed. *Rediscovering French Film*. New York: The Museum of Modern Art, 1983.

Barlow, Priscilla. "Surreal Symphonies: *L'Age d'or* and the Discreet Charms of Classical Music." In *Soundtrack Available: Essays on Film and Popular Music*, edited by Pamela Robertson Wojcik and Arthur Knight, 31–52. Durham: Duke University Press, 2001.

Barnier, Martin. *En route vers le parlant: Histoire d'une évolution technologique, économique et esthétique du cinéma (1926–1934)*. Liège: Éditions du Céfal, 2002.

Barrios, Richard. *A Song in the Dark: The Birth of the Musical Film*. New York: Oxford University Press, 1995.

Barrot, Olivier. *René Clair, ou Le Temps mesuré*. Paris: Hatier, 1985.

Basile, Giusy, and Chantal Gavouyère. *La Chanson française dans le cinéma des années trente: Discographie*. Paris: Bibliothèque Nationale de France, 1996.

Baxter, John. *Buñuel*. New York: Carroll & Graf, 1994.

Bazin, André. "The Case of Marcel Pagnol." Translated by Alain Piette and Bert Cardullo, edited by Bert Cardullo. *Literature/Film Quarterly* 23, no. 3 (1995): 204–8.

———. *Jean Renoir*. Translated by W. W. Halsey II and William H. Simon. New York: Simon and Schuster, 1973.

Bernier, Olivier. *Fireworks at Dusk: Paris in the Thirties*. Boston: Little, Brown and Company, 1993.

Billard, Pierre. *Le Mystère René Clair*. Paris: Plon, 1998.

Bordwell, David. "The Musical Analogy." *Yale French Studies*, no. 60 (1980): 141–56.

Bordwell, David, Janet Staiger, and Kristin Thompson. *The Classical Hollywood Cinema: Film Style and Mode of Production to 1960*. New York: Columbia University Press, 1985.

Boston, Richard. *Boudu Saved from Drowning*. London: BFI Publishing, 1994.

Bourgeois, Jacques. *René Clair*. Geneva: Editions Roulet, 1949.

Bourgeois, Nathalie, Bernard Benoliel, and Stéfani de Loppinot, eds. *L'Atalante: Un film de Jean Vigo*. Paris: Cinémathèque Française, 2000.

Bowles, Brett. *Marcel Pagnol*. Manchester and New York: Manchester University Press, 2012.

Breton, André. *Manifestoes of Surrealism*. Translated by Richard Seaver and Helen R. Lane. Ann Arbor: University of Michigan Press, 1969.

Brieu, Christian, Laurent Ikor, and J. Michel Viguier. *Joinville, le cinéma: Le Temps des studios*. Paris: Ramsay, 1985.

Brody, Elaine. *Paris: The Musical Kaleidoscope, 1870–1925*. New York: George Braziller, 1987.

Buache, Freddy. *The Cinema of Luis Buñuel*. Translated by Peter Graham. London: The Tantivy Press, 1973 (1970).

Buhler, James, Caryl Flinn, and David Neumeyer, eds. *Music and Cinema*. Hanover: Wesleyan University Press, 2000.

Buhler, James, and Hannah Lewis. "Evolving Practices for Film Music and Sound, 1925–1935." In *The Cambridge Companion to Film Music*, edited by Mervyn Cooke and Fiona Ford, 7–28. Cambridge: Cambridge University Press, 2016.

Buhler, James, and David Neumeyer. *Hearing the Movies: Music and Sound in Film History*. Second edition. New York: Oxford University Press, 2016.

Buñuel, Luis. *Classic Film Scripts: L'Age d'or/Un Chien andalou*. Translated by Marianne Alexandre. New York: Simon and Schuster, 1968.

———. *Mon dernier soupir*. Paris: Robert Laffont, 1994.

————. *My Last Sigh*. Translated by Abigail Israel. New York: Alfred A. Knopf, 1983.

Burke, Marina. "The Transition to Sound: A Critical Introduction." In *Sound and Music in Film and Visual Media: An Overview*, edited by Graeme Harper, Ruth Doughty, and Jochen Eisentraut, 58–86. New York: Continuum, 2009.

Caizergues, Pierre, ed. *Correspondance Georges Auric—Jean Cocteau*. Montpellier: Centre d'étude du XXe siècle, Université Paul-Valéry, 1999.

Caron, Sylvain, François de Médicis, and Michel Duchesneau, eds. *Musique et modernité en France (1900–1945)*. Montreal: Les Presses de L'Université de Montréal, 2006.

Charensol, Georges, and Roger Régent. *50 Ans de Cinéma avec René Clair*. Paris: La Table Ronde, 1979.

————. *Un maître du cinema: René Clair*. Paris: La Table Ronde, 1952.

Chion, Michel. *Audio-Vision: Sound on Screen*. Translated by Claudia Gorbman. New York: Columbia University Press, 1994.

————. *Film, a Sound Art*. Translated by Claudia Gorbman. New York: Columbia University Press, 2009.

————. *The Voice in Cinema*. Translated by Claudia Gorbman. New York: Columbia University Press, 1999.

Chirat, Raymond. *Catalogue des films français de long métrage: Films sonores de fiction 1929–1939*. Brussels: Cinémathèque Royale de Belgique, 1975.

Clair, René. *À nous la liberté: Entr'acte*. Translated by Richard Jacques and Nicola Hayden. New York: Simon and Schuster, 1970.

————. "The Art of Sound." In *Film Sound: Theory and Practice*, edited by Elisabeth Weis and John Belton, 92–95. New York: Columbia University Press, 1985.

————. *Cinema Yesterday and Today*. Translated by Stanley Appelbaum. New York: Dover, 1972.

————. *Reflections on the Cinema*. Translated by Vera Traill. London: William Kimber, 1953.

Clayton, Alex. "From Within: Music in the Style of Jean Renoir." *Cineaction* 66 (2005): 61–72.

Cocteau, Jean. *Opium: Diary of His Cure*. Translated by Margaret Crosland. London: Peter Owen, 1990 (1930).

————. *Le Sang d'un poète*. Monaco: Robert Marin, 1948.

————. *Two Screenplays: The Blood of a Poet; The Testament of Orpheus*. Translated by Carol Martin-Sperry. New York: The Orion Press, 1968.

Colina, José de la, and Tomás Pérez Turrent, eds. *Objects of Desire: Conversations with Luis Buñuel*. Translated by Paul Lenti. New York: Marsilio Publishers, 1992 (1986).

Conley, Tom. "Getting Lost on the Waterways of *L'Atalante*." In *Cinema and Modernity*, edited by Murray Pomerance, 253–72. New Brunswick, NJ: Rutgers University Press, 2006.

Conway, Kelley. *Chanteuse in the City: The Realist Singer in French Film*. Berkeley: University of California Press, 2004.

————. "France." In *The International Film Musical*, edited by Corey K. Creekmur and Linda Y. Mokdad, 29–44. Edinburgh: Edinburgh University Press, 2012.

————. "Popular Songs in Renoir's Films of the 1930s." In *A Companion to Jean Renoir*, edited by Alastair Phillips and Ginette Vincendeau, 199–218. West Sussex: Blackwell, 2013.

Cooke, Mervyn. *A History of Film Music*. New York: Cambridge University Press, 2008.

Courtade, Francis. *Les Malédictions du cinéma français*. Paris: Alain Moreau, 1978.

Crafton, Donald. *The Talkies: American Cinema's Transition to Sound, 1926–1931*. Berkeley: University of California Press, 1997.

Creekmur, Corey K., and Linda Y. Mokdad, eds. *The International Film Musical.* Edinburgh: Edinburgh University Press, 2012.

Crisp, Colin. *The Classic French Cinema, 1930–1960.* Bloomington: Indiana University Press, 1993.

———. *French Cinema: A Critical Filmography. Volume 1: 1929–1939.* Bloomington: Indiana University Press, 2015.

———. *Genre, Myth, and Convention in the French Cinema, 1929–1939.* Bloomington: Indiana University Press, 2002.

Dale, R. C. *The Films of René Clair. Vol. I: Exposition and Analysis.* Metuchen, NJ: Scarecrow Press, 1986.

———. *The Films of René Clair. Vol. II: Documentation.* Metuchen, NJ: Scarecrow Press, 1986.

Danan, Martine. "Hollywood's Hegemonic Strategies: Overcoming French Nationalism with the Advent of Sound." In *"Film Europe" and "Film America": Cinema, Commerce and Cultural Exchange 1920–1939,* edited by Andrew Higson and Richard Maltby, 225–48. Exeter: University of Exeter Press, 1999.

Davis, Colin. *Scenes of Love and Murder: Renoir, Film and Philosophy.* London: Wallflower Press, 2009.

Davis, Mary E. *Classic Chic: Music, Fashion, and Modernism.* Berkeley: University of California Press, 2006.

Deaville, James, and Simon Wood. "Synchronization by the Grace of God? The Film/Music Collaboration of Jean Cocteau and Georges Auric." *Canadian University Music Review* 22, no. 1 (2001): 105–26.

Doane, Mary Ann. "The Voice in the Cinema: The Articulation of Body and Space." *Yale French Studies,* no. 60 (1980): 33–50.

Duchesneau, Michel. *L'Avant-garde musicale à Paris de 1871 à 1939.* Liège: Pierre Mardaga, 1997.

Dumesnil, René. *La Musique contemporaine en France.* 2 vols. Paris: Armand Colin, 1930.

———. *La Musique en France entre les deux guerres (1919–1939).* Geneva: Editions du Milieu du Monde, 1946.

Durgnat, Raymond. *Jean Renoir.* Berkeley: University of California Press, 1974.

———. *Luis Buñuel.* Berkeley: University of California Press, 1977.

Durovicová, Nataša, and Kathleen Newman, eds. *World Cinemas, Transnational Perspectives.* New York: Routledge, 2010.

Duteurtre, Benoît. *L'Opérette en France.* Paris: Fayard, 2009.

Edwards, Gwynne. *A Companion to Luis Buñuel.* Woodbridge: Tamesis, 2005.

Eisenschitz, Bernard. "Los *Atalante.*" *Archivos de la Filmoteca,* 52 (February 2006): 104–20.

Evans, Arthur B. *Jean Cocteau and His Films of Orphic Identity.* Philadelphia: Art Alliance Press, 1977.

Evans, Peter William. *The Films of Luis Buñuel: Subjectivity and Desire.* Oxford: Clarendon Press, 1995.

Faulkner, Christopher. "René Clair, Marcel Pagnol and the Social Dimension of Speech." *Screen* 35, no. 2 (Summer 1994): 157–70.

———. *The Social Cinema of Jean Renoir.* Princeton: Princeton University Press, 1986.

Fischer, Lucy. "René Clair, *Le Million,* and the Coming of Sound." *Cinema Journal* 16, no. 2 (Spring 1977): 34–50.

Fleeger, Jennifer. *Mismatched Women: The Siren's Song through the Machine.* New York: Oxford University Press, 2014.

———. *Sounding American: Hollywood, Opera, and Jazz.* New York: Oxford University Press, 2014.

Fulcher, Jane F. *The Composer as Intellectual: Music and Ideology in France 1914–1940*. New York: Oxford University Press, 2005.

Garafola, Lynn. *Diaghilev's Ballets Russes*. New York: Oxford University Press, 1989.

Gendron, Bernard. *Between Montmartre and the Mudd Club: Popular Music and the Avant-Garde*. Chicago: University of Chicago Press, 2002.

Gomery, Douglas. *The Coming of Sound: A History*. New York: Routledge, 2005.

———. "Economic Struggle and Hollywood Imperialism: Europe Converts to Sound." *Yale French Studies*, no. 60 (1980): 80–93.

Gorbman, Claudia. "Clair's Sound Hierarchy and the Creation of Auditory Space." *Purdue Film Studies Annual* (1976): 113–23.

———. *Unheard Melodies: Narrative Film Music*. Bloomington: Indiana University Press, 1987.

———. "Vigo/Jaubert." *Ciné-Tracts* 1, no. 2 (Summer 1977): 65–80.

Grover-Friedlander, Michal. *Vocal Apparitions: The Attraction of Cinema to Opera*. Princeton: Princeton University Press, 2005.

Gullentops, David, and Malou Haine, eds. *Jean Cocteau: Textes et musique*. Sprimont: Mardaga, 2005.

Hacquard, Georges, *La Musique et le cinéma*. Paris: Presses Universitaires de France, 1959.

Hammond, Paul. *L'Age d'or*. London: BFI Publishing, 1997.

Harding, James. *The Ox on the Roof: Scenes from Musical Life in Paris in the Twenties*. New York: St. Martin's Press, 1972.

Harper, Graeme, Ruth Doughty, and Jochen Eisentraut, eds. *Sound and Music in Film and Visual Media: An Overview*. New York: Continuum, 2009.

Hayward, Susan, and Ginette Vincendeau, eds. *French Film: Texts and Contexts*. London and New York: Routledge, 2000.

Herpe, Noël, and Emmanuelle Toulet, eds. *René Clair, ou Le Cinéma à la lettre*. Paris: Association Française de Recherche sur l'Histoire du Cinéma, 2000.

Higson, Andrew, and Richard Maltby, eds. *"Film Europe" and "Film America": Cinema, Commerce and Cultural Exchange 1920–1939*. Exeter: University of Exeter Press, 1999.

"Hommage à Maurice Jaubert." Montréal: La Cinémathèque canadienne, April 1967.

Icart, Roger. *La Révolution du parlant, vue par la presse française*. [Perpignan]: Institut Jean Vigo, 1988.

Jacobs, Lea. *Film Rhythm after Sound: Technology, Music, and Performance*. Berkeley: University of California Press, 2015.

Jaubert, Maurice. "Music on the Screen." In *Footnotes to the Film*, edited by Charles Davy, 101–15. London: Lovat Dickson, 1938.

Joe, Jeongwon, and Sander L. Gilman, eds. *Wagner and Cinema*. Bloomington: Indiana University Press, 2010.

Kahn, Douglas, and Gregory Whitehead, eds. *Wireless Imagination: Sound, Radio, and the Avant-Garde*. Cambridge, MA: MIT Press, 1992.

Kelly, Barbara, ed. *French Music, Culture, and National Identity, 1870–1939*. Rochester, NY: University of Rochester Press, 2008.

———. *Music and Ultra-Modernism in France: A Fragile Consensus, 1913–1939*. Woodbridge: Boydell Press, 2013.

Kovacs, Steven. *From Enchantment to Rage: The Story of Surrealist Cinema*. Rutherford: Fairleigh Dickinson University Press, 1980.

Kraft, James P. *Stage to Studio: Musicians and the Sound Revolution, 1890–1950*. Baltimore: Johns Hopkins University Press, 1996.

Kuenzli, Rudolf E., ed. *Dada and Surrealist Film*. New York: Willis Locker & Owens, 1987.

Lack, Russell. *Twenty Four Frames Under: A Buried History of Film Music*. London: Quartet Books, 1997.

Lacombe, Alain, and François Porcile. *Les Musiques du cinéma français*. Paris: Bordas, 1995.

Langlois, Philippe. *Les Cloches d'Atlantis: Musique electroacoustic et cinéma: Archéologie et histoire d'un art sonore*. Paris: Éditions MF, 2012.

Lastra, James. *Sound Technology and the American Cinema: Perception, Representation, Modernity*. New York: Columbia University Press, 2000.

Lewis, Hannah. "'The Music Has Something to Say': The Musical Revisions of *L'Atalante* (1934)." *Journal of the American Musicological Society* 68, no. 3 (2015): 559–603.

———. "'The Realm of Serious Art': Henry Hadley's Involvement in Early Sound Film." *Journal of the Society for American Music* 8, no. 3 (August 2014): 285–310.

Lherminier, Pierre. *Jean Vigo. Un cinéma singulier*. Paris: Éditions Ramsay, 2007.

Marie, Michel. "The Poacher's Aged Mother: On Speech in *La Chienne* by Jean Renoir." Translated by Marguerite Morley. *Yale French Studies*, no. 60 (1980): 219–32.

Marks, Martin Miller. *Music and the Silent Film: Contexts and Case Studies, 1895–1924*. New York: Oxford University Press, 1997.

Marvin, Carolyn. *When Old Technologies Were New: Thinking about Electric Communication in the Late Nineteenth Century*. New York: Oxford University Press, 1988.

Mawer, Deborah. "'Dancing on the Edge of the Volcano': French Music in the 1930s." In *French Music since Berlioz*, edited by Richard Langham Smith and Caroline Potter, 249–80. Aldershot: Ashgate, 2006.

McCann, Ben. "'(Under)Scoring Poetic Realism'—Maurice Jaubert and 1930s' French Cinema." *Studies in French Cinema* 9, no. 1 (2009): 37–48.

McDonald, Matthew. "Hitchcock's *Blackmail* and the Threat of Recorded Sound." *Music and the Moving Image* 8, no. 3 (Fall 2015): 40–51.

Mellen, Joan, ed. *The World of Luis Buñuel: Essays in Criticism*. New York: Oxford University Press, 1978.

Mera, Miguel, and David Burnand, eds. *European Film Music*. Aldershot: Ashgate, 2006.

Milhaud, Darius. "Experimenting with Sound Films." *Modern Music* 7, no. 2 (February–March 1930): 11–14.

Moore, Christopher. "Socialist Realism and the Music of the French Popular Front." *Journal of Musicology* 25, no. 4 (2008): 473–502.

Myers, Rollo. *Modern French Music: From Fauré to Boulez*. New York: Praeger, 1971.

Neumeyer, David. *Meaning and Interpretation of Music in Cinema*. Bloomington: Indiana University Press, 2015.

———, ed. *The Oxford Handbook of Film Music Studies*. New York: Oxford University Press, 2014.

Nichols, Roger. *The Harlequin Years: Music in Paris 1917–1929*. Berkeley: University of California Press, 2002.

O'Brien, Charles. *Cinema's Conversion to Sound: Technology and Film Style in France and the U.S.* Bloomington: Indiana University Press, 2005.

———. "Songs in French-Language Cinema: *Cœur de Lilas* (1932) in National and Transnational Context." *Studies in French Cinema* 11, no. 2 (2011): 101–10.

O'Shaughnessy, Martin. *Jean Renoir*. Manchester: Manchester University Press, 2000.

Parès, Philippe. *33 tours en arrière et notes en vrac*. Paris: Éditions du Vivarais, 1978.

Pasler, Jann. *Composing the Citizen: Music as Public Utility in Third Republic France*. Berkeley: University of California Press, 2009.

Paulin, Scott Douglas. "On the Chaplinesque in Music: Studies in the Cultural Reception of Charlie Chaplin." PhD diss., Princeton University, 2005.

Perloff, Nancy. *Art and the Everyday: Popular Entertainment and the Circle of Erik Satie.* Oxford: Clarendon Press, 1991.

Phillips, Alastair, and Ginette Vincendeau, eds. *A Companion to Jean Renoir.* West Sussex: Wiley-Blackwell, 2013.

Porcile, François. *Maurice Jaubert: Musicien populaire ou maudit?* Paris: Les Éditeurs Français Réunis, 1971.

———. *Présence de la musique à l'écran.* Paris: Les Éditions du Cerf, 1969.

Porst, Jennifer. "The Influence of Sound on Visual Style in Renoir's *Tire au flanc* and *La Chienne*." *Studies in French Cinema* 11, no. 3 (2011): 195–206.

Powrie, Phil, ed. *The Cinema of France.* London and New York: Wallflower Press, 2006.

———. *Music in Contemporary French Cinema: The Crystal-Song.* Cham, Switzerland: Palgrave-Macmillan, 2017.

Powrie, Phil, and Robynn Stilwell, eds. *Changing Tunes: The Use of Pre-Existing Music in Film.* Aldershot: Ashgate, 2006.

Ramirez, Francis, and Christian Rolot. *Jean Cocteau: Le Cinéma et son monde.* Paris: Non Lieu, 2009.

Redner, Gregg. *Deleuze and Film Music: Building a Methodological Bridge between Film Theory and Music.* Bristol, UK: Intellect, 2011.

Renoir, Jean. *Interviews.* Edited by Bert Cardullo. Jackson: University Press of Mississippi, 2005.

———. *My Life and My Films.* Translated by Norman Denny. New York: Da Capo Press, 1974.

———. *Renoir on Renoir: Interviews, Essays, and Remarks.* Translated by Carol Volk. Cambridge: Cambridge University Press, 1989.

Richards, Rashna Wadia. "Unsynched: The Contrapuntal Sounds of Luis Buñuel's *L'Age d'or*." *Film Criticism* 33, no. 2 (2008–2009): 23–43.

Rorem, Ned. "Cocteau and Music." In *Jean Cocteau and the French Scene*, edited by Alexandra Anderson and Carol Saltus, 153–83. New York: Abbeville Press, 1984.

Roust, Colin. "'Say It with Georges Auric': Film Music and the *esprit nouveau*." *Twentieth-Century Music* 6, no. 2 (2011): 133–53.

———. "Sounding French: The Film Music and Criticism of Georges Auric, 1919–1945." PhD diss., University of Michigan, 2007.

Salles Gomes, P. E. *Jean Vigo.* London: Faber and Faber, 1998 (1957).

Savedoff, Barbara. "*L'Atalante*: The Marriage of Music and Image." *Millennium Film Journal* 23–24 (1990): 26–35.

Schiff, Christopher. "Banging on the Windowpane: Sound in Early Surrealism." In *Wireless Imagination: Sound, Radio, and the Avant-Garde*, edited by Douglas Kahn and Gregory Whitehead, 139–89. Cambridge, MA: MIT Press, 1992.

Schmidt, Carl B., ed. *Écrits sur la musique de Georges Auric/Writings on Music by Georges Auric.* 4 Vols. Lewiston: Edwin Mellen Press, 2009.

Sesonske, Alexander. *Jean Renoir: The French Films, 1924–1939.* Cambridge, MA: Harvard University Press, 1980.

Short, Robert. *The Age of Gold, Dalí, Buñuel, Artaud: Surrealist Cinema.* Los Angeles: Solar, 2008.

Silverman, Kaja. *The Acoustic Mirror: The Female Body in Psychoanalysis and Cinema.* Bloomington: Indiana University Press, 1988.

Slowik, Michael. *After the Silents: Hollywood Film Music in the Early Sound Era, 1926–1934.* New York: Columbia University Press, 2014.

———. "Diegetic Withdrawal and Other Worlds: Film Music Strategies before *King Kong*, 1927–1933." *Cinema Journal* 53, no. 1 (Fall 2013): 1–25.

———. "Experiments in Early Sound Film Music: Strategies and Rerecording, 1928–1930." *American Music* 31, no. 4 (Winter 2013): 450–74.

Smith, Jeff. *The Sounds of Commerce: Marketing Popular Film Music*. New York: Columbia University Press, 1998.

Smith, Richard Langham, and Caroline Potter, eds. *French Music since Berlioz*. Aldershot: Ashgate, 2006.

Spadoni, Robert. *Uncanny Bodies: The Coming of Sound Film and the Origins of the Horror Genre*. Berkeley: University of California Press, 2007.

Spring, Katherine. "Pop Go the Warner Bros., et al.: Marketing Film Songs during the Coming of Sound." *Cinema Journal* 48, no. 1 (2008): 68–89.

———. *Saying It with Songs: Popular Music and the Coming of Sound to Hollywood Cinema*. New York: Oxford University Press, 2013.

Steegmuller, Francis. *Cocteau: A Biography*. Boston: Little, Brown and Company, 1970.

Surowiec, Catherine A. "Maurice Jaubert: Poet of Music." In *Rediscovering French Film*, edited by Mary Lea Bandy, 87–88. New York: Museum of Modern Art, 1983.

Taruskin, Richard. "The Cult of the Commonplace." In *Oxford History of Western Music, Vol. 4: Music in the Early Twentieth-Century*, 1066–133. New York: Oxford University Press, 2010 (2005).

Temple, Michael. *Jean Vigo*. Manchester: Manchester University Press, 2005.

Temple, Michael, and Michael Witt, eds. *The French Cinema Book*. London: BFI Publishing, 2004.

Thompson, Emily. "Wiring the World: Acoustical Engineers and the Empire of Sound in the Motion Picture Industry, 1927–1930." In *Hearing Cultures: Essays on Sound, Listening and Modernity*, edited by Veit Erlmann, 191–209. Oxford: Berg Publishers, 2004.

Thompson, Kristin. *Exporting Entertainment: America in the World Film Market, 1907–1934*. London: British Film Institute, 1985.

Turk, Edward Baron. *Child of Paradise: Marcel Carné and the Golden Age of French Cinema*. Cambridge, MA: Harvard University Press, 1989.

Turvey, Malcolm. *The Filming of Modern Life: European Avant-Garde Film of the 1920s*. Cambridge, MA: MIT Press, 2011.

Van Parys, Georges. *Les Jours comme ils viennent*. Paris: Plon, 1969.

Vincendeau, Ginette. "Hollywood Babel: The Coming of Sound and the Multiple Language Version." In *The Classical Hollywood Reader*, edited by Steve Neale, 137–46. London: Routledge, 2012.

———. *Stars and Stardom in French Cinema*. London and New York: Continuum, 2000.

Waldman, Harry. *Paramount in Paris: 300 Films Produced at the Joinville Studios, 1930–1933, with Credits and Biographies*. Lanham: Scarecrow Press, 1998.

Warner, Marina. *L'Atalante*. London: British Film Institute, 1993.

Watkins, Glenn. *Pyramids at the Louvre: Music, Culture, and Collage from Stravinsky to the Postmodernists*. Cambridge, MA: Harvard University Press, 1994.

Weber, Eugen. *The Hollow Years: France in the 1930s*. New York: W. W. Norton & Company, 1994.

Weis, Elisabeth, and John Belton, eds. *Film Sound: Theory and Practice*. New York: Columbia University Press, 1985.

Weiss, Allen S. "Between the Sign of the Scorpion and the Sign of the Cross: *L'Age d'or*." In *Dada and Surrealist Film*, edited by Rudolf E. Kuenzli, 159–75. New York: Willis Locker and Owens, 1987.

Wierzbicki, James. *Film Music: A History*. New York: Routledge, 2009.

Wild, Jennifer. *The Parisian Avant-Garde in the Age of Cinema, 1900–1923*. Oakland: University of California Press, 2015.

Williams, Alan. *Republic of Images: A History of French Filmmaking*. Cambridge, MA: Harvard University Press, 1992.

Williams, Linda. *Figures of Desire: A Theory and Analysis of Surrealist Film*. Berkeley: University of California Press, 1981.

Wojcik, Pamela Robertson, and Arthur Knight, eds. *Soundtrack Available: Essays on Film and Popular Music*. Durham: Duke University Press, 2001.

Wolfe, Charles. "Vitaphone Shorts and *The Jazz Singer*." *Wide Angle* 12, no. 3 (July 1990): 58–78.

Wurtzler, Steve J. *Electric Sounds: Technological Change and the Rise of Corporate Mass Media*. New York: Columbia University Press, 2007.

INDEX

critical concerns regarding, 20–24
demand for, 191n12
and musical analogy, 24–27
and *musique mécanique*, 27–33
objections to, 7–8, 19
produced by French film
    industry, 19–20
reception of, 16–17, 18
transition to, 2–4, 7–10, 191n2,
    192n14, 199n23
synchronized sound technology
development of, 3–4
French cinema before advent of, 4–7
French film industry's reaction to, 105
impact of, 187
patent rights for, 18–19
thematized by *Prix de beauté*, 2
Syndicat des Musiciens, 27–29

Talazac, Odette, 123
Taruskin, Richard, 39–40
Temple, Michael, 158
La Tête d'un homme, 134–35, 136, 226
Théâtre du Vieux Colombier, 7, 41
théâtre filmé, 110–12, 126
theatricality
    in *Boudu sauvé des eaux*, 151
    versus cinematic in *opérette filmée*, 72,
        77–78, 80–81, 83–84, 88–90, 95–96
    Clair on, 113, 114
    and Clair's adaptation of *Le Million* for
        screen, 114–16
    in *Il est charmant*, 202n6
    and Pagnol's approach to sound
        cinema, 104–6
theatrical adaptations, 21–22, 101,
    110–11, 114–16, 143, 192n19
Théodore et Cie, 110, 226
Theremin, 33
Thiele, Wilhelm, 72, 85, 91
Thierry, Gaston, 90
Tobis-Klangfilm, 18–19, 114
Tony, C., 99
La Tragédie de la mine, 74, 223
Tristan und Isolde (Wagner), 35, 42, 46,
    47, 50, 56, 57, 201n50
Les Trois Masques, 20, 110, 219
Truffaut, François, 183, 218nn74, 75

UFA, 72, 73, 74, 85
universality of cinema, 24, 26

Van Parys, Georges, 43, 50, 115, 117,
    118, 123, 199n28, 208–9n27
Varda, Agnès, 183
Vaucorbeil, Max de, 85
vaudeville, 78, 114–15, 127, 208n25
Vigo, Jean. See also *L'Atalante*
    on *Un Chien andalou*, 213n9
    death of, 176, 182
    illness of, 175
    influence of, on future
        filmmakers, 218n74
    influences on, 212n6, 213n10
    Jaubert and, 213n11
    surrealist audiovisual devices
        employed by, 70
    and synchronized sound, 160–63
    teams up with Nounez, 214–15n28
Vincendeau, Ginette, 74, 75, 110
violin, in *L'Age d'or*, 35, 55
Vitaphone, 3, 80, 214n27
Vuillermoz, Émile, 5–6, 30, 32,
    90–91, 99–100

Wagner, Richard
    as accompaniment for silent film, 57,
        200–201n50
    Buñuel and, 57–58, 201n53
    Tristan und Isolde, 35, 42, 46, 47, 50,
        56, 57, 201n50
Wahl, Lucien, 24
Warner, Marina, 168, 216n51,
    217n54
Weber, Eugen, 192n14
White Shadows in the South Seas, 30
Wiéner, Jean, 9
Wierzbicki, James, 212n5
Willemetz, Albert, 73, 76, 92, 93, 99
Williams, Alan, 130, 141, 212n29
Wood, Simon, 66

Yvain, Maurice, 132

Zéro de conduite, 161–62, 163,
    213–14nn19, 20, 226
Zouzou, 227